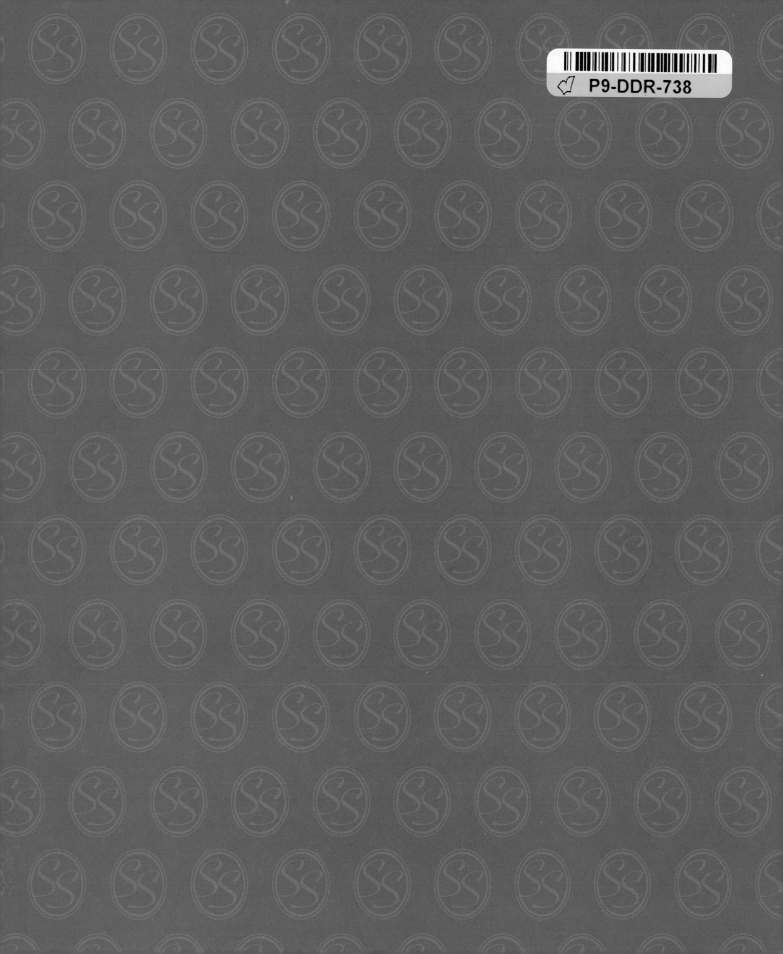

Southern

settings

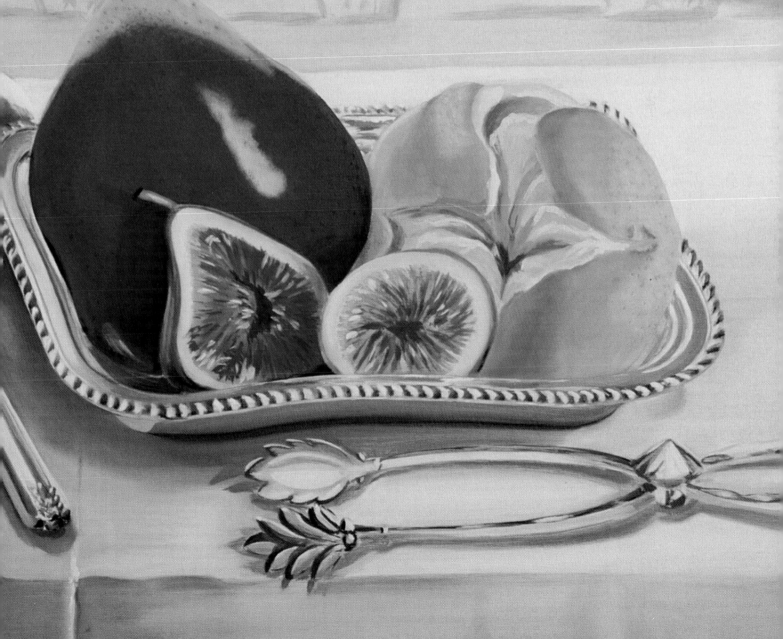

Southern
settings

The Decatur General Foundation is a charitable private not-for-profit corporation, established in 1984, whose mission is to develop, encourage, and accept funds for programs and services of Decatur General Hospital.

This cookbook is a collection of favorite recipes, which are not necessarily original recipes.

Published by: Decatur General Foundation

Copyright© 1996 Decatur General Foundation, Inc.
Post Office Box 2239
Decatur, Alabama 35609-2239
205-341-2187

ISBN: 0-9654734-0-6
Library of Congress Catalog Number: 96-92783

Edited, Designed, and Manufactured by:
FRP™
P.O. Box 305142
Nashville, Tennessee 37230
1-800-358-0560

Book design by Brad Whitfield

Photography: Ron Manville, YUM, Inc., and Wilson Craig, Decatur General Hospital
Chef and Food Stylist: James E. Griffin, YUM, Inc.
Prop Styling and Set Design: Christine Stamm, YUM, Inc.

Manufactured in the United States of America
First Printing: 1996   15,000 copies

For additional copies, use the order forms at the back of the book
or send a check for $24.95 plus $3.50 postage and handling
(Alabama residents add 8% sales tax) to:
Southern Settings
Decatur General Foundation
Post Office Box 1461
Decatur, Alabama 35602-1461
205-341-2187 • FAX: 205-341-2648
VISA/MasterCard accepted

Introduction

When we decided, after lengthy consideration, to call our cookbook
Southern Settings, we couldn't help congratulating ourselves
on the subtle brilliance of our choice. How clever we were, we thought, to
have come up with a word like *setting*, a word with so many layers of
meaning, and each of them relevant to our project.

The plan was to produce a cookbook that was more than a cookbook. While
eager to address the idea of *setting* as it applies to food and tables, we were
equally keen on exploring the term in its larger sense: *setting* as place,
backdrop, stage...as natural habitat and personality extension. A wonderful
word, *setting*, we thought. So rich in meaning, so flexible.

Ironically, it was that other word, *Southern*, that proved to be delightfully,
frustratingly flexible. What exactly did we mean by *Southern settings?* Were
we talking about the South of history, legend, and myth—a world of drawling
debutantes, kerchiefed mammies, spreading magnolias, and juleps on the
veranda? Or were we talking about the real South, the one that exists today—
a glorious hodgepodge of colorful contradictions, where old-fashioned meets
new-fangled, where tradition and heritage are the solid foundation for the
progress and vision of a new generation?

In search of an answer, we visited some of the homes—and tables—of
Decatur, Alabama, a typical *Southern* town with a firm foot in the past and a
bright eye on the future. From a stately antebellum mansion in the tiny hamlet
of Belle Mina, to a rustically refined house that "growed like Topsy"
on the banks of the Tennessee River, to a moody, Victorian mini-castle in the
heart of Old Decatur...we found the only thing these homes had in common,
besides the graciousness of their owners, was their general location, or *setting*,
if you will. But, oh, the *settings* within that *setting!*

And, oh, the culinary delights we found there. Cooking and feasting our
collective way through old favorites like Southern Fried Chicken, Turnip
Greens, and Corn Pudding and newer fare like Grilled Garlic Lime Pork with
Jalapeño Marmalade and Cashew Sesame Noodles, we sought to pin down the
elusive definition of the oft-used but little-understood phrase *Southern cuisine*.
In the end, we deemed it an utterly impossible task, and one at
which we had thoroughly enjoyed failing.

So now, it is with a great sense of joy and adventure that we invite
you to seek your own answers. Come gather where we gather, sup
where we sup. Come and lift a glass with us, celebrate with us. Come
and join us in our *Southern Settings*.

Contents

Special
Occasions

Belle Mina Hall

Belle Mina Hall was built in 1826 by
Thomas Bibb, Alabama's second
governor and brother of its first governor.
Today the home of Toby and Jack Sewell,
the beautiful Greek Revival mansion hardly
fits its billing as a farmhouse.
It is, however, the center of a working farm,
keeping watch over the surrounding cotton fields
and the pastures where the Sewells' band of
Hanoverian horses placidly graze.

*The free-standing staircase in the great hall
serves as a fitting backdrop for a sumptuous dinner of
Tenderloin of Beef with Green Peppercorn Sauce;
Mushroom Casserole;
Yellow Squash Stuffed with Spinach;
and Roasted Vidalia Onions with
Balsamic Apricot Glaze.*

Special Occasions

Like many of our recipes, Southern hospitality is passed down from one generation to the next. We invite you to browse through our menu and entertaining suggestions for your memorable occasions.

Plantation Dinner

Outside, the cotton bolls are opening, the cicadas are singing, and the sultry days of summer are coming to an end, as, inside, the candles are lit and your guests arrive for a magical evening.

Caponata (page 46) *in avocado halves*
Caesar Salad (page 104)
Tenderloin of Beef with Green Peppercorn Sauce (page 120)
Mushroom Casserole (page 182)
Yellow Squash Stuffed with Spinach (page 189)
Roasted Vidalia Onions with Balsamic Apricot Glaze (page 185)
Old English Trifle (page 249)

Wines

With appetizers:
*Gewürztraminer—Domaine Weinbach Reserve
Personnelle "Capucins 1994"*

With the entrée:
Cabernet Sauvignon—Silver Oak—Alexander Valley 1992

With dessert:
California Muscat—Bonny Doon—Vin de Glacieve 1995

The successful dinner party flows smoothly from appetizers to dessert. Avoid an awkward moment at the table by deciding ahead of time where each guest is to sit. Better yet, add the oft-forgotten elegance of place cards. They are especially helpful at large gatherings when the guests may be seated in different rooms, or at very long tables. Do not feel that you have to seat old friends together. Mixing the seating a little often enlivens the meal by sparking conversation and adding a sense of spontaneity to the occasion.

Evening Buffet

Begin this feast with soup served in Jefferson cups, and end with dessert and coffee on the porch. Add some soft music and watch your guests dance through the buffet line.

Cream of Squash Soup (page 93)
Chicken Curry (page 162) over rice with an assortment of condiments
Pineapple Casserole (page 197)
Mixed Greens with Goat Cheese (page 106)
Sour Cream Muffins (page 75)
Raspberry Cream Tart (page 232)

Wine
Domestic Riesling

Thanksgiving Dinner

Southerners enjoy smoking their turkeys as much as roasting them. Try your turkey cooked this way, and reserve the kitchen for fixing the rest of your dinner.

Cream of Shiitake Soup with Virginia Ham (page 92)
Smoked Turkey (page 168)
Corn Bread Dressing with Giblet Gravy (page 198)
Sweet Potato Soufflé (page 190)
Green Bean Bundles (page 177)
Scalloped Oysters (page 197)
Rolls
Pumpkin Pie Squares (page 231)
Pecan Pie (page 230)

Wine
French Red Burgundy

While the fresh flower centerpiece has always been considered requisite for the proper dinner table, and is indeed always right, there are certainly other ways to add color and texture to the setting. Consider the beauty of a bowl of fresh vegetables—eggplant, peppers, squash, onions—perhaps with a few flowers tucked in between. Hollow out a large, leafy green cabbage from the farmers market, insert a small glass jar in the hollow, and fill with Queen Anne's lace from the roadside. Or forget the centerpiece altogether and give each place its own small vase or basket of blossoms. There is one rule you must follow, however. Do not block your guests' view of each other. Keep your centerpiece low, or make it very tall—above eye level. And always remember the candles.

Cocktail Party

*This delightful assortment of hearty hors d'oeuvres together
with a selection of beers, wines, and mixed drinks
ensures a successful party. Make-ahead recipes allow you time to
come out of the kitchen and enjoy your guests.*

Boneless Pork Loin with Tangy Sauce (page 137)
Yeast Rolls (page 70)
Fresh Tomato Tart (page 49)
Mushrooms Stuffed with Spinach (page 48)
Kahlúa Pecan Brie (page 35)
Southern Caviar (page 29)
Oven-Baked Crab Dip (page 30)

Picnic

Sewell Farm

Anyone for a picnic?
Finding the right spot should be easy.
Spread your quilt anywhere—on the
riverbank at Rhodes Ferry Park or at
Point Mallard, in Delano Park in the Albany
district or Wilson Morgan Park further west,
or even on a tailgate at the football game.

*For our picnic, pictured here in front of an old corn crib
on the Sewell farm, not far from the cotton fields,
we've packed a barbecue lover's delight of
Ribs; Barbecued Chicken and Pork; buns;
Corn Salad, Three-Bean Baked Beans;
Coleslaw; Pickles; corn on the cob;
and a refreshing pitcher of iced tea.*

Sometimes a picnic in the park can be as relaxing as a weekend at the beach. Just getting out of the house, spreading your quilt on the ground, and enjoying the slow pace of the day can make the whole world seem a little friendlier. Take your time with a picnic and enjoy every moment. The right setting, good company, agreeable weather, and delicious food can make any hillside or open field your own little five-star world.

Barbecue Supper or Picnic

This spread of North Alabama's famous barbecue is featured fare in our special section, which begins on page 130.

Barbecued Chicken and Pork, Ribs, buns
Corn Salad (page 105)
Coleslaw (page 131)
Three-Bean Baked Beans (page 175)
Chocolate Pecan Crumble Bars (page 226)
Minted Iced Tea (page 51)

Wine
Côtes du Rhone

Picnic

Pack the baskets and a cooler with this fine array of portable palate pleasers, and head to the stadium, riverside, or woods for an afternoon of fun.

Hummus (page 32) *and tortilla chips*
Fried Chicken (page 163)
Broccoli Salad (page 103)
German Potato Salad (page 102)
Pimento Cheese Sandwiches (page 94)
Mayor's Chocolate Cake (page 215)
Cooler filled with favorite beverages

Wine
California Rhone-Style Red, e.g., Grenache

Afternoon Tea

Tea parties—still a Southern tradition—are usually given to honor a bride, greet a new neighbor, or receive an out-of-town friend.

Assorted gourmet teas
Iced Tea Punch (page 54)
Cheese Straws (page 39)
Scones (page 72) with Lemon Curd (page 246)
Chicken Salad Finger Sandwiches (page 110)
Cucumber Finger Sandwiches (page 89)
Fresh fruit with Orange Yogurt Dip (page 31)
Shortbread (page 227)
Praline Squares (page 227)

Wine
Sauvignon Blanc

Luncheon

Light and elegant, this menu produces a lovely Southern Setting for a bridesmaids' luncheon, bridge party, baby shower, or fond farewell.

Kir Royales (page 55)
Monterey Chicken Salad (page 111)
Frozen Fruit Salad (page 99) or Strawberry Pretzel Salad (page 101)
Marinated Asparagus (page 172)
Angel Biscuits (page 74)
Melon Sorbet (page 242)

Wine
Chardonnay

When planning a tea, give careful consideration to traffic flow. Since the dining room is often a dead end, think of alternative locations for the tea table, or perhaps set more than one. You might place additional serving trays on coffee tables or side tables throughout the house. Remember, too, to have replacement trays of food and drink ready in the kitchen.

Setting your table can be every bit as creative as painting a picture or writing a poem. Use your artistic vision. Do not confine yourself to traditional ideas of how a table should be set and how it should look. Don't be afraid to mix china patterns or patterns of flatware. Borrow ideas, and browse through garage sales and antique shops for unusual pieces and accessories. Set your table like you prepare your food, as an extension of your character and personality.

Dessert Buffet

The sweetest menu of them all is yours for a holiday open house, Valentine's Day party, after-the-game gathering, or mid-winter blues get-together.

Chocolate Toffee Torte (page 213)
Coconut-Glazed Pound Cake (page 216)
Dacquoise (page 240)
Poached Pears with Raspberry Sauce (page 243)
Chess Pie (page 229)
Lemon Cups (page 246)
Florentine Cookie Amaretto (page 223)
Bread Pudding with Jack Daniel's Sauce (page 235)
Toasted Pecans (page 48)
Liqueurs
Coffee/tea

Wines
Champagne, Late Harvest Riesling, or California Muscat

A nice complement to a table of sweet treats is a tray of assorted fresh fruits and cheeses. Generous wedges of Brie, Camembert, Havarti, or any other cheese—at room temperature—with apples, pears, and red grapes—chilled—add to the beauty of the setting.

Brunch

Pearce Guest House

*T*ucked away out of sight and sound
in the very middle of a block in the Albany
Historical District of Decatur,
is the new guest house which
Hank and Beth Pearce have built behind
their home—their very own secret garden.
While the cat chases dragonflies and
dreams longingly of a goldfish dinner,
the two of you, or more if you wish,
can enjoy brunch here in
the warmth and quiet of a
summer morning.

Pictured are Eggs Benedict with Cheese Scones;
sliced melon; Banana Bread;
Broccoli Corn Bread Muffins;
Cheese Herb Biscuits; bacon;
and Spicy Bloody Marys.

Brunch is perhaps the perfect party. A most versatile way to entertain, it can be dressed up and elegant, or dressed down and low-key, very large or quite small, winter or summer. Brunch has several advantages over other types of parties. Generally, brunch fare is less expensive, so you can serve more for less. Your guests aren't tired, and neither are you—since you've done all the work the day before—so everyone is relaxed and has a good time. And if you begin around noon, nobody has to worry about food for the rest of the day. There are two requirements for success: plenty of food, since guests will want seconds, and lots of freshly ground coffee.

Brunch

Make a stay-at-home weekend an occasion with this delicious brunch.

Spicy Bloody Marys (page 55)
Eggs Benedict (page 202)
Sliced cantaloupe, honeydew melon and watermelon
Cheese Scones (page 73)
Bacon and sliced ham
Broccoli Corn Bread Muffins (page 77)
Banana Bread (page 60)

Wine
Champagne

Brunch

This make-ahead brunch menu is sure to please your weekend company.

Mimosas
Elegant Eggs (page 201)
Truck Stop Potatoes (page 187)
Bacon
Fruit Verde (page 98)
Strawberry Bread (page 67) with orange or strawberry butter

Wine
California Sparkling

Brunch

Your family and guests will love this assortment of old-fashioned favorites for weekends at the beach, the lake, or at home on the screened-in porch.

Vegetable Frittata (page 193)
Country Ham (page 139)
Cheese Herb Biscuits (page 76)
Sausage Grits Casserole (page 205)
Fresh fruit or Candied Apples (page 196)
Speedy Orange Rolls (page 70)
Hot Spiced Cider (page 52)

Wine
Pinot Noir

Christmas Morning Brunch

After a late night of playing Santa and the certain early wakeup call, this delectable breakfast is sure to satisfy the ravenous appetites you've all worked up opening gifts.

Holiday Eggnog (page 53)
Oeufs aux Champignons (page 204)
Cranberry Apple Bake (page 196)
Garlic Cheese Grits Casserole (page 205)
Macadamia Nut Muffins (page 77)
Sour Cream Coffee Cake (page 79)

Wine
French Champagne

Wedding Reception

Whether you cook it yourself or have it catered, you will welcome help choosing selections for a memorable table for this most special day! May we help you?

Toasted Pecans (page 48)
Cheese Straws (page 39)
Chicken Salad (page 110) *in toast cups*
Fresh Fruit with Amaretto Dip (page 31)
Tea Punch
Bride's cake
Groom's cake

If your reception is closer to mealtime, consider these additions:

Baked Artichoke Dip (page 28)
Toast Points (page 30)
Baked Brie (page 34) *or Kahlúa Pecan Brie* (page 35)
Sliced Tenderloin of Beef (page120) *or Pork Tenderloin* (page 137)
Mustard Caper Sauce or Horseradish Sauce (page 121)
Yeast Rolls (page70)
Assorted cocktails

Wine
Champagne

It is not necessary to serve a great deal of food at a wedding reception. The amount depends on the hour the reception is held. A very light menu could be planned for a two o'clock or three o'clock wedding. Add some or all of the more substantial foods to your menu if the hour is later.

Appetizers & Beverages

Neville Home

New and thoroughly modern, Joan and Frank
Neville's home on the north bank of the Tennessee
River is a grand place for beginnings. Frank, an
architect, designed the house to take best
advantage of the incredible riverscape.
One wall is made entirely of glass, and the view
of a sunset over the mile and a half of water
takes one's breath.
The crystal chandelier over the dining table,
which once hung in the home of Governor
and Mrs. George Wallace, adds the patina of
something old. Join us for a drink
in the living room, or, if you'd prefer,
we'll meet you at the dock.

For a start, try our Fresh Tomato Tart;
Mushrooms Stuffed with Spinach;
Hot Turnip Green Dip with Jalapeño Corn Muffins;
Baked Brie; and Cocktail Meatballs with a sip of Sangria,
a Kir Royale, a Martini, or a Mint Julep.

Baked Artichoke Dip

May substitute mayonnaise for sour cream in this recipe

1 can artichoke hearts, chopped
1 can chopped green chiles
1 cup grated Parmesan cheese or
mozzarella cheese

1 cup sour cream
2 tablespoons hot sauce
(not Tabasco sauce)

*Combine the artichoke hearts, green chiles, cheese, sour cream and hot sauce in
a bowl and mix well. Spoon into a baking dish.
Bake at 350 degrees for 25 to 30 minutes or until heated through.
Serve with tortilla chips or crackers.*
Yield: Three Cups

Layered Mexican Bean Dip

*Watching your fat grams? Substitute no-fat ingredients
in this party pleaser! Olé!*

2 cans refried beans
1 (10-ounce) can chopped
jalapeños
3 avocados
Freshly squeezed juice of 1/2 lemon
1 1/2 cups sour cream
1/2 cup mayonnaise

1 envelope taco mix
1 bunch green onions, chopped
3 tomatoes, chopped
2 small cans sliced black olives, very
finely chopped
Shredded Cheddar cheese

*Spread the beans in a 9x13-inch glass dish. Sprinkle with the jalapeños.
Cut the avocados into halves and scoop out the pulp. Mix the pulp and lemon
juice in a bowl. Spread over the jalapeños.
Mix the sour cream, mayonnaise and taco mix in a bowl. Spread over the
avocado mixture. Layer the green onions, tomatoes and olives over the
mayonnaise mixture. Sprinkle with the cheese.
Chill thoroughly. Let stand at room temperature for 1 hour before serving.
Serve with tortilla chips.*
Yield: Fifteen to Twenty Servings

Black Bean Salsa

Salsa takes a colorful twist with this recipe from Anne Pollard of the Green Bottle Grill. Serve with blue corn chips or tortilla chips or as a spicy side dish with your favorite Mexican meal.

1 (15-ounce) can black beans or
   equivalent amount of cooked
   dried beans, drained
cup prepared medium or hot salsa
1/4 cup chopped green onions
1/4 cup chopped red pepper
1/4 cup chopped red onion

1 tablespoon lime juice
1 tablespoon olive oil
2 cloves of garlic, minced
1/4 teaspoon ground cumin
2 tablespoons chopped fresh
   cilantro or parsley
1 avocado

Combine the beans, salsa, green onions, red pepper, red onion, lime juice, olive oil, garlic, cumin and cilantro in a bowl and mix well. Chop the avocado at serving time. Stir into the bean mixture.
Yield: Two to Three Cups
Anne Pollard, Green Bottle Grill

Southern Caviar

Shoe Peg corn and black-eyed peas are regional staples that combine nicely in this vegetable dip. It can also be used as a dressing on a salad of mixed greens. Men love this!

cans black-eyed peas without pork,
   drained, rinsed
1 small can white Shoe Peg corn,
   drained
1 large firm tomato, chopped
4 green onions, chopped
1 small onion, chopped

1 green pepper, chopped
1 cup chopped parsley
1 tablespoon cilantro
2 cloves of garlic, minced
1 bottle Italian salad dressing or
   no-oil herb vinaigrette

Combine the peas, corn, tomato, green onions, onion, green pepper, parsley, cilantro and garlic in a large bowl. Add the salad dressing and toss lightly. Marinate in the refrigerator for 8 to 10 hours. Serve over white corn chips.
Yield: Sixteen Servings

Margaritas

The drink of choice for Mexican dining. Serve plenty of tortilla chips on the side.

Rub the rims of 10 wide-mouthed glasses with lime wedges. Place some margarita salt in a saucer and spin the rim of each glass in the salt. Mix 2 1/4 cups tequila, 2 1/4 cups Triple Sec, 1 cup freshly squeezed lime or lemon juice and a 7-ounce bottle of lime juice in a pitcher. Add ice to the glasses and pour the tequila mixture over the ice. Garnish each glass with a lime wedge.
Yield: Ten Servings

Fiery Cajun Shrimp

Superb flavor, but definitely not for the faint of heart!

1 cup melted butter
1 cup melted margarine
6 to 8 tablespoons
Worcestershire sauce
1/4 cup ground pepper
1 teaspoon ground rosemary
2 teaspoons Tabasco sauce
2 teaspoons sea salt or salt
3 cloves of garlic, minced
Juice of 2 lemons
5 to 6 pounds uncooked shrimp
in the shell
2 lemons, sliced

Mix the butter, margarine, Worcestershire sauce, pepper, rosemary, Tabasco sauce, sea salt, garlic and lemon juice in a bowl. Pour 1/2 cup into a large baking dish. Alternate layers of the shrimp and lemon slices in the baking dish until 1 inch headspace remains. Pour the remaining sauce over the shrimp. Bake at 400 degrees for 15 to 20 minutes or until the shrimp are cooked through, stirring once or twice. Serve with baguettes of hot French bread.

Yield: Eight to Ten Servings

Oven-Baked Crab Dip

For an elegant presentation, serve in a silver chafing dish.

Sliced white bread, crusts trimmed
16 ounces cream cheese, softened
1/3 cup mayonnaise
1 tablespoon confectioners' sugar
1 tablespoon chablis or other dry white wine
1/2 teaspoon onion juice
1/2 teaspoon prepared mustard
1/4 teaspoon garlic salt
1/4 teaspoon salt
6 ounces canned or fresh crab meat, drained, flaked
Chopped fresh parsley

For toast points, cut each bread slice into 4 triangles, allowing 2 triangles per guest. Place on a baking sheet. Bake at 250 degrees for 45 minutes; do not brown.

For the dip, combine the cream cheese, mayonnaise, confectioners' sugar, chablis, onion juice, mustard, garlic salt and salt in a bowl and mix well.

Stir in the crab meat gently.

Spoon the mixture into a lightly greased 1-quart baking dish. Bake at 375 degrees for 15 minutes. Sprinkle with the parsley.

Serve with the toast points.

Yield: Twelve to Fifteen Servings

Dips for Fruit

Fresh fruits such as red or green apples or pears, berries, oranges, grapes and pineapple make wonderful arrangements on a buffet table. Use a cake or trivet stand to give some vertical dimension to your arrangement and/or drape the grapes. Be creative! Alongside, prepare a platter of individual fruit slices with one of these delectable dips.

Amaretto Dip

8 ounces cream cheese, softened
2 cups confectioners' sugar

Amaretto to taste

Blend the cream cheese and confectioners' sugar in a bowl until smooth. Add the amaretto 1 tablespoon at a time to taste or to desired consistency.

Yield: Three Cups

Orange Yogurt Dip

1 cup vanilla yogurt
Grated zest of 1 small orange

1/4 cup frozen orange juice concentrate, thawed

Mix the yogurt and orange zest in a small bowl. Stir in the concentrate gradually until blended. Pour into a small serving bowl. Chill, covered, until serving time.

Yield: One Cup

Apple Dip

8 ounces cream cheese, softened
3/4 cup packed brown sugar

1/4 cup sugar
1 teaspoon vanilla extract

Combine the cream cheese, brown sugar, sugar and vanilla in a bowl and mix well. At serving time, rinse, core and slice some tart crisp apples. Sprinkle the slices with lemon juice to prevent browning.

Yield: Two Cups

About Hummus

Old from the Middle East, new in the U.S., hummus gained popularity during the health food craze and has stayed with us since then. The base is made from chick-peas (garbanzo beans) and tahini, a peanut butter-type paste made from ground sesame seeds. (Tahini is usually found in the Greek section of the supermarket or with the olives.) When puréed and seasoned, the flavor is best described as tangy and nutty. For an extra-creamy texture, this dish is best made in a food processor fitted with a steel blade.

Hummus

1 (16-ounce) can chick-peas or garbanzo beans
2 cloves of garlic, crushed, or to taste
3/4 cup tahini
1/2 cup lemon juice, or to taste

Salt to taste
1/8 teaspoon cayenne, or to taste
2 tablespoons chopped parsley

Drain the chick-peas, reserving the liquid. Set aside 1/2 cup chick-peas. Purée the remaining chick-peas in a food processor fitted with a steel blade. Add the garlic, tahini and lemon juice. Process until smooth and creamy, adding the reserved liquid as needed. Season with salt. Top with the cayenne, parsley and reserved chick-peas. Serve with a small piece of pita bread or as a dip for carrots, celery sticks and peppers. May also be used as a spread inside pita pocket sandwiches of your favorite meat and vegetable combo.
Yield: Eight to Twelve Servings

Southwestern Dip

Plain old onion dip no longer stands a chance once you've tried this one. Make copies of this recipe. Your friends will ask for this favorite recipe of John Harris.

1 cup mayonnaise
1 cup sour cream
2 tablespoons grated onion
1 teaspoon ground cumin seeds
2 (11-ounce) cans Mexicorn

1 (8-ounce) jar medium-hot salsa, drained
1 can chopped green chiles, drained
3 cups shredded sharp Cheddar cheese

Mix the mayonnaise, sour cream, onion and cumin seeds in a medium bowl. Mix the Mexicorn, salsa, green chiles and cheese in a large bowl. Stir in the mayonnaise mixture. Chill, covered, for 2 hours or longer.
May be prepared 1 day ahead. Serve with king-size corn chips.
Yield: Twenty to Thirty Servings
John R. Harris, Jr.

Hot Turnip Green Dip with Jalapeño Corn Muffins

Turnip greens will always be a regional favorite, and great hostesses will always find innovative ways to serve them. This recipe is one of the best and is pictured on page 26.

1 (10-ounce) package frozen chopped turnip greens, thawed, drained
1/4 teaspoon grated lemon peel
1/2 cup finely chopped onion
1/2 cup finely chopped celery
2 tablespoons melted butter
2 to 3 ounces fresh mushrooms, sliced
1 (10-ounce) can cream of mushroom soup
1 (6-ounce) roll process cheese food with garlic
1 teaspoon Worcestershire sauce
5 drops of hot sauce

Combine the turnip greens and lemon peel in a food processor fitted with a knife blade. Process until finely chopped. Cook the onion and celery in the butter in a Dutch oven over medium heat until tender, stirring constantly. Stir in the turnip green mixture, mushrooms, soup, cheese food, Worcestershire sauce and hot sauce. Cook until heated through. Serve from a chafing dish. Garnish with cherry tomato slices and fresh parsley sprigs. Serve with Jalapeño Corn Muffins.
Yield: Three Cups

Jalapeño Corn Muffins

2 cups jalapeño corn bread mix
1 large egg, slightly beaten
1 cup milk
2 tablespoons vegetable oil

Grease miniature muffin cups and heat in a 400-degree oven for 5 minutes. Place the corn bread mix in a bowl and make a well in the center. Add a mixture of the egg, milk and oil, stirring just until moistened. Fill the prepared muffin cups 2/3 full with the batter. Bake at 400 degrees for 11 minutes.
Yield: Twenty-Eight Muffins

Phyllo Dough

Phyllo dough (sometimes spelled filo) is a paper-thin flour and water pastry dough that is formed into sheets. It is used most often in Greek and Middle Eastern cooking. When buttered, stacked, and baked, its thin layers puff up and brown, similarly to a strudel or puff pastry. Its popularity today has made it commonly available in the frozen food section of the supermarket, usually with the frozen pie shells and bread. Fresh phyllo is usually available only in Greek or Middle Eastern specialty groceries or bakeries. Because the pastry is so thin, it dries very quickly when exposed to air, so it must be carefully handled. It is extremely important to follow the thawing instructions on the box. If

Baked Brie

This recipe is for a large Brie, but a smaller Brie, as pictured on page 26, can be used as well. Gather the ends of the phyllo and "tie" with a strip of pleated phyllo. When baked, tie with a strip of green onion dipped in boiling water. A Brie dressed to impress!

12 sheets phyllo dough, thawed
2 cups melted unsalted butter
1 (5-pound) Brie, not fully ripe

Layer 5 sheets of the phyllo on a buttered baking sheet, brushing each sheet with melted butter. Place the Brie in the center and fold the edges of the phyllo up around the cheese. Cover the top of the cheese with 6 sheets of phyllo, brushing each sheet with melted butter. Tuck the ends of the pastry under the cheese. Brush the top and sides with melted butter. Fold the last sheet of phyllo lengthwise into a 1-inch wide strip and brush with melted butter. Roll up from the short side, beginning tightly to form a flower "bud" and loosening the strip as you continue rolling, flattening to make it resemble "petals." Center over the Brie and brush with melted butter. Bake at 350 degrees for 20 to 30 minutes or until golden brown. Let stand for 30 minutes before serving. As a variation, add parsley or other herbs to the butter for more color; brush the Brie with apricot preserves before covering with the phyllo.

Yield: Twenty Servings

Kahlúa Pecan Brie

Incredible taste combinations! And you thought gingersnaps were just for kids!

1 (15-ounce) miniature Brie
¹/₂ cup toasted finely chopped pecans
2 tablespoons Kahlúa or other coffee-flavored liqueur
1¹/₂ tablespoons brown sugar
Apple slices or gingersnaps

Remove the rind from the top of the cheese, cutting to within ¹/₂ inch of the outside edge. Place on an ovenproof dish.
Mix the pecans, Kahlúa and brown sugar in a bowl. Spread over the cheese.
Bake at 350 degrees for 3 to 5 minutes or just until soft.
Serve immediately with apple slices or gingersnaps.
May be assembled and chilled for up to 4 hours before serving. Let stand at room temperature for 10 to 15 minutes before baking.
Yield: Twelve to Fifteen Servings

Horseradish Cheese Spread

Great to have on hand for drop-in company, this spread keeps for two weeks in the refrigerator, making it the perfect "make-ahead" hors d'oeuvre.

1 (2-pound) block of Velveeta cheese
1 cup mayonnaise
1 small jar prepared horseradish

Place the cheese in a microwave-safe bowl. Microwave on High for 5 to 7 minutes or until melted. Add the mayonnaise and horseradish, stirring until blended. Pour into 1 large crock or 3 small ones.
Chill, covered tightly, until needed.
Serve with firm crackers. May use low-fat Velveeta cheese.
Yield: Eighteen Servings

improperly stored or thawed, the pastry layers may stick to themselves or the edges may become brittle and dry, making it very difficult to work with. Before beginning any recipe prepared with phyllo, carefully unroll the dough onto a tray and cover completely with waxed paper or plastic wrap, then a damp (not wet) cloth; remove only one sheet at a time as needed. Leftover phyllo can be rewrapped and stored in the refrigerator or refrozen if it still retains its moisture. Phyllo can be easily trimmed with scissors or a sharp knife and folded into various shapes as called for. Always remember to butter the top layer before baking.

Jeweled Cheese Ball

Yes, there are enough cheese ball recipes to fill volumes, but they are still great for parties, holiday baskets, and snacking. Try one of these favorites to suit your taste buds! If wrapped tightly and refrigerated, cheese balls will keep for weeks.

2 cups shredded Cheddar cheese
1 cup chopped pitted dates
1/2 cup butter, softened
1 tablespoon brandy
1/2 cup toasted sliced almonds

Combine the cheese, dates, butter and brandy in a 1 1/2-quart mixer bowl. Beat at medium speed until well mixed. Shape into a ball and roll in the almonds. Cover and chill thoroughly. Let stand at room temperature for 30 minutes before serving.
Yield: Thirty Servings

Beefy Cheese Ball

8 ounces cream cheese, softened
1 package dried beef
3 to 4 green onions, chopped, or 1 cup snipped or dried chives
1 teaspoon garlic salt or flavor enhancer
1 tablespoon Worcestershire sauce (optional)
1 cup chopped pecans

Combine the cream cheese, dried beef, green onions, garlic salt and Worcestershire sauce in a bowl and mix well. Shape into a ball or log with wet hands or plastic wrap. Roll in the pecans. Chill thoroughly. Serve with crackers. May roll in finely chopped or dried parsley flakes instead of pecans; may substitute 1 small can deviled ham for the dried beef, adding a dash of hot sauce and omitting the Worcestershire sauce; may substitute 1 cup chopped smoked turkey for the dried beef and green onions, adding 3 tablespoons mayonnaise and omitting the garlic salt; may add 1 pound shredded American cheese to the mixture and shape into 2 logs—roll the logs in pecans and sprinkle with chili powder.
Yield: Twenty Servings

Liver Pâté

A simple chicken liver pâté for pâté lovers. Add a tablespoon of brandy or sherry for additional zip.

1 pound chicken livers
1/4 cup finely chopped onion
1/4 teaspoon ground cloves
1/2 teaspoon nutmeg

2 teaspoons dry mustard
2 teaspoons salt
1 cup unsalted butter
1/8 teaspoon cayenne, or to taste

Combine the chicken livers with water to cover in a saucepan. Bring to a boil. Simmer, covered, for 15 to 20 minutes or just until tender; drain well. Combine the chicken livers, onion, cloves, nutmeg, dry mustard, salt, butter and cayenne in a blender container. Process until smooth. Spoon into a crock and store in the refrigerator.

Yield: Two Cups

Mushroom Pâté

Is there anything more elegant than pâté? Betty Sims, founder of Johnston Street Cafe in Decatur, suggests serving with Bremner wafers on a bed of red curly lettuce. This mushroom version will surely delight you and your guests.

1 tablespoon unflavored gelatin
1/4 cup cold water
1 pound mushrooms, sliced

2 tablespoons butter
16 ounces cream cheese, softened
1 teaspoon garlic salt

Soften the gelatin in the cold water in a small glass cup for 5 minutes. Place the small cup in a larger cup half filled with boiling water, stirring until the gelatin is dissolved. Sauté the mushrooms in the butter in a skillet; drain well. Combine the mushrooms, gelatin, cream cheese and garlic salt in a food processor container. Process until smooth. Chill thoroughly. Garnish as desired.

Yield: Six Cups

Betty Brandon Sims, Johnston Street Cafe

Shrimply Divine

The name says it all.

8 ounces cream cheese, softened
1/4 cup sour cream
3 tablespoons chopped scallions
1 tablespoon lemon juice
1/2 teaspoon cayenne
1 tablespoon milk
Tabasco sauce to taste
12 ounces shrimp, chopped, cooked

Mix the cream cheese, sour cream, scallions, lemon juice, cayenne, milk and Tabasco sauce in a bowl. Add the shrimp and mix well. Chill, covered, for 2 hours or longer. Serve with crackers.
Yield: Six Servings

Cheese Krispies

Similar to cheese straws, these tidbits do not require a cookie press. They are wonderful for every special occasion or family get-together. Delicious and addictive!

1 cup margarine or butter, softened
2 cups flour, sifted
2 cups shredded Cheddar cheese
1 teaspoon salt
1/8 teaspoon cayenne, or to taste
1/8 teaspoon Tabasco sauce, or to taste
2 cups Rice Krispies

Combine the margarine, flour, cheese, salt, cayenne and Tabasco sauce in a bowl and mix well. Stir in the cereal. Shape into small balls. Place on a nonstick baking sheet. Crisscross each ball with a fork. Bake at 350 degrees for 15 minutes.
Yield: Four to Five Dozen
"Corn" Chef David Tanis

Cheese Straws

*Cheese straws separate great cooks from good cooks and, here in the
South, recipes are passed down with reverence from generation to generation.
This recipe was given by a mother to her son's wife with the admonition,
"A heavy-duty cheese press is a must!"*

1 pound New York sharp cheese, shredded
2 cups flour
2 teaspoons baking powder
2 teaspoons salt
1/4 teaspoon red pepper
12 to 14 tablespoons butter, softened

*Let the cheese stand until it reaches room temperature.
Sift the flour, baking powder, salt and red pepper together 3 times. Combine
with the cheese and butter in a large bowl and mix well.
Combine the "star" and "teeth" plates in a cookie press. Run the cheese
straws lengthwise on a foil-covered baking sheet. Bake at 350 degrees for
10 1/2 to 11 minutes. May add 1 1/2 ounces bleu cheese for a tangy flavor.
Note: The baking time must be watched carefully for each sheet of cheese
straws. If the edges become brown, the cheese straws are too well done. They
need to be crisp after cooling just enough to taste. Do not attempt to
bake 2 batches at the same time.*
Yield: Thirty Servings

Cheese Phyllo Turnovers

*These tasty little triangles would make a wonderful beginning
for your next dinner party.*

8 ounces Muenster cheese, shredded, or
8 ounces feta cheese, crumbled
1/3 cup chopped parsley
1/2 teaspoon salt
1/2 teaspoon pepper
2 tablespoons butter, softened
1 small egg
1 package frozen chopped spinach, thawed, drained (optional)
1 package phyllo dough sheets, thawed
2 to 3 tablespoons butter, softened

*Combine the cheese, parsley, salt, pepper, 2 tablespoons butter, egg and
spinach in a large bowl and mix well.
Cut the phyllo sheets into halves; work with only 1 piece at a time. Place 1/2 to
1 tablespoon of the spinach mixture in 1 corner of the piece. Fold this
corner over and over into a small triangle shape. Repeat the process
with the remaining phyllo and filling.
Arrange the triangles in a lightly buttered baking pan.
Brush the tops with 2 to 3 tablespoons butter.
Bake at 375 degrees for 20 to 25 minutes or until lightly browned.
Drain the excess butter from the pan immediately.
Serve hot.
May be frozen before baking. Bake as directed above without thawing.
Yield: Twelve Servings*

Cornmeal Blini with Smoked Salmon and Crème Fraîche

A Southernized version of the Russian classic uses cornmeal pancakes instead of the traditional buckwheat. A real gourmet treat.

1/2 cup unbleached flour
1/2 cup fine yellow cornmeal
2 teaspoons baking powder
1/2 teaspoon salt
3/4 cup milk
1 egg
2 tablespoons melted unsalted butter
1/2 cup Crème Fraîche (page 236) or sour cream
8 ounces smoked salmon, cut into slivers

Combine the flour, cornmeal, baking powder and salt in a large bowl and mix well.
Beat the milk and egg in a medium bowl. Pour over the flour mixture.
Mix lightly to make a medium-thick pancake batter, thinning with a small
amount of additional milk if needed. Stir in the butter.
Heat a nonstick skillet or griddle or a lightly oiled cast-iron skillet over medium heat.
Ladle in 2 teaspoons of the batter for each pancake. Bake for 2 minutes or until
the tops are bubbly. Turn and bake for 1 minute longer or until lightly brown. Remove
to an ovenproof dish and keep warm as the remaining batter is cooked.
To serve, place 1 heaping teaspoon Crème Fraîche on each pancake. Top with
salmon slivers. Garnish with capers, pickled onions, freshly ground black pepper,
red or black caviar, and/or snipped chives.
To prepare for an entrée, bake 2 tablespoons of the batter for each pancake. Arrange
3 or 4 blini on each of 4 warmed plates. Drape the salmon around the blini.
Dot each blini with Crème Fraîche. Garnish as above.
Yield: Twelve to Sixteen Servings

Cocktail Meatballs

Pictured on page 26, this quick and easy recipe for a large crowd will leave you time to attend to your guests! Serve on a platter with wooden picks or in a casserole or chafing dish.

1 large package frozen Italian meatballs
(approximately 150)
6 (10-ounce) cans tomato soup
1 cup packed brown sugar
1 (10-ounce) bottle Worcestershire sauce

1/3 cup mustard
1/3 cup vinegar
2/3 cup chopped onion
2/3 cup chopped green pepper
1 tablespoon butter

Brown the meatballs in the oven using the package directions. Bring the soup, brown sugar, Worcestershire sauce, mustard and vinegar to a boil in a 6-quart saucepan. Sauté the onion and green pepper in the butter in a skillet. Add the meatballs and onion mixture to the soup mixture. Simmer for 1 hour or longer. May substitute 1 package frozen stir-fry onions and peppers for the fresh onion and green pepper.
Yield: One Hundred Fifty Servings

Snappy Chicken Balls

Taste the flavors of the Caribbean in these savory nibbles. For those special parties, serve in a glass dish garnished with small yellow or white flowers or candied orange peel. Keeps well for three days.

2 cups chopped cooked chicken
1 1/2 cups almonds
1 tablespoon chopped green onions
1/4 cup chopped chutney
8 ounces cream cheese, softened

1/4 cup mayonnaise
2 teaspoons curry powder
Salt to taste
1 cup grated coconut

Process the chicken, almonds and green onions separately in a food processor fitted with a steel blade until very finely chopped. Mix the chicken, almonds, green onions and chutney in a medium bowl. Blend the cream cheese, mayonnaise, curry powder and salt in a large bowl. Stir in the chicken mixture. Chill thoroughly. Shape the mixture into bite-size balls. Roll in the coconut. Chill, covered, until serving time.
Yield: Eighty to Ninety Servings

Japanese Chicken Wings

Supply lots of napkins—the taste is well worth the sticky hands!

3 tablespoons soy sauce
3 tablespoons water
1 cup sugar
½ cup vinegar
1 teaspoon MSG

½ teaspoon salt
3 pounds chicken wings, cut into halves
1 egg, slightly beaten
1 cup flour
1 cup butter

Combine the soy sauce, water, sugar, vinegar, MSG and salt in a bowl and mix well.
Rinse the chicken and pat dry. Dip the chicken in the egg, then in the flour.
Fry the chicken in the butter in a skillet until deep brown and crispy. Arrange the
chicken in a shallow baking pan. Pour the soy sauce mixture over the chicken.
Bake at 350 degrees for 30 minutes or until the chicken is cooked through,
basting with the pan juices occasionally.
Yield: Sixteen to Eighteen Servings

Ham Party Rolls

Pop-in-your-mouth delicious!

1 (8-ounce) jar Dijon mustard
1/2 cup butter or margarine, softened
2 tablespoons poppy seeds
Worcestershire sauce to taste
2 packages party rolls
12 ounces thinly sliced cooked ham, cut into short pieces
8 ounces thinly sliced Swiss cheese

Mix the Dijon mustard, butter, poppy seeds and Worcestershire sauce in a bowl. Split the rolls horizontally into 2 layers, leaving the bottom halves in the foil pans. Spread each tray of rolls with 1/4 of the mustard mixture. Cover with the ham and cheese. Spread with the remaining mustard mixture. Replace the tops of the rolls. Bake at 375 degrees for 15 minutes or until heated through.
Yield: Twenty-Four Servings

Sesame Pork Strips

Meaty tidbits to enjoy with your guests' favorite cocktails.

1 1/2 pounds pork steak or pork fillets, cut into 1/2-inch slices, trimmed
1/4 cup soy sauce
1 tablespoon honey
2 to 3 tablespoons dry sherry
Freshly ground pepper to taste
1/2 teaspoon powdered ginger
1 clove of garlic, crushed
2 tablespoons toasted sesame seeds
Chicken broth

Place the pork in a shallow glass dish. Mix the next 7 ingredients in a bowl. Pour over the pork. Marinate at room temperature for 2 to 3 hours, turning frequently. Drain the marinade, reserving the sesame seeds. Discard the marinade. Place the pork in a roasting pan. Top with the reserved seeds. Roast at 350 degrees for 45 minutes or until cooked through, turning frequently and basting with the chicken broth. Cut the pork into small diagonal slices. Spear with cocktail picks and serve at room temperature.
Yield: Six to Eight Servings

Baked Oysters with Italian Herbs

This wonderful appetizer can also serve six as an entrée.

1 ⅓ cups Italian bread crumbs
½ cup grated Parmesan cheese
¼ teaspoon salt
½ teaspoon coarsely ground black pepper
¼ teaspoon cayenne
1 teaspoon dried basil
1 teaspoon dried oregano
4 pints oysters
½ cup butter
½ cup olive oil
½ cup chopped green onions
¼ cup chopped fresh parsley
2 tablespoons minced garlic

Combine the bread crumbs, cheese, salt, black pepper, cayenne,
basil and oregano in a bowl and mix well.
Drain the oysters well on paper towels.
Heat the butter and olive oil in a large skillet. Add the green onions,
parsley and garlic. Sauté until tender.
Add the bread crumb mixture to the skillet and mix well. Remove from the heat.
Stir in the oysters gently. Spoon into a large shallow baking dish.
Bake at 425 degrees for 20 minutes or until browned.
Serve immediately.
Yield: Eight to Ten Servings

Caponata

Be sure to prepare this dish a few hours before serving to allow the flavors to blend and you'll discover a zesty appetizer.

1/2 cup olive oil
1 (1-pound) eggplant, cut into 1/2-inch cubes
1 medium onion, coarsely chopped
1/2 cup thinly sliced celery
3/4 cup tomato purée
3/4 cup water
1/4 cup tomato paste
1 teaspoon salt
1/8 teaspoon pepper
1 1/2 teaspoons brown sugar
1/2 cup thinly sliced pimento-stuffed olives
1/4 cup sliced black olives (optional)

Heat the olive oil in a 10-inch skillet over medium heat. Add the eggplant. Cook until tender-crisp, stirring frequently. Remove the eggplant with a slotted spoon and set aside. Cook the onion in the remaining olive oil in the skillet until golden brown. Add the eggplant, celery, tomato purée, water, tomato paste, salt, pepper, brown sugar, stuffed olives and black olives and mix well. Simmer, covered, for 35 to 40 minutes or until the eggplant is tender and the sauce has thickened, stirring occasionally. Serve in peeled avocado halves.

May use as an omelet filling. May serve warm, at room temperature or cold as a spread with crackers.

Yield: Three to Four Cups

Fried Dill Pickles

*It may sound strange, but this tantalizing Mississippi creation is
great when served with catfish. For best results, be sure to
buy the crispest dills you can find.*

1½ cups flour
Salt and black pepper to taste
1 egg
1 cup milk
2 teaspoons Worcestershire sauce
¼ teaspoon hot pepper sauce
¼ teaspoon ground cayenne
¼ teaspoon garlic powder
Vegetable oil for frying
10 baby dill pickles, cut crosswise into ¼-inch slices

*Combine the flour, salt and black pepper in a small bowl and mix well.
Beat the egg and milk in a medium bowl. Add the Worcestershire sauce, hot pepper
sauce, cayenne, garlic powder and additional salt and black pepper and mix well.
Pour enough oil into a large heavy saucepan to measure 2 inches. Heat over medium-
high heat until a deep-fry thermometer inserted into the oil registers 350 degrees.
Dip the pickle slices a few at a time into the egg mixture, then into the seasoned flour.
Drop carefully into the hot oil. Move the pickles around with a slotted spoon for 1
minute or until evenly browned. Remove to paper towels to drain.
Keep each batch warm as the other batches are cooking.*

Serve hot.

Yield: Four Servings

Toasted Pecans

No truly Southern occasion is complete without lots of these on hand!

Heat 1 quart pecans, ¹/₂ cup butter and salt to taste in a heavy skillet, stirring to mix well. Pour the mixture onto a nonstick baking sheet. Bake at 325 degrees for 30 minutes. Adjust the seasoning.
Yield: 1 quart

Mushrooms Stuffed with Spinach

This superb taste combination, pictured on page 26, is great for a fir: course or a vegetable serving at a formal dinner. Use smaller mushroom caps for an hors d'oeuvre tray at your next party.

2 small packages frozen chopped spinach
16 ounces cream cheese, softened
¹/₄ cup grated Parmesan cheese
Salt and pepper to taste
24 giant mushroom caps
¹/₂ cup melted butter

Cook the spinach using the package directions; drain well.
Combine the spinach, cream cheese, Parmesan cheese, salt and pepper in a large bowl and mix well.
Brush the mushroom caps with some of the butter. Arrange in a 9x13-inch glass baking dish sprayed with nonstick cooking spray.
Spoon the spinach mixture into the mushroom caps. Sprinkle with additiona Parmesan cheese. Drizzle with the remaining butter.
Broil for 3 to 5 minutes or until the spinach mixture is bubbly and the Parmesan cheese begins to brown.
Yield: Twenty-Four Servings

Fresh Tomato Tart

*Pictured on page 26 with sweet orange-cherry tomatoes—a great way to
enjoy any tomato as an appetizer or side dish.*

Basic Pastry Dough
8 ounces mozzarella cheese, shredded
2 tablespoons chopped fresh basil
4 to 5 ripe tomatoes, cut into 1/2-inch slices
1/2 teaspoon salt
1/4 teaspoon pepper
1/4 cup extra-virgin olive oil

*Line a tart pan with the pastry. Spread with the cheese. Sprinkle with the basil.
Arrange the tomato slices evenly over the cheese. Sprinkle with the salt
and pepper. Drizzle with the olive oil.
Bake at 400 degrees for 30 to 40 minutes or until bubbly and heated through.
Slice into wedges and serve hot, garnished with additional chopped fresh basil.*
Yield: Eight to Ten Servings

Basic Pastry Dough

1 1/2 cups flour
1/2 teaspoon salt
1/2 cup shortening
1/2 cup cold water

*Combine the flour and salt in a bowl. Cut in the shortening until crumbly. Add
the cold water gradually, mixing until a stiff dough forms. Roll on a
floured surface to desired thickness.*
Yield: One Pastry

Flavored Coffees

These special coffees are sophisticated finales to elegant dinner parties. The Irish Coffee could actually serve as a dessert, and the Café Brûlot is a dramatic way to end an evening.

Irish Coffee

1 cup hot dark roast drip coffee
1 ounce Irish whiskey
2 teaspoons sugar
Whipped cream

Pour the coffee into a 6-ounce stemmed wine glass until it is 1 inch from the rim. Add the whiskey and stir in the sugar. Mound whipped cream over the coffee until it rises 1 inch above the rim of the glass.
Yield: One Serving

Café Brûlot

2 ounces brandy or Cognac
2 sugar cubes
2 cinnamon sticks
2 allspice seeds
2 whole cloves
1 small piece of lemon peel
1 small piece of orange peel
2 cups freshly brewed dark roast drip coffee

Combine the brandy, sugar, cinnamon sticks, allspice, cloves, lemon peel and orange peel in a silver bowl. Ignite and stir until the sugar is dissolved. Add the coffee. Ladle into demitasse cups or Café Brûlot cups.
Yield: Four to Six Servings

Perfect Tea

The English will constantly remind Americans that they cannot make a proper pot of tea. Southerners will constantly remind their Northern neighbors that they cannot make a proper glass of tea, iced that is. No matter what your roots, here are directions for hot, iced, and mint tea.

Loose tea leaves or tea bags
Freshly drawn water

Fill a teapot with boiling water. Let stand until the teapot is thoroughly heated; pour off the water. Place in the teapot 1 rounded teaspoon tea leaves or 1 tea bag for each cup to be brewed. Bring the fresh water to a boil in a tea kettle or saucepan. Pour into the teapot 1 cup of water for each cup of tea. Brew, covered, for 3 to 5 minutes or to desired strength. Remove the tea bags and strain the tea into a preheated pot or cups. Sweeten to taste. Serve immediately with thin lemon, orange or lime slices; lemon, orange or lime juice; whole cloves; sprigs of fresh mint; cream; sugar; and/or sugar syrup.

For Iced Tea, brew as directed above, using 1 tablespoon tea leaves or 2 tea bags for each 8 ounces of boiling water. Strain or remove the tea bags and pour the hot tea into tall glasses filled with crushed ice or ice cubes. Sweeten to taste.

For Minted Iced Tea, brew as directed above, using 1 tablespoon tea leaves or 2 tea bags for each 8 ounces of boiling water. Strain or remove tea bags. For each 2 cups of hot tea, add 2 sprigs of fresh mint, leaves bruised, and 3 tablespoons lemon juice. Let stand for 30 to 60 minutes. Strain into tall glasses filled with crushed ice or ice cubes. Sweeten to taste.

Yield: Variable

Spiced Tea

Make this spicy tea hot for cold winter days or chill it for summer.

1 quart water
1 cinnamon stick
1 teaspoon whole cloves
6 tea bags
1 (46-ounce) can unsweetened pineapple juice
1 (46-ounce) can unsweetened orange juice
1/2 cup lemon juice
1 1/2 cups sugar

*Combine the water, cinnamon stick and cloves in a large saucepan. Boil for 5 minutes.
Remove from the heat and add the tea bags. Let steep for 10 minutes.
Strain through a sieve into a large container. Add the pineapple juice, orange juice,
lemon juice and sugar and mix well.*
Yield: One Gallon

Hot Spiced Cider

*A great drink for an evening meeting, after the game, after caroling, or as a
prelude to a winter's meal. It's especially good for the aroma it emits while
brewing. Add a peppermint swizzle stick for additional flavor and garnish.*

2 quarts apple cider
3 cinnamon sticks
2 teaspoons freshly grated nutmeg
2 teaspoons whole cloves
1/4 teaspoon ground allspice
1/4 cup sugar
1/2 cup fresh lemon juice
2 cups orange juice

*Combine the cider, cinnamon sticks, nutmeg, cloves, allspice,
sugar, lemon juice and orange juice in a large saucepan. Cook until heated
through. Strain into a large container. Serve garnished with orange slices.
May be prepared ahead and reheated.*
Yield: Sixteen Servings

Champagne Punch

A classic for baby showers and Christenings.

2 cups maraschino cherries with stems
1½ cups superfine sugar
2 cups lemon juice
5 cups cold water
2 quarts dry Champagne or sparkling grape juice
1 quart ginger ale

Fill an ice ring mold half full with cherries. Add enough water to fill. Freeze until solid.
Mix the sugar, lemon juice and cold water in a large bowl. Pour into a punch bowl.
Add the Champagne and ginger ale and mix well. Add the ice ring.
The sugar mixture may be prepared several days ahead and refrigerated until needed.
Yield: Twenty-Five Servings

Holiday Eggnog

Guaranteed to liven up any holiday gathering. If this doesn't
get your party going, nothing will! Equally good without the alcohol.

6 egg yolks
2 cups sugar
1 pint bourbon
1 cup Jamaican rum
1 cup brandy
3 pints heavy cream
2 cups milk
6 egg whites
Ground nutmeg to taste

Beat the egg yolks and sugar in a bowl until thick. Add the bourbon, rum and
brandy gradually, stirring constantly. Blend in the cream and milk.
Beat the egg whites in a mixer bowl until stiff but not dry peaks form. Fold into
the eggnog. Pour into a punch bowl. Cover and chill thoroughly.
Ladle into punch cups. Sprinkle with nutmeg.
Yield: Twenty-Five Servings

Iced Tea Punch

The blend of juices makes this iced tea drink a refreshing change for summer afternoons on the porch. Garnish with some fresh mint from the garden.

6 small tea bags
4 cups boiling water
1 (6-ounce) can frozen orange juice concentrate, thawed
1 (6-ounce) can frozen lemonade concentrate, thawed
1 cup pineapple juice
1½ cups sugar
10 cups cold water

Steep the tea bags in boiling water for 5 minutes or until of desired strength. Discard the tea bags. Combine the tea, concentrates, pineapple juice, sugar and cold water in a large container and mix well. Pour into a punch bowl. Serve over ice and a sprig of fresh mint.
Yield: One Gallon

Sangria

This wine punch favorite originated in Spain and is the perfect starter for an elegant Sunday brunch.

5 tablespoons chilled orange juice
3 tablespoons chilled lemon juice
1 cup chilled water
2 tablespoons superfine sugar
1 quart cabernet or merlot, chilled
1 cup chilled brandy
1 (12-ounce) bottle club soda, chilled
1 lemon, thinly sliced, seeded
1 orange, thinly sliced, seeded

Combine the orange juice, lemon juice, water and sugar in a punch bowl or large pitcher and stir until the sugar is dissolved. Add the wine, brandy and club soda and stir gently. Add the fruit. Chill for several hours to allow the flavors to blend. Serve in punch cups with at least 1 slice of fruit or a twist.
Yield: Sixteen Servings

Spicy Bloody Marys

The spiciest Bloody Mary you'll ever love to drink! And, yes, the Worcestershire sauce measurement is correct! Pictured on page 20.

1 (46-ounce) can tomato juice
1 cup vodka
½ cup Worcestershire sauce
½ cup lemon juice
4 to 6 drops of Tabasco sauce
1 teaspoon celery salt
1 teaspoon celery seeds (optional)

Combine the tomato juice, vodka, Worcestershire sauce, lemon juice, Tabasco sauce, celery salt and celery seeds in a large pitcher and mix well. Chill, covered, for 24 hours. Serve over ice cubes. Garnish with celery sticks.
Yield: Eight Servings

Martini

Pictured on page 26. James Bond (maybe he was from Southern England) likes them stirred, not shaken—or was it shaken, not stirred? Don't forget the olives, or, if you prefer, a twist of lemon zest!

3 ounces gin
Sweet vermouth
Olives or twist of lemon zest

Chill and frost a 9-ounce clear stemmed goblet in the freezer. Place 5 ice cubes in the frosted glass. Pour the gin over the ice. Pass the shadow of the vermouth bottle over the glass. Stir very gently; do not bruise the gin. Top with the olives. Drink carefully.
One Serving

Kir Royale

The delectable flavor of raspberries comes through in this Champagne cocktail.

Pour 2 tablespoons chambourd (raspberry liqueur) into a Champagne glass. Fill with your favorite chilled Champagne. Garnish with a fresh raspberry.
Yield: One Serving

Mint Julep

The Mint Julep is to Southern libations as grits are to a proper Southern breakfast. A must on Derby Day, this bourbon cocktail is prepared in a sterling silver julep cup (pictured on page 26) and sipped most enjoyably on hot summer days.

20 large sprigs of fresh mint
2 cups sugar
2 cups water
2¹/₂ cups aged Kentucky bourbon

Rinse the mint and pat dry. Select and reserve 10 sprigs for a garnish. Place the remaining sprigs between double layers of paper towels. Roll with a rolling pin until the mint is bruised. Combine the sugar, water and mint in a medium saucepan. Bring to a boil over low heat; reduce the heat to very low. Simmer for 5 minutes, stirring until the sugar dissolves. Remove from the heat and let cool completely. Discard the mint. To serve, pour ¹/₄ cup of the mint syrup into each silver cup or glass goblet. Fill with finely crushed ice. Let stand until a frost forms on the outside of the cups. Add the bourbon. Stir with a chopping motion with a long-handled spoon. Garnish with the reserved mint.
Yield: Ten Servings

Peach Smash

Fresh ripe peaches are plentiful in the South each summer. Enjoy them in this smashing peach daiquiri.

2 ripe peaches, pitted, cut into chunks
1 (6-ounce) can frozen limeade concentrate, thawed
1 limeade can rum
2 teaspoons confectioners' sugar
¹/₂ teaspoon almond extract
6 ice cubes

Combine the peaches, concentrate, rum, confectioners' sugar, flavoring and ice cubes in a blender container. Process until puréed. Serve immediately.
Yield: Four Servings

Breads

Sims Home

Bill and Betty Sims' home, "Sunshine,"
aptly named for both its sunny color and the
disposition of its owners, is centered in a lovely
rural space just outside the city.
Dr. Bill mends bones as an occupation and works
wood in his spare time. Betty is one of Decatur's
best known cooks and caterers.
Bread is a staple of the Southern diet, and rarely
is a meal served without it. What better setting
for our selection—perhaps straight from Betty's
kitchen—than a bench from Bill's workshop.

*Pictured are Boules; Croissants;
French Baguettes; Spoon Bread;
Corn Pones; and Honey Wheat Bread.*

Banana Bread

For special breakfasts or brunch, serve this bread with a variety of muffins, bagels, and other breads in a large basket lined with colorful cloth napkins. Added ribbons and bows make it a centerpiece! Pictured on page 20.

1³/₄ cups flour
1 teaspoon baking soda
¹/₂ teaspoon salt
¹/₂ cup melted butter

1 cup sugar
2 eggs
1 teaspoon vanilla extract
2 very ripe bananas, mashed

Mix the flour, baking soda and salt together. Combine the butter and sugar in a mixer bowl and mix well. Beat in the eggs 1 at a time. Stir in the vanilla. Add the flour mixture gradually, beating well after each addition. Stir in the bananas. Pour into a greased and floured loaf pan. Bake at 375 degrees for 45 to 60 minutes or until the loaf tests done.
Yield: Twelve Servings

Cheddar-Olive Bread

Here's a flavorful bread for modern cooks with bread machines.

³/₄ cup water
2 cups flour
³/₄ cup shredded sharp Cheddar cheese
1 tablespoon sugar

¹/₂ teaspoon salt
³/₄ teaspoon quick-acting yeast
¹/₂ cup small pimento-stuffed
olives, drained

Measure the water, flour, cheese, sugar, salt and yeast into the bread machine pan in the order the manufacturer suggests. Add the olives at the time of the raisin/nut signal or 5 to 10 minutes before the last kneading cycle ends. Bake using the regular or rapid-bake cycle; do not use the delayed bake cycle. Remove to a wire rack to cool. For a large loaf, increase the water to 1 cup plus 2 tablespoons, the flour to 3 cups, the cheese to 1¹/₄ cups, the sugar to 1¹/₂ tablespoons, the salt to ³/₄ teaspoon, the yeast to 1¹/₄ teaspoons and the olives to ³/₄ cup.
Yield: Twelve to Fifteen Servings

Dill Bread

This is wonderful with soups in the winter and makes a real summer statement as part of a cold roast beef sandwich.

1 envelope dry yeast
¼ cup warm (105 to 115 degrees) water
1 cup creamed cottage cheese
1 tablespoon minced onion
2 teaspoons dillseed
1 teaspoon salt
¼ teaspoon baking soda
1 egg, beaten
2 tablespoons honey
1 tablespoon butter or margarine
2½ cups flour

Dissolve the yeast in the warm water.
Heat the cottage cheese to lukewarm in a saucepan. Add the onion, dillseed, salt, baking soda, egg, honey and butter. Cook until the mixture is heated through and the butter is melted.
Combine the flour, yeast and cottage cheese mixture in a large bowl and mix until a soft dough forms. Cover and let rise in a warm place for 1 hour or until doubled in bulk.
Place in a greased 5x9-inch loaf pan. Let rise in a warm place for 30 minutes.
Bake at 350 degrees for 35 minutes or until golden brown.
Yield: Twelve Servings

Dill

A versatile herb, dill is found in everything from potato salad to basting sauces. Its name originated from the Norse word "dilla," which means "to lull," and it has been known to soothe an upset stomach, relieve gas, and stimulate milk production in nursing mothers. The plant's delicate green stems are snipped and used fresh or dried (dillweed). Flowers are often placed in pickle jars for added flavor and eye appeal. The seeds, which are produced after flowering, are also used in breads and salads.

French Baguettes

Crusty French bread, or baguettes (pictured on page 58), are long, slender golden loaves full of flavor and fragrance and bakeable in your very own oven.

1 envelope dry yeast
1/4 cup warm (110 to 115 degrees) water
2 tablespoons butter, softened
1 tablespoon sugar
1 1/2 teaspoons salt

3/4 cup hot water
3 3/4 cups sifted flour
1 egg white, slightly beaten
1 tablespoon water

Soften the yeast in the warm water. Let stand for 5 to 10 minutes or until dissolved. Combine the butter, sugar and salt in a large bowl and mix well. Pour the hot water over the mixture, stirring constantly until the butter is melted and the mixture is lukewarm. Blend in 1/2 cup of the flour, beating until smooth. Stir the yeast mixture and add to the sugar mixture, beating well.

Add approximately half the remaining flour to the yeast mixture and beat until quite smooth. Add enough of the remaining flour to make a soft dough. Turn onto a lightly floured surface. Let rest for 5 to 10 minutes. Knead the dough for 5 to 8 minutes or until smooth and elastic, using as little additional flour as possible.

Warm a deep bowl with hot water. Dry the bowl and butter lightly.

Shape the dough into a smooth ball. Place in the bowl, turning to grease the surface of the dough. Cover with waxed paper and a towel. Let rise in a warm place for 1 1/2 to 2 hours or until doubled in bulk.

Punch the dough down. Fold the edge toward the center and turn the dough over. Cover and let rise for 45 minutes or until almost doubled in bulk. Punch down again and turn onto a lightly floured surface. Roll into an 8x14-inch rectangle. Roll up tightly into a long slender loaf, pinching the ends to seal. Roll the dough back and forth between the palms of the hands, pulling to lengthen and taper the ends.

Butter lightly a 12x15-inch baking sheet; sprinkle with cornmeal or farina.

Place the dough diagonally on the prepared baking sheet. Make diagonal cuts 1/4 inch deep at 2-inch intervals with a sharp knife.

Mix the egg white and 1 tablespoon water in a bowl. Brush part of the mixture over the loaf. Cover the loaf with a towel. Let rise in a warm place until doubled in bulk. Brush with some of the egg white mixture. Bake at 425 degrees for 15 minutes. Brush with the remaining egg white mixture. Bake for 20 minutes longer or until golden brown.

Yield: Fifteen to Eighteen Servings

Boules

Many area food connoisseurs enjoy dining at the Green Bottle Grill in Huntsville. Enjoy their luscious loaves, pictured on page 58.

1/4 teaspoon sugar
2 teaspoons salt
2 cups water
2 envelopes dry yeast
6 cups bread flour
1 egg white, slightly beaten
1 tablespoon water

Dissolve the sugar and salt in 2 cups water in a glass measure.
Sprinkle with the yeast and stir. Let stand for 5 minutes or
until the yeast begins to foam.
Pour into a heavy-duty mixer bowl.
Add 4 cups of the flour and mix until blended. Add the remaining 2 cups flour
gradually, mixing with a dough hook or by hand until thoroughly blended.
Knead for 5 minutes longer or until smooth and elastic.
Place the dough in a clean bowl or on a wooden board. Cover with a damp
cloth. Let rise for 30 to 45 minutes or until doubled in bulk.
Divide the dough into 4 equal portions and shape into round balls.
Place on a nonstick baking sheet.
Mix the egg white with 1 tablespoon water. Brush over the tops of the loaves.
Let rise for 1 hour or until doubled in bulk.
Bake at 425 degrees for 20 minutes or until golden brown.
Yield: Four Round Loaves
Green Bottle Grill

French Bread

French bread is characterized by a crisp and golden outside and a moist and soft inside. In France, this is produced by the hot brick floors of their huge baking ovens—hardly an American appliance these days! This procedure can be somewhat replicated in one of two ways: (1) by placing a large baking stone on the bottom of the oven and preheating it for 30 minutes or (2) by placing a flat heatproof pan or cast-iron skillet on the bottom of the oven and filling it with boiling water at the beginning of the baking period. For even crustier bread, mist lightly with a spray bottle of water halfway through the baking time.

Hawaiian Sweet Bread

Pineapple juice and ginger add a tropical flavor to this sweet yeast bread. Wrap in a pretty napkin, tie with a ribbon, or place in a basket to welcome a new neighbor—aloha!

7 cups bread flour
3/4 cup instant potato flakes
2/3 cup sugar
1 teaspoon salt
1/2 teaspoon ginger
2 teaspoons vanilla extract
2 envelopes quick-acting yeast
1 cup milk
1/2 cup margarine
1/2 cup water
1 cup pineapple juice, at room temperature
3 eggs

Combine 3 cups of the flour, potato flakes, sugar, salt, ginger, vanilla and yeast in a large mixer bowl and mix well.
Heat the milk, margarine and water in a saucepan until very warm (120 to 130 degrees).
Add the milk mixture, pineapple juice and eggs to the flour mixture. Blend at low speed just until moistened. Beat at medium speed for 4 minutes.
Stir in 3 cups of the flour gradually, mixing until a stiff dough forms.
Turn onto a floured surface. Knead in the remaining flour for 5 to 8 minutes or until the dough is smooth and elastic.
Place the dough in a greased bowl, turning to grease the surface. Cover loosely with plastic wrap and a towel. Let rise in a warm place for 1 to 1 1/2 hours or until doubled in bulk.
Punch the dough down. Divide into 3 equal portions; shape each portion into a ball. Place in 3 greased 8- or 9-inch round baking pans. Cover and let rise in a warm place for 1 hour or until doubled in bulk.
Bake at 375 degrees for 25 to 35 minutes or until golden brown.
Remove from the pans immediately.
Yield: Thirty-Six Servings

Honey Wheat Bread

A good hearty loaf for sandwiches or with soups. Pictured on page 58.

1½ cups nonfat dry milk
2 teaspoons salt
7 to 8 cups whole wheat flour
2 tablespoons dry yeast

3 cups warm (105 to 115 degrees) water
½ cup vegetable oil or melted butter
½ cup honey

Combine the dry milk powder, salt and 3 cups of the flour in a bowl and mix well. Dissolve the yeast in the water in a large bowl. Add the oil and honey. Add the dry milk mixture. Beat for 150 strokes. Add enough of the remaining flour to make a stiff dough.

Turn onto a floured surface. Knead for 5 minutes or until smooth and elastic.

Let rise, covered, in a warm place until doubled in bulk.

Punch the dough down. Shape into 3 loaves and place in oiled loaf pans.

Let rise in a warm place until the dough rises 1 inch above the top of the pans.

Bake at 350 degrees for 30 minutes or until golden brown.

Note: If you measure the oil first and then measure the honey without washing the measuring cup, the honey will slide right out without sticking.

Yield: Forty-Five Servings

Rye Bread

A hearty bread, great with soups and Reuben sandwiches.

1 cup milk
2 tablespoons honey
1 tablespoon sugar
1 tablespoon salt
1 tablespoon butter
1 envelope dry yeast
3/4 cup warm water
1 tablespoon caraway seeds
2 1/2 cups rye flour
2 1/2 cups all-purpose flour
1/4 cup cornmeal
1 egg white
2 tablespoons water

*Scald the milk in a saucepan. Add the honey, sugar, salt and butter
and mix well. Cool to lukewarm.
Sprinkle the yeast over the warm water in a large warm bowl,
stirring until dissolved. Add the milk mixture.
Add the caraway seeds and rye flour and beat well. Add enough
of the all-purpose flour to make a soft dough.
Turn onto a lightly floured board. Knead for 7 minutes or until smooth and
elastic. Place in a greased bowl, turning to grease the surface. Let rise, covered,
in a warm place for 1 1/2 hours or until doubled in bulk.
Turn onto a lightly floured board. Divide the dough into 2 equal portions.
Shape each piece into a smooth ball. Flatten each piece slightly.
Roll lightly to form loaves. Sprinkle 2 baking sheets with the cornmeal.
Place the loaves on the prepared baking sheets.
Beat the egg white and 2 tablespoons water in a cup. Brush over the loaves.
Let rise, uncovered, in a warm place for 35 minutes.
Bake at 400 degrees for 25 minutes. Cool on wire racks.*
Yield: Twenty-Four Servings

Strawberry Bread

Strawberries are not just for breakfast anymore! Whip up two of these colorful loaves and share one with a new neighbor or a sick friend.

3 cups flour
2 cups sugar
1 tablespoon cinnamon
1 teaspoon baking soda
1 teaspoon salt

1 cup chopped pecans or walnuts
2 (10-ounce) packages frozen
strawberries, thawed
4 eggs
1 1/4 cups vegetable oil

*Combine the flour, sugar, cinnamon, baking soda, salt and pecans
in a large bowl and mix well.
Mix the strawberries, eggs and oil in a medium bowl. Add to the flour mixture
and mix well. Pour into 2 greased and floured loaf pans.
Bake at 350 degrees for 1 hour or until the loaves test done.*
Yield: Twenty-Four Servings

Zucchini Bread

*If you have a garden, you'll be relieved to discover another use for this most
prolific squash. If you don't, you'll happily purchase zucchini or gladly accept
some from a neighbor's surplus to make this moist, delicious bread.*

3 eggs
1 cup vegetable oil
2 cups sugar
1 tablespoon vanilla extract
2 cups grated zucchini
3 cups flour

1 teaspoon salt
1 teaspoon baking soda
2 teaspoons cinnamon
1/2 teaspoon baking powder
1/2 cup chopped pecans or walnuts

*Combine the eggs, oil, sugar, vanilla, zucchini, flour, salt, baking soda,
cinnamon, baking powder and pecans in a large bowl and mix well.
Pour into 2 greased loaf pans.
Bake at 350 degrees for 1 hour or until the loaves test done.*
Yield: Twenty-Four Servings

Jalapeño Corn Bread

Serve this colorful corn bread alongside a steaming pot of chili for the perfect weekend supper for friends and family.

3 cups self-rising cornmeal or
corn bread mix
3 tablespoons sugar
1 teaspoon salt
1 1/2 cups grated medium-sharp
Cheddar cheese

1 large onion, chopped
1 cup vegetable oil
1 1/2 cups milk
3 eggs
1 small can whole kernel corn
3 jalapeños, chopped

*Combine the cornmeal, sugar and salt in a large bowl and mix well.
Add the cheese, onion, oil, milk, eggs, corn and jalapeños and mix well.
Pour into a greased 9x13-inch baking pan.
Bake at 400 degrees for 30 to 40 minutes or until the corn bread tests done.*
Yield: Fifteen to Eighteen Servings

Cinnamon Rolls

*These longtime bake sale favorites will enliven any family breakfast
and are pretty enough for company brunch.*

1 cup scalded milk, cooled to lukewarm
6 tablespoons melted margarine,
cooled to lukewarm
1/2 cup sugar
2 envelopes dry yeast
1 tablespoon sugar
1 teaspoon salt
1 cup lukewarm water
3 eggs, beaten

7 cups flour
3 tablespoons melted margarine
1 1/2 cups packed brown sugar
1/2 cup sugar
1 tablespoon cinnamon
2 cups confectioners' sugar
2 tablespoons vegetable oil
2 tablespoons light corn syrup
3 tablespoons hot water

Combine the milk, 6 tablespoons margarine and 1/2 cup sugar in a
medium bowl and mix well.
Combine the yeast, 1 tablespoon sugar, salt and lukewarm water in a large bowl,
stirring until the yeast is dissolved. Add the milk mixture and mix well.
Add the eggs and 2 cups of the flour, beating well. Add enough of the
remaining flour, stirring to make a smooth dough.
Turn onto a floured surface. Knead in remaining flour until smooth and elastic.
Place in a greased bowl, turning to grease the surface. Let rise, covered,
in a warm place until doubled in bulk.
Divide the dough into 4 equal portions. Roll each portion 1/2 inch thick on a floured
surface. Spread each with the remaining margarine. Sprinkle with a
mixture of the brown sugar, 1/2 cup sugar and cinnamon. Roll as for jelly rolls;
cut each roll into 1/2-inch slices.
Place the slices in four greased 9-inch round baking pans. Let rise, covered,
in a warm place until doubled in bulk.
Bake at 350 degrees for 20 to 25 minutes or until golden brown.
Combine the confectioners' sugar, oil, corn syrup and hot water in a
bowl and mix well. Spread over the rolls.
Yield: Four Dozen

Yeast Rolls

There is nothing in the world like the smell of freshly baked rolls. Try this simple recipe or one of the variations and enjoy the aroma!

1 package dry yeast	1 to 3½ tablespoons sugar
¼ cup lukewarm water	1 cup boiling water
¼ cup shortening	1 egg, beaten
1¼ teaspoons salt	3 cups flour

Dissolve the yeast in the lukewarm water. Combine the shortening, salt and sugar in a large bowl. Add the boiling water, stirring until dissolved. Let cool to lukewarm. Add the yeast mixture and egg and mix well. Add the flour, beating until a smooth dough forms. Place the dough in a greased large bowl, turning to grease the surface. Chill, covered, overnight. Pinch off pieces of the dough and shape into small balls. Place 3 balls in each greased muffin cup. Let rise in a warm place for 1 hour. Bake at 425 degrees for 15 minutes.

Yield: Two Dozen

For *Speedy Orange Rolls*, mix 1½ cups confectioners' sugar, ½ tablespoon grated orange peel, 3 tablespoons melted butter or margarine and 2 tablespoons orange juice in a bowl. Knead the dough on a lightly floured surface for 2 minutes or until smooth. Let stand, covered, for 15 minutes. Roll the dough into a 7x14-inch rectangle. Spread with half the orange filling, leaving a 1-inch margin on the long sides. Roll as for a jelly roll, beginning on the long side. Pinch the seam to seal; do not seal the ends. Cut into 12 equal slices. Place the slices cut side down in greased muffin cups. Let rise, covered, in a warm place for 30 minutes. Bake at 400 degrees for 16 to 18 minutes or until lightly browned. Spread with the remaining orange filling.

Yield: One Dozen

For *Onion Twist Rolls*, mix 1 cup sour cream with 1 envelope onion instant soup mix in a bowl. Knead the dough on a lightly floured surface for 8 minutes or until smooth and elastic. Divide into halves. Roll each half into a 6x12-inch rectangle. Spread half the sour cream mixture on each piece. Fold each rectangle into halves lengthwise and cut into 1-inch strips. Twist each strip and place on a greased baking sheet. Brush with a mixture of 1 slightly beaten egg and 1 tablespoon water. Sprinkle with sesame seeds to taste. Let rise, covered, in a warm place for 1 to 1½ hours or until doubled in bulk. Bake at 375 degrees for 20 minutes or until lightly browned.

Yield: Two Dozen

Croissants

With jams or preserves at breakfast, as a sandwich bread for lunch, or just plain with soup, salad or supper, these melt-in-your-mouth buttery French rolls (pictured on page 58) are delicious anytime.

2 cups flour
1/2 cup cold unsalted butter, cut into slices
1 envelope dry yeast
2/3 cup warm (105 to 115 degrees) skim milk
1/4 teaspoon salt
2 tablespoons sugar
1/4 cup flour
1/4 cup melted unsalted butter
1 egg
1 tablespoon water

Process 2 cups flour and 1/2 cup butter in a food processor until coarse crumbs form. Remove to a large bowl.

Mix the yeast and skim milk in the food processor container. Add the salt, sugar, 1/4 cup flour and 1/4 cup butter. Process until smooth. Combine with the first mixture, stirring just until moistened.

Chill, covered with plastic wrap, overnight or for a few days.

Shape into a ball, adding additional flour if needed for handling.

Divide the dough into 2 equal portions.

Roll each portion into a 14-inch circle on a lightly floured board. Cut each circle into 10 wedges for smaller croissants or 8 wedges for larger rolls. Roll up each wedge from the wide end.

Place the rolls point side down 1 inch apart in a lightly greased baking pan, curving the sides to form a crescent shape. Let rise, covered, in a warm place for 1 to 1 1/2 hours or until doubled in bulk.

Mix the egg and water in a cup. Brush some of the mixture lightly over the rolls. Bake at 400 degrees for 10 minutes. Brush with the remaining egg mixture. Bake for 5 minutes longer or until golden brown.

Yield: Sixteen to Twenty Servings

Scones

This British delicacy is traditionally baked in a cast-iron skillet or griddle. This baking sheet version bakes just as well in a hot oven and will be ready just in time for tea. Serve on a silver platter. Oh, yes, one lump or two?

2¹/₂ cups flour
1 tablespoon baking powder
¹/₂ teaspoon salt
¹/₂ cup cold unsalted butter, cut into pieces
¹/₄ to ¹/₃ cup sugar
²/₃ cup milk or cream

Combine the flour, baking powder and salt in a large bowl and mix well. Cut in the butter until crumbly. Add the sugar, tossing to mix. Add the milk, stirring with a fork until a soft dough forms. Shape the dough into a ball. Knead on a lightly floured surface 10 to 12 times or until smooth and elastic. Cut the dough into halves. Knead each half lightly into a ball. Turn the smooth side up and pat or roll into a 6-inch circle. Cut each circle into 6 to 8 wedges. Place the wedges on a nonstick baking sheet. For crisp sides, separate the wedges slightly; for soft sides, allow the wedges to touch. Bake at 425 degrees for 12 minutes or until the tops are medium brown. Remove to a wire rack lined with a linen or cotton towel. Cover the scones loosely with the cloth and cool completely.
Yield: Twelve to Sixteen Servings

For Whole Wheat Scones, substitute 1¹/₂ cups whole wheat flour for 1¹/₂ cups of the all-purpose flour. Bake at 375 degrees for 15 minutes.

For Lemon Scones, add 1 tablespoon freshly grated lemon peel to the flour mixture. Mix 2 teaspoons fresh lemon juice with 2 tablespoons sugar. Top each scone with ¹/₄ teaspoonful of the lemon juice mixture before baking.

For Lavender Scones, bring the milk and 1 tablespoon dried lavender flowers to a boil in a saucepan. Cool to lukewarm and strain into a measuring cup. Add enough milk to measure ²/₃ cup. Serve the scones plain or filled with whipped cream and sliced peaches or green grape halves.

For Scented Geranium Scones, add 4 or 5 very finely chopped scented geranium leaves (not regular geranium leaves) with the sugar or chop the leaves with the flour before adding the butter.

Cheese Scones

Try this variation of the scone for a brunch bread. Can't you just taste it with a spicy fruit dish? Pictured on page 20.

1 1/2 cups flour
1 1/2 teaspoons cream of tartar
1/2 teaspoon baking soda
1 teaspoon dry mustard
1/2 teaspoon salt
1/4 cup cold unsalted butter, cut into pieces
1 cup shredded sharp Cheddar cheese
2 tablespoons grated Parmesan cheese
1 large egg
1/2 cup milk or cream

Combine the flour, cream of tartar, baking soda, dry mustard and salt in a large bowl and mix well.
Cut in the butter until crumbly. Add the Cheddar cheese and Parmesan cheese and mix well.
Add the egg and milk and mix well. Shape the dough into a ball.
Turn onto a lightly floured board. Knead 10 to 12 times or until the dough is smooth and elastic. Cut the dough into halves. Knead each half lightly and turn the smooth side up. Pat or roll each into a 6-inch circle. Cut each circle into 6 to 8 wedges.
Place on a nonstick baking sheet.
Bake at 400 degrees for 12 minutes or until medium brown.
Yield: Twelve to Sixteen Servings

Angel Biscuits

Originally known as Alabama biscuits, the Heart of Dixie
state lays claim to these yeast and baking powder creations that were renamed
"Riz Biscuits" when the recipe appeared sometime in the 1950s on a
Martha White flour bag. Sometime after that, the title "angel biscuits" was
attached and the rest is history. A supreme advantage of the recipe
is that the dough can be stored in the refrigerator for approximately a week or
more and used as needed. Angel biscuits are delicious sliced while
warm and served with herb- or fruit-filled butter or filled with slivers
of country ham, smoked turkey, or smoked salmon.

2 envelopes dry yeast
1/4 cup warm (105 to 115 degrees) water
5 cups flour
1 tablespoon baking powder
1 teaspoon baking soda
2 1/2 tablespoons sugar
1 teaspoon salt
1 cup unsalted butter, cut into small pieces
2 cups buttermilk
1/2 cup melted unsalted butter, cooled to lukewarm

Butter a baking sheet or line with parchment paper.
Dissolve the yeast in the warm water. Let stand until the yeast begins to foam.
Sift the flour, baking powder, baking soda, sugar and salt into a large bowl. Cut in
1 cup butter until crumbly. Stir in the yeast and buttermilk.
Turn onto a floured board. Knead until the dough is smooth and no longer sticky. Roll
1 inch thick on a floured surface. Cut with a 1 1/2-inch biscuit cutter. Place the biscuits
2 inches apart on the prepared baking sheet. Brush the tops with 1/2 cup butter.
Bake at 450 degrees for 10 to 12 minutes or until light golden brown.
The recipe may be doubled. Unbaked biscuits that are cut out may be frozen on a
baking sheet until firm, stored in the freezer in a plastic bag, and baked as needed.
How wonderful to have weeks' worth of biscuit dough with only one dirty bowl!
Yield: Four Dozen

"Is That All There Is?" Sour Cream Muffins

Aptly titled after the inevitable question when this recipe is shared. These are a dependable standby when there are no homemade rolls in the freezer. There's nothing like fresh bread from the oven to keep a meal from looking thrown together or deli purchased!

1 cup sour cream
2 cups self-rising flour
1 cup melted butter

Mix the sour cream and flour in a bowl. Stir in the butter. Fill nonstick muffin cups almost to the top with the batter. Bake at 375 degrees for 10 to 15 minutes or until lightly browned.
Yield: One Dozen

"Done Buttered" Biscuits

This variation of the "Is that all there is?" makes preparation even easier if you have baking mix on hand.

1 cup sour cream
1/2 cup melted butter or margarine
2 cups baking mix

Mix the sour cream and butter in a bowl. Add the baking mix and mix well. Spoon batter into greased small muffin cups. Bake at 425 degrees for 12 to 14 minutes or until golden brown.
Yield: One Dozen

Self-Rising Flour

When the recipe calls for self-rising flour and it is not in the pantry, mix or sift together 3/4 cup all-purpose flour, 1 teaspoon baking powder and 1/4 teaspoon salt.

Cheese Herb Biscuits

Some great cooks insist that the secret to high-rising, tender biscuits is to pat out, rather than roll, the dough, and to press, not twist, the biscuit cutter into the dough. Pictured on page 20 with brunch, for a gourmet biscuit treat.

2 cups flour
1 tablespoon baking powder
1 teaspoon salt
1/4 cup shortening

3/4 cup shredded Gruyère cheese
1/4 cup chopped fresh dill
1 cup milk
2 tablespoons melted unsalted butter

Mix the flour, baking powder and salt with a fork in a bowl. Cut in the shortening until crumbly. Stir in the cheese and dill. Add the milk, stirring until a soft dough forms. Turn onto a lightly floured board. Knead quickly just until thoroughly mixed. Roll out 1/2 inch thick. Cut with a heart-shaped biscuit cutter. Place the biscuits on a nonstick baking sheet. Brush the tops with the butter. Bake at 450 degrees for 12 to 15 minutes or until golden brown.
Yield: One Dozen

Spoon Bread

Spoon bread (pictured on page 58) is a delicate and fluffy variation of corn bread. Properly served, it is ladled onto the plate. Properly eaten, it is dripping in butter!

1 cup white cornmeal
1 teaspoon salt
1 cup water

2 cups hot milk
2 eggs, beaten
3 tablespoons melted butter

Combine the cornmeal and salt in a 2-quart saucepan. Stir in the water. Stir in the milk gradually. Cook over low heat until thickened and smooth, stirring frequently. Stir a small amount of the hot mixture into the eggs; stir the eggs into the hot mixture. Add the butter, stirring constantly. Pour into a greased shallow 1 1/2-quart baking dish. Bake at 375 degrees for 40 to 50 minutes or until browned. Serve at once.
Yield: Six to Eight Servings

Broccoli Corn Bread Muffins

Pictured on page 20. Yes, local cooks from all around tell us you can't beat this Jiffy recipe. Who will argue these busy days?

1/2 (10-ounce) package frozen chopped broccoli
1 package Jiffy corn bread mix
1 onion, chopped

6 tablespoons melted butter
4 eggs
2 cups shredded Cheddar cheese
1/4 teaspoon salt (optional)

Cook the broccoli using the package directions and drain well. Combine with the corn bread mix, onion, butter, eggs and cheese in a bowl and mix well. Pour into a greased 8x8-inch baking pan. Bake at 350 degrees for 20 to 25 minutes or until golden brown. May be baked in muffin cups.
Yield: Eight to Ten Servings

Macadamia Nut Muffins

Macadamia nuts are one of many outstanding contributions from the islands of Hawaii. These melt-in-your-mouth morsels from caterer Lyla Peebles carry their smooth flavor into these moist and delicious muffins. Savor every bite!

1 cup flour
1 1/4 teaspoons baking powder
1/2 teaspoon salt
1/2 cup unsalted butter, softened
1 cup packed brown sugar
3 large eggs

3/4 teaspoon almond extract
1/2 teaspoon vanilla extract
1/4 cup whipping cream
3/4 cup coarsely chopped macadamia nuts
1/3 cup whole macadamia nuts

Sift the flour, baking powder and salt into a bowl. Cream the butter and brown sugar in a mixer bowl until light and fluffy. Beat in the eggs 1 at a time. Stir in the flavorings. Add the flour mixture gradually, beating well after each addition. Add the whipping cream, beating just until smooth. Fold in the chopped nuts. Spoon the batter into paper-lined muffin cups. Sprinkle each muffin with whole nuts. Bake at 350 degrees for 25 minutes or until a wooden pick inserted near the center comes out clean. Serve warm or at room temperature.
Yield: Ten Servings
Lyla Peebles, Lyla's Flowers and Fine Food

Raisin Bran Muffins

*Applesauce and buttermilk make this a good low-fat
way to have your muffin and eat it, too.*

1 (15-ounce) package Raisin Bran
5 cups flour
3 cups sugar
1 cup chopped pecans (optional)
5 teaspoons baking soda

4 eggs, beaten, or equivalent amount of
egg substitute
1 quart buttermilk
1 cup applesauce

*Combine the cereal, flour, sugar, pecans and baking soda in a large container and mix
well. Mix the eggs, buttermilk and applesauce in a bowl. Pour over the flour mixture,
stirring to mix well. Pour into greased muffin cups. Bake at 350 degrees for 20 minutes.*

Yield: Four to Five Dozen

Corn Pones

*Corn pone got its name from the Algonquin word "pone," which means bread
without milk or eggs. This regional treat is also sometimes known as
"hot water bread" for the same reason. Whatever the reason, it is a favorite
Southern staple of old, and it may be illegal to serve turnip
greens without it! Pictured on page 58.*

2 to 3 tablespoons shortening
1 cup white cornmeal, preferable
water-ground

1/2 teaspoon salt
Boiling water

*Melt the shortening in a heavy cast-iron skillet in a 450-degree oven. Mix the
cornmeal and salt in a bowl. Add enough boiling water to form a stiff dough. Remove
the skillet from the oven, tilting to coat the surface. Stir the unmelted shortening into the
cornmeal mixture. Shape the dough into small patties. Place in the hot skillet. Bake at
450 degrees for 20 to 30 minutes or until lightly browned and crisp. Note: The patties
may be placed in 1/4 inch melted shortening or bacon drippings in a skillet and cooked
on the stovetop. Fry the patties until golden brown, turning once. These pones will be
crisp on the outside but soft inside; the oven-baked pones are more crisp throughout.*

Yield: Eight to Ten Servings

Hush Puppies

2 cups white cornmeal
1 tablespoon flour
1 teaspoon baking soda
1 teaspoon baking powder
1 teaspoon salt

6 tablespoons finely chopped onion
1 egg, beaten
1 cup buttermilk
Vegetable oil or melted shortening for frying

Sift the cornmeal, flour, baking soda, baking powder and salt into a bowl. Add the onion and mix well. Stir in a mixture of the egg and buttermilk. Heat the oil to 375 degrees in a deep skillet or deep fryer. Drop the cornmeal mixture by teaspoonfuls into the hot oil. Deep fry until golden brown; when cooked through, the hush puppies will float. Drain on paper towels or on a brown paper bag.
Yield: Fifteen to Twenty Servings

Sour Cream Coffee Cake

Serve this sugar and spice coffee cake for a weekend morning treat, or make it a special part of a brunch menu.

2 cups flour
1 teaspoon baking soda
1 teaspoon baking powder
1 cup butter, softened
1 cup sugar
3 eggs
1 cup sour cream

1 teaspoon vanilla extract
1 cup packed brown sugar
2 tablespoons flour
2 tablespoons butter, softened
1 cup chopped pecans
1 teaspoon cinnamon

Mix 2 cups flour, baking soda and baking powder in a bowl. Cream 1 cup butter and 1 cup sugar in a mixer bowl until light and fluffy. Beat in the eggs 1 at a time. Beat in the sour cream and vanilla. Add the flour mixture gradually, beating well after each addition. Mix the brown sugar, 2 tablespoons flour, 2 tablespoons butter, pecans and cinnamon in a bowl. Layer the batter and brown sugar mixture ½ at a time in a nonstick tube pan. Bake at 350 degrees for 45 minutes. Cool slightly. Invert onto a serving plate.
Yield: Sixteen Servings

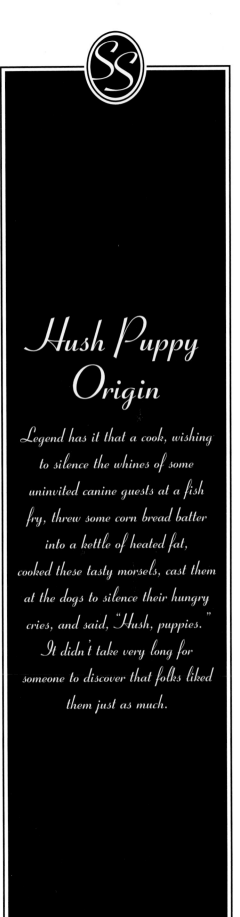

Hush Puppy Origin

Legend has it that a cook, wishing to silence the whines of some uninvited canine guests at a fish fry, threw some corn bread batter into a kettle of heated fat, cooked these tasty morsels, cast them at the dogs to silence their hungry cries, and said, "Hush, puppies." It didn't take very long for someone to discover that folks liked them just as much.

Cranberry Sour Cream Crumble

Delicious and attractive twist on a coffee cake. Good for brunch.

1/4 cup chopped almonds
1/2 cup flour
1/3 cup sugar
1/4 cup chopped almonds
1/4 cup melted butter
1/4 teaspoon vanilla extract
2 cups flour
1 1/4 teaspoons baking powder
1/2 teaspoon baking soda
1/4 teaspoon salt
1 cup sugar
1/2 cup butter, softened
1 teaspoon vanilla extract
2 eggs
1 cup light sour cream or nonfat sour cream
1 cup whole cranberry sauce

*Sprinkle 1/4 cup almonds in a greased 9-inch springform
pan or 10-inch tube pan; set aside.
For the topping, combine 1/2 cup flour, 1/3 cup sugar, 1/4 cup almonds, 1/4 cup
butter and 1/4 teaspoon vanilla in a small bowl and mix until crumbly; set aside.
Combine 2 cups flour, baking powder, baking soda and
salt in a large bowl and mix well; set aside.
For the batter, combine 1 cup sugar, 1/2 cup butter and 1 teaspoon vanilla in a mixer
bowl. Beat at medium speed for 1 to 2 minutes or until well mixed, scraping the bowl
frequently. Add the eggs, beating constantly for 1 to 2 minutes or until well mixed,
scraping the bowl frequently. Add the flour mixture and sour cream alternately,
beating constantly for 1 to 2 minutes or until well mixed.
Spread half the batter in the prepared pan. Cover with the cranberry
sauce, spreading the sauce to the edge. Spread with the remaining batter.
Sprinkle the topping over the batter.
Bake at 350 degrees for 70 to 85 minutes or until a wooden pick inserted
near the center comes out clean.
Cool in the pan on a wire rack for 10 minutes. Remove the sides of the pan.
Yield: Twelve Servings*

Soups & Salads

Fort Nash

When Papa Nash, in 1938, engaged an
Auburn architect to design the house on Oak
Street for himself and his wife, he envisioned
a modern wonder in the middle of Decatur's
oldest neighborhood.
He died before the house was completed in 1940,
however, and Mrs. Nash presented it to their older
daughter as a wedding present. Surrounded still
by Victorian cottages and larger homes of that era,
the Nash house is something to see even today.
Though it has been through several interior
incarnations, its current owners,
Beth and Dr. Mike Twente, have returned it to
its original Art Deco glory.
They have assembled an amazing collection
of furnishings and accessories from
the period, including the glass and elephant
tusk table pictured here that was used
as a desk by Alexis Carrington on the set
of the television series *Dynasty*.

On the Alexis table are
Cream of Artichoke Soup; Fruit Verde;
Black Bean and Rice Salad; and Tomato,
Goat Cheese and Pasta Salad.

Cream of Artichoke Soup

*Served hot or cold, this to-die-for soup is a local
favorite and is pictured on page 82.*

4 large or 6 medium artichokes
1/2 cup finely chopped onion
1/2 cup finely chopped celery
6 tablespoons butter
6 tablespoons flour
6 cups clear chicken broth
1/4 cup fresh lemon juice
1 bay leaf
1 teaspoon salt
1/4 teaspoon pepper
1/4 teaspoon dried thyme
2 egg yolks, beaten
2 cups light cream

*Boil the artichokes in water to cover in a saucepan for 1 hour.
Scrape the leaves and finely chop the base of each artichoke.
Sauté the onion and celery in the butter in a stockpot until tender but not
browned. Add the flour. Cook for 1 minute, stirring constantly.
Add the chicken broth and lemon juice and mix well. Add the bay leaf, salt, pepper,
thyme, artichoke scrapings and chopped artichokes. Simmer, covered, for 20 minutes or
until slightly thickened. At this point, the soup may be puréed in a blender for a smooth
creamy consistency. Beat the egg yolks and cream in a mixer bowl.
To serve hot, bring the soup to the boiling point; remove from the heat. Stir in
the egg mixture. Adjust the seasonings. Set over hot water to keep warm.
To serve cold, stir the egg mixture into the soup. Adjust the
seasonings. Chill until serving time.
Garnish with thin lemon slices and chopped parsley.
May substitute 1 can top-quality artichoke hearts for the fresh artichokes.
Note: It is important to use homemade chicken broth for the best results.
Yield: Six to Ten Servings*

Black Bean Soup Olé

Very low in fat, this soup is good hot or cold. It's easy to serve on a boat, or when skiers return home too exhausted to cook or eat out.

1 onion, chopped
½ cup chopped celery
½ cup grated carrot
½ cup chopped green bell pepper (optional)
1 to 2 tablespoons olive oil
2 (15-ounce) cans black beans, rinsed, drained

⅓ to 1 can tomatoes with green chiles
1 (14-ounce) can diced tomatoes
½ cup beef broth
¼ teaspoon garlic powder
½ teaspoon ground cumin
½ teaspoon pepper
1 cup water

Sauté the onion, celery, carrot and green pepper in the olive oil in a Dutch oven. Add the beans, tomatoes with green chiles, diced tomatoes, beef broth, garlic powder, cumin, pepper and water and mix well. Bring to a boil; remove from the heat.

Yield: Six Servings

White Chili

Lower in fat, but just as spicy, this variation takes most of the "red" out of this Southern favorite.

6 to 8 chicken breasts
9 cups water
1½ cups chopped onions
Salt and pepper to taste
1½ cups chopped onions
1½ tablespoons vegetable oil
1 (8-ounce) can chopped green chiles
½ teaspoon ground cloves
1 tablespoon ground cumin
½ teaspoon cayenne
1 tablespoon dried oregano
6 cans Great Northern beans
2 cans tomatoes with green chiles
Shredded Monterey Jack cheese to taste
Shredded sharp Cheddar cheese to taste

Rinse the chicken. Combine the chicken, water, 1½ cups onions, salt and pepper in a stockpot. Cook until the chicken is tender. Remove the chicken from the broth. Reserve 8 cups of the broth. Cut the chicken into bite-size pieces. Sauté 1½ cups onions in the oil in a skillet. Combine the sautéed onions, reserved broth, green chiles, cloves, cumin, cayenne and oregano in a stockpot. Add the beans and mix well. Simmer for 30 to 35 minutes or until heated through. Add the chicken. Simmer for 30 minutes longer. Add the tomatoes with green chiles. Heat to serving temperature. Ladle into soup bowls. Top with the Monterey Jack cheese and Cheddar cheese. Yield: Six to Eight Servings

Corn and Crab Meat Bisque

Betty tells us guests are always impressed by the rich flavor of this simply prepared bisque.

1/4 cup chopped onion
1/4 cup butter
2 tablespoons flour
4 cups fresh or frozen corn
4 cups milk

1 cup whipping cream
Salt and pepper to taste
1 pound crab meat
Crumbled crisp-fried bacon

Sauté the onion in the butter in a large saucepan. Add the flour. Cook for 2 minutes, stirring constantly.
Purée the corn in a food processor. Add to the onion mixture. Cook for 5 minutes. Add the milk, cream, salt and pepper. Bring to a boil.
Stir in the crab meat.
Heat to serving temperature. Ladle into soup bowls. Top with the bacon.
Yield: Six Servings
Betty Brandon Sims, Johnston Street Cafe

Old-Time Courtland Stew

This is an often-praised entrée or side dish (a close relative of Brunswick stew) and a complement to any barbecue dinner. It is, however, quite time-consuming and involved. Therefore, since it freezes so well, a large quantity should be prepared and stored in several containers in your freezer (the time investment in this large recipe is the same as with a small quantity). Sealable plastic bags or plastic containers with tight flexible lids are excellent for storage. The stew can be microwaved in the storage containers for almost instant future use. This makes four gallons, so be sure your stockpot is large enough.

12 pounds fresh chicken
8 (29-ounce) cans tomatoes
10 large onions, chopped
3 (10-ounce) packages frozen okra, or 2 pounds fresh
10 medium to large potatoes, sliced
2 pounds butter
6 cans cream-style corn
2 teaspoons pepper, or to taste
1/2 teaspoon Tabasco sauce
2 teaspoons salt
6 whole cloves

Rinse the chicken. Combine the chicken with water to cover in a stockpot. Cook until the chicken can be easily removed from the bone. Remove chicken from the broth, reserving the broth. Let the chicken stand to cool. Remove the skin and bones and cut the chicken into bite-size pieces with kitchen shears.
Return the chicken to the stockpot. Add the undrained tomatoes, onions, okra and potatoes. Cook slowly for 8 to 10 hours. (I tend to take a chance and leave it cooking on low heat overnight. Watching a pot boil for 10 hours is less than stimulating.)
Cook for 2 to 6 hours longer or until the potatoes are very soft.
Add the butter, corn, pepper, Tabasco sauce, salt and cloves. Cook over medium heat for 30 minutes, stirring frequently. Remove cloves before serving.
Note: Without any change in the recipe, the meat of two to four squirrels may be added for an even hardier stew without a "gamy" flavor.
Yield: Sixty-Four Servings

Cucumber Soup

Rich, rich, rich!

1 small onion, chopped
3 medium cucumbers, peeled, seeded, chopped
3 tablespoons butter
1/4 cup flour
3 cups chicken broth
1 cup whipping cream

Sauté the onion and cucumbers in the butter in a saucepan.
Simmer, covered, for 15 minutes.
Stir in the flour. Add the chicken broth and cream. Cook until thickened
and bubbly, stirring constantly. Let cool.
Pour into a blender container. Process until smooth.
Serve chilled. Top with sliced cucumbers.
Yield: Four Servings

Cucumber Cheese Spread

A simple spread for luncheons or canapés.

2 medium cucumbers, peeled, seeded, chopped
Salt to taste
1/4 to 1/2 medium onion, very finely grated
16 ounces cream cheese, softened
1 tablespoon mayonnaise

Sprinkle the cucumbers with salt. Drain in a colander for 30 minutes, patting dry if needed. Mix the undrained onion, cream cheese and mayonnaise in a bowl. Stir in the cucumbers.
Yield: Three Cups

Making a Roux

Many inexperienced cooks may shy away from trying recipes that call for a roux, a combination of oil and flour found in all gumbos. The objective is to make a nice brown paste without burning. This is best accomplished by heating the oil in a heavy pot or cast-iron skillet and slowly adding an equal amount of flour while stirring constantly (very important!). Once the flour is added, reduce the heat to very low, continuing to stir constantly until golden brown. Those with electric stovetops may have more trouble controlling the heat, so remove the pan and continue to stir while the burner cools down. When the roux is golden brown, pour the mixture into another container until ready to use; it will get too dark if it remains in the pan in which it was prepared. For gumbos, pour the excess oil off the top of the roux to prevent the gumbo from becoming too rich.

Duck Gumbo Filé

Game or frozen duck works well in this traditional gumbo. The filé powder can be found boxed, bottled, or canned in the herb and spice section of the supermarket or in gourmet shops that feature Creole cuisine.

1 pound smoked Italian
sausage links
4 duck breasts
Salt and black pepper to taste
1 cup vegetable oil
1 cup flour
2 large onions, chopped
3 ribs celery, chopped
1/2 red or green bell pepper, chopped
2 bunches green onions, chopped
2 large cloves of garlic, minced

1/2 cup white wine
4 to 6 cups water
Lemon pepper to taste
1/8 teaspoon crushed red pepper, o
to taste
1/8 teaspoon Worcestershire sauc
1/8 teaspoon Tabasco sauce,
or to taste
1 bay leaf
1 teaspoon filé powder

Boil the sausage briefly in water to cover in a saucepan to remove some of the fat. Remove from the saucepan and cut into bite-size pieces. Rinse the duck. Combine the duck, salt, black pepper and water to cover in saucepan. Cook until the duck is tender. Remove the duck from the broth, reserving 4 to 6 cups of the broth. Remove the meat from the bones and shred, discarding the skin and bones.

Make a roux (at left) of the oil and flour in a heavy stockpot. Add the onions, celery, bell pepper, green onions and garlic to the roux.

Cook over low heat until the roux is golden brown and onions are tender; discard and start over if the roux smokes. Add the sausage. Cook for 5 minutes. Add the wine and reserved broth. Cook over low heat for 2 hours. Add the water, additional salt, lemon pepper, red pepper, Worcestershire sauce, Tabasco sauce, bay leaf and filé powder. Cook over low heat for 2 hours longer. Remove the bay leaf before serving. Serve gumbo filé over long grain rice.

Note: May prepare the roux in the microwave with 2/3 cup vegetable oil and 1 cup flour. Microwave until golden brown, stirring approximately once per minute.

Yield: Twelve to Fifteen Servings

Frogmore Stew

Named after an old fishing community off the Carolina coast, Frogmore Stew, a.k.a. Low Country Boil, is almost a Southern equivalent to the New England clambake and is equally delicious cooked outdoors or in. Variations may include the addition of whole crabs or cooking in beer.

1/4 cup Old Bay seasoning
4 pounds small red potatoes
2 pounds kielbasa or hot smoked link sausage, cut into 1 1/2-inch slices
6 ears of fresh corn, cut into halves
4 pounds large fresh shrimp

Fill a large outdoor cooker halfway with water. Add the
Old Bay seasoning. Bring to a boil.
Add the potatoes. Return to a boil. Cook for 10 minutes. Add the sausage and
corn. Return to a boil. Cook for 10 minutes or until the potatoes are tender.
Add the shrimp. Cook for 3 to 5 minutes or until the shrimp turn pink.
Remove the stew with a slotted spoon to a serving platter.
Serve with additional Old Bay seasoning and cocktail sauce.
Note: The stew may be cooked indoors in a large Dutch oven over high heat.
Yield: Twelve Servings

Cream of Shiitake Soup with Virginia Ham

From Atlanta, Scott Curry, Decatur's newest chef, pairs shiitake mushrooms with Virginia ham in this fabulous soup recipe.

1/3 cup extra-virgin olive oil
2 pounds shiitake mushrooms, stems removed, cut into 1/4-inch slices
Salt and freshly ground pepper to taste
2 teaspoons minced garlic
1/4 cup finely chopped shallots
3 cups chicken stock

1/2 cup finely chopped shallots
1 cup chopped onion
1 tablespoon extra-virgin olive oil
1 cup dry white wine
2 cups chicken stock
2 cups whipping cream
3 ounces Virginia ham, julienned

Heat 1/3 cup olive oil in a large heavy saucepan over medium heat. Add the mushrooms. Cook for 15 seconds, stirring constantly. Add the salt, pepper, garlic and 1/4 cup shallots. Cook for 1 minute, stirring constantly; do not allow the vegetables to color or burn. Add 3 cups chicken stock and mix well. Reduce the heat to low. Simmer for 4 to 5 minutes or until the mushrooms begin to soften. Remove from the heat and cool slightly. Purée in a food processor fitted with a metal blade or in a blender; set aside.

Combine 1/2 cup shallots, onion and 1 tablespoon olive oil in a large saucepan over medium-high heat. Cook for 4 minutes or until the onion is translucent, stirring constantly. Add the wine. Cook for 15 minutes or until the liquid is reduced by 2/3. Add 2 cups chicken stock. Cook for 15 minutes or until the liquid is reduced to 1/2 cup. Add the cream. Reduce the heat to medium. Cook for 10 minutes, stirring constantly. Remove from the heat.

Strain the reduced liquid through a sieve. Return to the saucepan. Add the puréed mixture. Increase the heat to medium-low. Heat to serving temperature, stirring to combine the ingredients. Adjust the salt and pepper.

Add additional chicken stock if the soup is too thick.

Ladle into soup bowls. Top with the ham.

Yield: Eight Servings

Scott Curry, Johnston Street Cafe

French Onion Soup

Easy and delicious for a first course, or with French bread and a salad for a meal.

4 large onions, thinly sliced
1/2 cup margarine
1 (10-ounce) can beef broth
1 (10-ounce) can chicken broth
Salt and pepper to taste
4 slices French bread
4 slices mozzarella cheese or Gruyère cheese

Cook the onions in the margarine in a skillet until tender. Remove the onions with a slotted spoon to a large stockpot. Add the beef broth and chicken broth gradually. Season with salt and pepper. Bring to a boil. Simmer for 15 minutes. Place 1 slice of bread in each of 4 ovenproof soup bowls. Pour the soup over the bread. Top with the cheese. Arrange the bowls on a baking sheet. Bake at 350 degrees until the cheese is melted.
Yield: Four Servings

Cream of Squash Soup

1 quart chicken stock
1 large onion, finely chopped
3 pounds zucchini, julienned
3 pounds yellow squash, julienned
1 tablespoon tarragon
1 quart heavy cream
1/4 cup cornstarch
1/4 cup water

Bring the chicken stock to a boil in a stockpot. Add the onion, zucchini and squash. Cook for 5 minutes. Add the tarragon and cream. Stir in a mixture of the cornstarch and water. Cook until thickened, stirring frequently.
Yield: Twelve to Fifteen Servings

Pimento Cheese Spread

An old Southern favorite—pack it along with a bucket of chicken for your Sunday picnic or a football tailgate party.

2 cups finely shredded cheese
1 small jar chopped pimentos
1 small onion, finely chopped
3 jalapeños, finely chopped
Juice of 1/2 lemon
1/4 to 1/2 cup mayonnaise,
or to taste
Salt and black pepper to taste
Crushed red pepper to taste

Combine the cheese, undrained pimentos, onion, jalapeños and lemon juice in a bowl. Stir in the mayonnaise. Season with salt, black pepper and red pepper. Serve as a spread for sandwiches or celery or as a dip.
Yield: Three Cups

Deluxe Potato Soup

Warm up a cold night with a bowl of this hearty soup, a tossed salad, and some home-baked bread.

3 cups chopped potatoes
1/2 cup chopped celery
1/2 cup chopped onion
3 cups chicken broth
2 cups scalded milk
3 tablespoons butter
1 (12-ounce) can chopped light chicken, or
1 1/2 to 2 cups chopped cooked chicken (optional)
1 cup sour cream
1 tablespoon flour
Salt to taste
1/4 teaspoon pepper
4 slices bacon, crisp-fried, crumbled (optional)

Combine the potatoes, celery, onion and chicken broth in a 3- to 4-quart saucepan. Cook until the vegetables are tender. Remove the vegetables from broth; press through a sieve or purée in a food processor fitted with a steel blade. Return the vegetables to the broth. Add the milk and butter. Simmer 20 minutes. Add the chicken. Stir in a mixture of the sour cream and flour. Simmer until thickened, stirring frequently. Season with salt and pepper. Ladle into soup bowls. Top with the bacon.
Note: This recipe can be made lower in fat by omitting the butter and sour cream and substituting 3 cups nonfat buttermilk for the 2 cups scalded milk.
Yield: Six Servings

Tortellini Soup

Tortellini, tiny cheese-filled or meat-filled pasta creations, are wonderful in soups. This is a meaty sausage-based soup from a true Southern Italian family.

1 pound Italian sausage
1 cup chopped onion
3 cloves of garlic, chopped
3 (14-ounce) cans beef broth
1 cup Lambrusco wine
1 (15-ounce) can tomatoes
3 carrots, thinly sliced
2 to 3 zucchini, sliced
1 (8-ounce) can tomato sauce
1/2 teaspoon dried basil
1/2 teaspoon dried oregano
3 tablespoons chopped fresh parsley
1 (8-ounce) package cheese tortellini
Freshly grated Parmesan cheese to taste

Remove the casing from the sausage. Brown the sausage in a skillet, stirring until crumbly. Remove with a slotted spoon.
Sauté the onion and garlic in the pan drippings.
Combine the beef broth, wine, undrained tomatoes, carrots, zucchini, tomato sauce, onion mixture, sausage, basil, oregano and parsley in a large stockpot and mix well. Bring to a boil. Simmer for 1 hour.
Add the tortellini. Simmer for 1 hour.
Arrange on individual plates. Sprinkle with the cheese.
Serve with sweet Italian bread.
May use a 14-ounce package of tortellini and increase the beef broth to 4 cans.
Yield: Six to Eight Servings

Gumbos

Southern soups are so hearty they are often meals in themselves. Creole cuisine's gumbo has been written about, sung about, and tasted all over the country. The name was derived from the Choctaw word for okra, a common ingredient used to thicken this type of soup. Although gumbos do not always contain okra, they may contain filé, a powder made from ground sassafras leaves that serves the same function. If this is the case, the soup should be properly called a "gumbo filé." This gumbo is great after Thanksgiving.

Turkey Gumbo

Just imagine the aroma of simmering turkey stock and the scent of sizzling onions and peppers browning slowly in a large pot over an open fire.

1 turkey carcass	2 quarts water
2 turkey legs or thighs	½ cup Worcestershire sauce
3 quarts water	Tabasco sauce to taste
1 teaspoon salt	1 (15-ounce) can tomatoes
¼ cup olive oil	1½ tablespoons salt
1 cup flour	4 ounces sliced ham, cut into
8 ribs celery, chopped	small pieces
3 large onions, chopped	1 to 2 bay leaves
1 green bell pepper, chopped	Cayenne to taste
2 cloves of garlic, minced	1 teaspoon brown sugar
½ cup chopped parsley	1 tablespoon lemon juice
1 pound okra, sliced	4 cups rice, cooked
1 cup sliced smoked low-fat	
turkey sausage	

Rinse the turkey. Break the turkey carcass into several pieces. Combine with the turkey legs, 3 quarts water and 1 teaspoon salt in a stockpot. Boil for hour. Remove the turkey carcass and legs and let cool. Remove the meat from the bones, discarding the bones. Reserve 2 quarts of the stock and the meat. Heat the olive oil in a heavy Dutch oven over medium heat. Stir in the flour. Cook until dark golden brown, stirring constantly. Add the celery, onions, green pepper, garlic and parsley. Cook for 15 to 20 minutes or until the vegetables are tender, stirring constantly.

Add the okra and sausage. Cook for 5 minutes. Add the reserved turkey stock, 2 quarts water, Worcestershire sauce, Tabasco sauce, tomatoes, 1½ tablespoons salt, ham, bay leaves and cayenne. Simmer, covered, for 2½ to 3 hours or until the flavors have blended, stirring occasionally.

Add the turkey meat. Simmer for 30 minutes longer. Stir in the brown sugar and lemon juice just before serving time. Remove and discard the bay leaves. Spoon the rice into heated gumbo bowls. Ladle the gumbo over the rice.

Yield: Sixteen to Eighteen Servings

Vegetable Beef TLC Soup

This easy beef and vegetable soup recipe makes one gallon and can easily be multiplied to pass along to friends.

1 pound ground chuck
1 large onion, chopped
3 (16-ounce) packages frozen mixed vegetables with potatoes, thawed, or
3 (15-ounce) cans mixed vegetables with potatoes, drained
2¹/₂ to 3 cups chopped fresh tomatoes, or 2 (14-ounce) cans
1 to 1¹/₂ cups corn kernels, or 1 (11-ounce) can, drained
1 (8-ounce) can tomato sauce
¹/₂ cup catsup
1 tablespoon sugar
1 teaspoon salt
1 teaspoon pepper
1 (7-ounce) package vermicelli, broken into 2-inch pieces

Brown the ground chuck in a skillet and drain well.
Combine the ground chuck, onion, mixed vegetables, tomatoes, corn, tomato sauce,
catsup, sugar, salt and pepper in a large Dutch oven and mix well. Add
enough water to bring to the desired consistency.
Bring to a gentle boil; reduce the heat. Simmer, covered, for 1¹/₂ to 3¹/₂ hours
or until the tomatoes and corn are tender and the flavors have blended.
Add the vermicelli during the last 15 minutes of cooking time.
Yield: Ten Servings

Fruit Verde

Pictured on page 82, this fruit salad can also be beautifully served in carved cantaloupe or honeydew melon halves.

1 cup small honeydew balls or cubes
1 cup seedless white grapes
2 medium kiwifruit, peeled, thinly sliced
1 pear, cored, cut into 1/2-inch pieces

1 kiwifruit, peeled
1/2 cup white grape juice
1/2 cup fresh mint leaves

Combine the honeydew, grapes, 2 kiwifruit and pear in a large bowl and mix gently. Chill, covered, until serving time.
Combine 1 kiwifruit, grape juice and mint leaves in a blender container.
Process until puréed. Chill, covered, for 1 hour.
Strain the grape juice mixture through a sieve. Pour over the chilled fruit. Toss gently to combine.
Garnish with fresh mint leaves.
Yield: Eight Servings

Frozen Fruit Salad

An icy variation of the popular Southern ambrosia dessert. Good to keep in the freezer for company, these are frozen in individual servings. They are a great Southern favorite, especially with children.

³/4 cup sugar
4¹/2 cups water
2 cups apricot nectar
1 (10-ounce) package frozen strawberries
in syrup, thawed

1 (8-ounce) can crushed pineapple
in juice
4 medium bananas, sliced
¹/8 teaspoon salt, or to taste

Combine the sugar and water in a small saucepan. Bring to a boil; reduce the heat. Simmer for 8 minutes or until syrupy. Let cool.

Combine the apricot nectar, undrained strawberries, undrained pineapple, bananas and salt in a large bowl and mix gently. Stir in the cooled syrup.

Spoon into foil-lined muffin cups. Freeze for 4 hours to overnight.

Let stand for 5 minutes before serving.

Yield: Eighteen Servings

Cranberry Topiary Tree

Fresh cranberries are great for making a topiary tree for the holidays. Just hot glue cranberries to your favorite styrofoam shape. The cranberries will last for approximately two weeks. Add ivy for a nice touch.

Fresh Cranberry Salad

Lyla Peebles of Mooresville gives us two great suggestions for cranberries—for both eyes and taste buds. This beautiful congealed salad may be served along with your favorite chicken salad or poultry dish.

1 pound fresh cranberries
2 cups water
2 cups sugar
1 (3-ounce) package cherry gelatin
1 (3-ounce) package strawberry gelatin
1 large orange, cut into pieces
1 (20-ounce) can crushed pineapple
1 cup chopped pecans

Combine the cranberries, water and sugar in a saucepan. Cook over medium heat until the cranberries burst, stirring frequently. Add the cherry gelatin and strawberry gelatin, stirring until the gelatins are dissolved. Add the orange and pineapple and mix gently. Stir in the pecans. Pour into desired molds. Chill until set.
Yield: Twelve to Fifteen Servings
Lyla Peebles, Lyla's Flowers and Fine Food

Strawberry Pretzel Salad

Salad or dessert? People serve this versatile
refrigerator concoction both ways.

2²/₃ cups small pretzels, crushed
3 tablespoons sugar
³/₄ cup melted butter
1 cup sugar
8 ounces cream cheese, softened
8 ounces whipped topping
2 (3-ounce) packages strawberry gelatin
2 cups boiling water
1 (16-ounce) package frozen strawberries, thawed

Combine the pretzels, 3 tablespoons sugar and butter in a bowl
and mix well. Pour into a 9x13-inch baking dish.
Bake at 350 degrees for 10 minutes. Cool completely.
Cream 1 cup sugar and cream cheese in a mixer bowl until
light and fluffy. Spoon into the prepared crust.
Combine the gelatin and boiling water in a bowl, stirring until the gelatin is
dissolved. Stir in the strawberries. Chill until partially set.
Pour the gelatin mixture over the cream cheese mixture. Chill overnight.
Yield: Twelve to Fifteen Servings

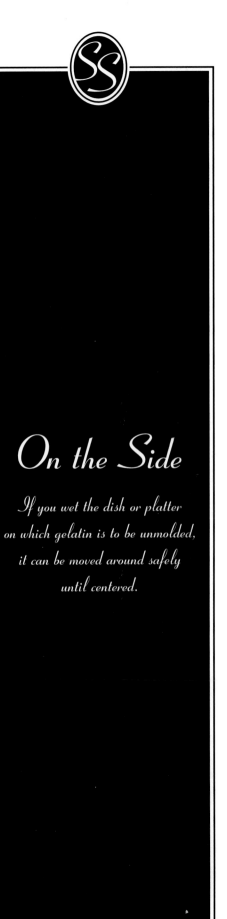

On the Side

If you wet the dish or platter
on which gelatin is to be unmolded,
it can be moved around safely
until centered.

German Potato Salad

Great for picnics and football tailgating, this is a variation of the traditional German-style potato salad.

8 to 10 Idaho potatoes
1/4 cup red wine vinegar
2 tablespoons sugar
1 cucumber, peeled, sliced
1 head iceberg lettuce, torn into bite-size
pieces

3/4 to 1 cup (or more) mayonnaise
Salt and pepper to taste
6 slices bacon, crisp-fried, crumbled
(optional)

Combine the potatoes with water to cover in a saucepan. Boil until the potatoes are tender when pierced with a fork; drain well. Peel the potatoes and cut into 1/4-inch slices. Pour the vinegar over the potatoes in a large bowl. Sprinkle with the sugar. Let stand to cool slightly. Add the cucumber and lettuce to the potatoes and mix gently. Add the mayonnaise, salt and pepper and mix well. Top with the bacon.
Chill until serving time. May be served warm.
Yield: Eight to Ten Servings

Black Bean and Rice Salad

A quick, easy, and healthy combination of vegetables and grains, pictured on page 82. A wonderful main dish for vegetarians or a great side dish for all.

1 package boil-in-the-bag rice
1 can black beans, drained, rinsed
1 can Shoe Peg corn, drained
1 purple onion, chopped
1 tomato, chopped
1/4 cup vinaigrette

Prepare the rice using the package directions. Combine the rice, beans, corn, onion, tomato and vinaigrette in a large bowl and mix well. Chill for several hours to overnight.
Note: Can sizes are not particularly important in this recipe.
Yield: Eight Servings

Broccoli Salad

A sweet-and-sour dressing with nuts and raisins for the vegetable that made George Bush famous.

1 cup mayonnaise
1/2 cup sugar
Wine vinegar
1 bunch fresh broccoli, chopped
12 slices bacon, crisp-fried, crumbled
1/2 cup raisins
1/2 cup chopped red onion
1/2 cup chopped pecans

Mix the mayonnaise and sugar in a medium bowl. Stir in enough vinegar to make of the desired consistency. Chill thoroughly.
Combine the broccoli, bacon, raisins, onion and pecans in a large bowl and mix gently. Add the mayonnaise mixture, tossing to coat.
Chill for 2 hours.
Yield: Six Servings

Caesar Salad

The king (or emperor?) of tossed salads with homemade croutons toasted in garlic oil.

1 clove of garlic, cut into halves
1/2 cup olive oil
1 cup 1/2-inch French bread cubes, crusts removed
3/4 teaspoon salt
1/4 teaspoon freshly ground pepper
1/4 teaspoon dry mustard
1 1/2 teaspoons Worcestershire sauce
3 anchovies, drained, chopped
1 egg (optional)
1 large head romaine, trimmed, rinsed, dried
2 tablespoons freshly grated Parmesan cheese
Juice of 1/2 lemon (about 2 tablespoons)

Crush 1 garlic half. Combine with the olive oil in a tightly covered jar. Chill for 1 hour or longer.
Heat 2 tablespoons of the garlic oil in a skillet. Add the bread cubes. Sauté until browned. Set aside.
Add the salt, pepper, dry mustard, Worcestershire sauce and anchovies to the remaining garlic oil in the jar. Shake vigorously to mix. Chill until needed.
Bring 2 inches of water to a boil in a small saucepan. Turn off the heat.
Lower the egg carefully into the water. Let stand for 1 minute.
Remove the egg carefully. Let cool.
At serving time, rub the remaining piece of garlic over the inside of a large wooden bowl. Discard the garlic.
Cut out the coarse ribs from the lettuce leaves. Tear the leaves into bite-size pieces into the prepared bowl. Shake the dressing and pour carefully over the lettuce. Sprinkle with the cheese. Toss until all leaves are coated. Break the egg over the center of the salad. Pour the lemon juice over the egg and toss well. Sprinkle with the croutons. Toss quickly and serve immediately.
Note: Freshly grated imported Parmesan cheese makes a big difference in taste. Have extra on hand to grate over individual servings if desired.
Yield: Four Servings

Corn Salad

This local favorite from Betty Sims has been served by the ton over the years. A definite must at a barbecue picnic (pictured on page 14) or with other grilled entrées.

1 quart frozen Shoe Peg corn,
cooked, drained
1 green bell pepper, seeded, chopped
1 cup sliced cherry tomatoes
1/2 cup chopped purple onion
3/4 cup chopped cucumber

1/2 cup mayonnaise
1/4 cup sour cream
1 tablespoon apple cider vinegar
1/2 teaspoon celery salt
1/2 teaspoon white pepper
Salt to taste

Combine the corn, green pepper, cherry tomatoes, onion, cucumber, mayonnaise, sour cream, vinegar, celery salt, white pepper and salt in a large bowl and mix gently.

Chill, covered, for 3 hours or longer.

Yield: Six to Eight Servings

Betty Brandon Sims, Johnston Street Cafe

Mixed Greens with Goat Cheese and Pomegranate Vinaigrette

A recipe for the well-developed palate and the adventuresome, the combination of these special ingredients makes a lovely plated salad for your most special guests. Pomegranates are available in the fall, with a peak in October.

5 ounces goat cheese
2 cloves of garlic, minced
1/2 teaspoon minced fresh tarragon
1/2 teaspoon minced fresh basil
4 small heads Belgian endive
10 cups mixed greens such as frisée, lamb's lettuce and arugula
Pomegranate Vinaigrette

Combine the cheese, garlic, tarragon and basil in a bowl, stirring until the mixture is blended and soft.
Separate the endive into leaves. Rinse and dry the endive leaves and mixed greens.
Arrange the mixed greens on 6 salad plates. Fill the endive leaves with small amounts of the cheese mixture. Divide among the plates.
Sprinkle each salad with Pomegranate Vinaigrette. Garnish each with 1/2 teaspoon pomegranate seeds.
Yield: Six Servings

Pomegranate Vinaigrette

6 tablespoons olive oil
2 teaspoons sherry vinegar
4 teaspoons red wine vinegar
1 tablespoon pomegranate juice
Salt and freshly ground pepper to taste

Whisk the olive oil, sherry vinegar, wine vinegar, pomegranate juice, salt and pepper lightly in a small bowl.
Note: To obtain fresh pomegranate juice and seeds, rinse the pomegranate and cut into halves. Ream 1 half as you would an orange. Reserve the other half to use as a garnish if desired.
Yield: One-Half Cup

Snow Pea and Napa Cabbage Slaw

Napa, or Chinese, cabbage has long, pale yellow-green to white leaves that can be eaten cooked or uncooked. Recent popularity has now made this vegetable widely available in the supermarket. This slaw takes an Oriental twist with snow peas and a dressing made with rice vinegar.

8 ounces snow peas, trimmed
1½ pounds napa cabbage, shredded
2 medium carrots, shredded
1 medium yellow bell pepper,
 cut into thin strips

3 scallions, finely chopped
1 tablespoon freshly squeezed lemon juice
1 tablespoon rice vinegar
3 tablespoons olive oil
Salt and pepper to taste

Blanch the snow peas in boiling water in a large saucepan for 15 seconds. Remove with a slotted spoon to a bowl of ice water to stop the cooking. Drain well and cut diagonally into thin slices. Combine the snow peas, cabbage, carrots, yellow pepper, scallions, lemon juice, vinegar, olive oil, salt and pepper in a large bowl and toss well.

Yield: Six Servings

Fumi Salad

A delicious Oriental-style slaw. The ramen noodles add a delicate crunch.

2 packages Oriental-flavor ramen noodles
½ cup slivered almonds
½ cup sesame seeds
¼ cup sugar
2 teaspoons salt
1 teaspoon pepper

¾ cup vegetable oil
¼ cup sesame oil
6 tablespoons rice wine vinegar
1 head Chinese cabbage, chopped
4 green onions, chopped

Crush the noodles in the package and set aside.
Place the almonds and sesame seeds on a nonstick baking sheet. Bake at 250 degrees for 15 to 20 minutes or until browned. Set aside.
Combine the sugar, salt, pepper, vegetable oil, sesame oil, vinegar and contents of the noodle seasoning packets in a jar and shake to mix well. Set aside.
Combine the cabbage and green onions in a large bowl and mix well. Add the noodles, almonds, sesame seeds and dressing at serving time. Toss lightly.

Yield: Eight to Ten Servings

Mediterranean Pasta Salad

This colorful medley of pasta and peppers is wonderful for picnics or light lunches, or as an accompaniment to your favorite grilled meats. It keeps well in the refrigerator for several days.

2/3 cup olive oil
3 tablespoons red wine vinegar
2 tablespoons chopped fresh basil
2 tablespoons chopped green onions
2 tablespoons grated Parmesan cheese
1 1/4 teaspoons salt
1/4 teaspoon freshly ground pepper
1 small red bell pepper
1 small green bell pepper
1 small yellow bell pepper

12 to 16 ounces rotelle pasta, cooked, drained
1 medium tomato, chopped
1/4 cup toasted pignoli (pine nuts)
1/4 cup Greek-style olives or pitted black olives
8 ounces feta cheese or mozzarella cheese, cut into cubes
2 tablespoons chopped fresh basil
1/4 teaspoon crumbled dried oregano

For the dressing, combine the olive oil, vinegar, 2 tablespoons basil, green onions, Parmesan cheese, salt and pepper in a food processor or blender container. Process until smooth.

For the salad, cut the bell peppers into halves lengthwise. Cut each half crosswise into strips.

Combine the bell peppers, pasta, tomato, pignoli and olives in a large bowl. Add the dressing, tossing to mix.

Roll the cheese cubes in 2 tablespoons basil. Add to the salad. Sprinkle with the oregano. Toss lightly.

Serve at room temperature.

Yield: Four Servings

Tomato, Goat Cheese and Pasta Salad

The perfect ladies lunch entrée, best prepared in summer with fresh garden-ripe tomatoes. Invite your mother to lunch and share this delightful salad, pictured on page 82.

5 large tomatoes, chopped, drained
2 jalapeños, seeded, chopped
2 cloves of garlic, minced
1 tablespoon salt
1/4 cup olive oil
Juice of 1 lime
1/8 teaspoon Tabasco sauce, or to taste
Chili powder to taste
12 ounces bow tie pasta or orrechiette pasta
2 tablespoons lightly toasted pignoli (pine nuts)
4 to 5 ounces goat cheese, crumbled

Combine the tomatoes, jalapeños, garlic, salt, olive oil, lime juice, Tabasco sauce and chili powder in a large bowl and mix well.
Let stand for 2 hours to allow the flavors to blend.
Cook the pasta using the package directions; drain well.
Combine the tomato mixture, pasta, pine nuts and cheese in a large salad bowl and toss gently.
Serve warm. Garnish with chopped fresh cilantro.
Yield: Four to Six Servings

Goat Cheese

Goat cheese, also called chèvre, is now commonly found in the imported cheese section of the deli or supermarket, although it is being successfully produced domestically. Flavors range from white, soft, and mild (Montrachet) to hard, dark, shriveled, and strong. Some are seasoned with herbs for more distinctive flavors. Experiment with different types in salads and hors d'oeuvre, and enjoy!

Chicken Salad

No self-respecting Southern cookbook would be complete without this classic preparation of the ladies' favorite luncheon entrée.

½ cup slivered almonds
4 cups chopped cooked chicken breasts
1 cup chopped celery
1 cup white or red seedless grapes, cut into halves
½ cup mayonnaise
½ cup Cooked Salad Dressing
Salt and pepper to taste
Lettuce leaves

*Place the almonds on a nonstick baking sheet. Bake at 300
degrees for 10 to 12 minutes or until lightly toasted.
Combine the chicken, almonds, celery, grapes, mayonnaise, Cooked Salad Dressing,
salt and pepper in a large bowl. Toss lightly but thoroughly, trying to avoid
breaking the chicken pieces. Chill until serving time.
Serve over the lettuce leaves.*
Yield: Eight Servings

Cooked Salad Dressing

3 tablespoons sugar
2 tablespoons flour
1 teaspoon dry mustard
¼ teaspoon salt
1 egg
¾ cup milk or skim milk
¼ cup cider vinegar

*Combine the sugar, flour, dry mustard and salt in a saucepan. Beat in the egg.
Add the milk gradually, stirring to blend. Cook over low heat until thickened, stirring
constantly. Remove from the heat. Stir in the vinegar. Let cool before using.
May instead be microwaved on High for 3 minutes, stirring 3 to 4 times.
Keeps well in the refrigerator for up to 3 weeks.*
Yield: One and One-Half Cups

Monterey Chicken Salad

Grapes, pasta, and vegetables tossed with chicken in a sweet dressing make a light and lively version of this Southern favorite.

5 cups chopped cooked chicken breasts
2 cups white grape halves
1 cup snow peas
2 cups packed torn spinach
7 ounces rigatoni, cooked, drained
1 can artichokes, drained, rinsed, quartered
3 green onion tops, sliced
1/2 large cucumber, sliced
2 1/2 cups sliced celery
1/2 cup vegetable oil
1/4 cup sugar
2 tablespoons cider vinegar
1 teaspoon salt
1/2 teaspoon lemon juice
2 tablespoons minced fresh flat-leaf parsley

For the salad, combine the chicken, grapes, snow peas, spinach, rigatoni, artichokes, green onions, cucumber and celery in a large bowl and mix well. Chill until serving time.
For the dressing, combine the oil, sugar, vinegar, salt, lemon juice and parsley in a jar and shake well to mix.
Add the dressing to the salad and toss lightly.
Garnish with navel orange slices.
Note: Cooking the chicken with a carrot, an onion and some celery leaves improves the flavor of this salad.
Yield: Twelve Servings

Choosing Papayas

The papaya is a large tropical fruit with a smooth skin that ripens from green to yellow or orange. The flesh is melon-like, sweet, and juicy, and contains many black seeds. Well-stocked produce sections in the supermarket will have them all year, but the peak season is May and June. Choose medium-sized fruit with the skin at least half yellow. Do not buy fruit with bruised or broken skins.

Polynesian Chicken Salad

This chicken salad is a complete meal, featuring tropical fruits and a curry dressing. Try it for luncheons, daytime card parties, or cold summer suppers.

6 chicken breasts, skinned
Salt to taste
1/2 cup toasted slivered almonds
2 to 3 green onions, chopped
8 ounces frozen green peas, thawed
3 ribs celery, chopped
2 papayas, chopped
1/2 cup shredded coconut
3 to 4 fresh mushrooms, sliced
Curry Dressing
Lettuce leaves

Rinse the chicken. Cook the chicken in boiling salted water in a large saucepan until tender. Let cool. Debone the chicken and chop into bite-size pieces. Combine the chicken, almonds, green onions, peas, celery, papayas, coconut and mushrooms in a large bowl and mix well.
Pour the Curry Dressing over the salad and toss lightly. Chill until serving time. Serve over lettuce leaves. Garnish with sliced avocados.
Yield: Six Servings

Curry Dressing

1/2 to 1 cup mayonnaise
1 cup chutney
1 to 2 tablespoons curry powder
Freshly ground pepper to taste
Juice of 1 lemon

Combine the mayonnaise, chutney, curry powder, pepper and lemon juice in a bowl and mix well. Chill until needed.
Yield: One and One-Half to Two Cups

Taco Salad

This variation of the popular dish is tossed with tortilla chips instead of being served in tortilla bowls—easier as well as economical for this main dish salad. Make sure more chips and salsa are on hand for additional munching! Good for a crowd.

1 pound ground beef
1 onion, chopped
1 head lettuce, torn into bite-size pieces
3 to 4 tomatoes, chopped
1 (16-ounce) can kidney beans, drained, rinsed
1 (15-ounce) can chick-peas, drained
1 (8-ounce) package shredded medium-sharp Cheddar cheese
1 (10-ounce) package taco chips or other salsa chips
1 bottle Thousand Island salad dressing
Tabasco sauce or hot sauce to taste (optional)

Brown the ground beef with the onion in a skillet, stirring until crumbly; drain and let cool.
Combine the ground beef mixture, lettuce, tomatoes, kidney beans, chick-peas, cheese and taco chips in a large bowl and mix well.
Add a mixture of the salad dressing and Tabasco sauce, just before serving.
May boil dry-roasted peanuts from a jar and substitute to taste for the chick-peas.
Yield: Ten to Twelve Servings

Raspberry Vinaigrette

½ cup vegetable oil
½ cup raspberry vinegar
1 tablespoon raspberry mustard
Freshly ground pepper to taste

Combine the oil, vinegar, mustard and pepper in a jar. Shake well to mix.
Serve over mixed greens such as romaine, endive, arugula, chicory, spinach or red lettuce.
Yield: One Cup

Balsamic Vinaigrette

Balsamic vinegar is made from grapes and aged in wooden barrels. The color and flavor are derived from the woods during the aging process. The casks of oak, juniper, and other specially selected woods impart their own unique scent to the process as the vinegar is transferred from one type of barrel to the next over a ten-year period of time. Once you've tried it, you'll always keep a bottle around for dressings or marinades, or to use by itself to add zip to any dish.

1 clove of garlic
1 tablespoon Dijon mustard
3 tablespoons balsamic vinegar
Salt and pepper to taste
1 cup extra-virgin olive oil

Cut the garlic into halves. Rub the pieces over the inside of a small bowl. Set aside the garlic.
Whisk the Dijon mustard and vinegar in the prepared bowl.
Season with the salt and pepper.
Drizzle the olive oil into the bowl in a steady stream, whisking constantly until the dressing is creamy and thickened and all the olive oil has been added.
Adjust the seasonings. Add the garlic.
Let stand at room temperature until serving time.
Remove the garlic and whisk again.
Yield: One and One-Fourth Cups

Zorba's Five-Star Feta Cream Dressing

One bite of this tangy feta dressing and you will be tempted to hop around waving a white handkerchief as the Greeks do.

2 tablespoons finely chopped sun-dried tomatoes
Olive oil
1 cup homemade or plain yogurt
2 ounces cream cheese, softened
2 cloves of garlic, crushed
2 tablespoons balsamic vinegar

1 tablespoon tomato paste
8 ounces feta cheese, crumbled
3 sprigs of fresh rosemary, chopped
1 tablespoon chopped fresh basil
3 large olives, chopped
1/2 tablespoon capers, drained

Soak the tomatoes in olive oil to cover for 1 hour.
Combine the yogurt, cream cheese, garlic, vinegar, tomato paste and half the feta cheese in a large bowl, stirring until mixed.
Add the remaining feta cheese, rosemary, basil, olives and capers and mix gently.
Drain the tomatoes. Stir into the dressing.
Serve over romaine lettuce.
Yield: One and Three-Fourths Cups

Honey Dressing

A sweet dressing for fruit salads.

2 tablespoons sugar
1 teaspoon salt
1 teaspoon paprika
1 teaspoon dry mustard
1/4 teaspoon pepper
1/4 cup freshly squeezed lemon juice

3/4 cup vegetable oil
2 to 3 drops of onion juice or
1/2 teaspoon grated onion
1/3 cup honey
1 teaspoon celery seeds

Combine the sugar, salt, paprika, dry mustard, pepper, lemon juice, oil, onion juice, honey and celery seeds in a jar. Shake vigorously until thoroughly mixed. Chill until serving time.
May increase the honey to 1/2 cup and omit the sugar.
Yield: One and One-Half Cups

Lemon Mustard Dressing

A great tangy flavor for mixed greens or traditional salads with lettuce, celery, green onions, and carrots. Best made in the morning for evening suppers. Keeps well in the refrigerator.

6 tablespoons vegetable oil
2¹/₂ tablespoons freshly squeezed lemon juice
1 teaspoon sugar
1 teaspoon salt
¹/₂ teaspoon freshly ground pepper
¹/₂ teaspoon Dijon mustard
1 small clove of garlic, crushed

Combine the oil, lemon juice, sugar, salt, pepper, Dijon mustard and garlic in a jar. Shake vigorously until well mixed.
Yield: One-Half Cup

Homemade Mayonnaise

If refrigerated, this mayonnaise will keep for up to 5 days. Let it return to room temperature before serving.

2 egg yolks
1 egg
1 tablespoon Dijon mustard
¹/₈ teaspoon salt, or to taste
Freshly ground pepper to taste
¹/₄ cup freshly squeezed lemon juice
2 cups corn oil or extra-virgin olive oil

Combine the egg yolks, egg, Dijon mustard, salt, pepper and half the lemon juice in a food processor container fitted with a steel blade. Process for 1 minute. Add the oil in a fine stream with the food processor running. Turn off the food processor and scrape the sides of the container. Adjust the seasonings. If the corn oil was used, the remaining lemon juice will probably need to be added. Spoon into a covered container. Chill until needed.
Yield: Three Cups

Meat & Game

McCrary Home

*J*ust minutes from Decatur, Mooresville is indeed a little gem in its setting of old oaks and pecans. Incorporated in 1818, before Alabama was even a state, this charming little village (population 54) is hidden away just off Interstate 65. With several original buildings still in use, including a slave-built church, the old post office, and a small number of homes, it has retained its early American charm.

It is not surprising that Mooresville was selected as the locale for the most recent film version of *Tom Sawyer.* The original section of George and Shirley McCrary's Federal farmhouse was built in 1826. Each successive generation has added to the house, and it has been continuously occupied since 1880 by members of George's family.

*Pictured in front of the McCrarys' home on
High Street—with Tom's picket fence in the
mid-ground—is our presentation of veal, pork,
and beef dishes for you to try:
Grilled Garlic Lime Pork with Jalapeño Onion Marmalade;
Lemon Veal Parmesan;
Grilled Steak with Red Pepper Coulis;
and Ratatouille.*

Green Peppercorns

Green peppercorns are a milder variety of the spicy black peppercorn and are used in sauces such as the one at right. They are usually found bottled in gourmet food stores, but can sometimes be found freeze-dried in the spice aisle of the grocery store.

Tenderloin of Beef with Green Peppercorn Sauce

Beef tenderloin makes an extraordinary main event for special occasions and dinner parties. This oh-so-tender roast is pictured on page 8.

1 (4- to 5-pound) beef tenderloin	1 bunch thyme
3 cloves of garlic, minced	Salt to taste
Coarsely ground pepper to taste	Green Peppercorn Sauce
1 bunch rosemary	

Trim and tie the tenderloin. Sprinkle the garlic and pepper over the beef and pat into the beef. Place in a shallow roasting pan. Cover with the rosemary and thyme. Roast at 425 degrees for 10 minutes. Reduce the oven temperature to 350 degrees. Roast for 25 to 35 minutes or until a meat thermometer registers 140 to 145 degrees for medium. Remove from the oven. Sprinkle with salt. Let stand for 10 minutes before slicing. Top each serving with some of the Green Peppercorn Sauce. Serve the remaining sauce on the side.

Yield: Ten to Fifteen Servings

Green Peppercorn Sauce

3 tablespoons minced shallots	Salt and pepper to taste
2 tablespoons butter	2 tablespoons green
1/2 cup burgundy	peppercorns, drained
1/2 cup cream	1 tablespoon butter
1 teaspoon Dijon mustard	

Sauté the shallots in 2 tablespoons butter in a saucepan over medium-high heat for 2 to 3 minutes or until tender. Add the burgundy. Cook until reduced by 1/2. Stir in the cream, mustard, salt and pepper. Keep warm over low heat. Sauté the peppercorns in 1 tablespoon butter in a skillet. Stir into the sauce.

Yield: One and One-Half Cups

Grilled Steak with Red Pepper Coulis

Dress up your next steak cookout with this colorful relish/sauce, pronounced coo-lee. Red peppers can be expensive, but aren't your guests worth it? Pictured on page 118.

3 pounds sirloin, top round or flank steak
Salt and freshly ground pepper to taste
Red Pepper Coulis

*S*prinkle the steak with salt and pepper. Grill over hot mesquite coals to desired degree of doneness. Cut into slices.
Spoon the Red Pepper Coulis over the slices to serve.
Yield: Six Servings

Red Pepper Coulis

1/2 cup olive oil
6 sweet red peppers, cored, seeded, cut into 1/2-inch cubes
12 large cloves of garlic, cut into halves lengthwise
2 tablespoons balsamic vinegar
1 tablespoon sugar
1/8 teaspoon red pepper flakes, or to taste
Salt and freshly ground black pepper to taste
3 tablespoons finely chopped oil-pack sun-dried tomatoes
16 whole basil leaves

*H*eat the olive oil in a large skillet over medium heat. Add the red peppers and garlic. Sauté for 15 minutes.
Stir in the vinegar and sugar. Add the red pepper flakes, salt and black pepper. Cook for 15 minutes, stirring occasionally.
Stir in the tomatoes and basil. Simmer for 10 minutes. Serve hot.
Yield: Two Cups

Mustard Caper Sauce

Mix 3 cups mayonnaise, 1 cup sour cream, 1 drained small bottle of capers, 3 tablespoons Dijon mustard and 1/2 teaspoon cayenne in a bowl. Serve with sliced beef or pork tenderloin and yeast rolls.
Yield: Four Cups

Horseradish Sauce

A Southern favorite made even more delicious with a vermouth basting sauce. The best for celebrations and that extra-special meal.

Beat 1 quart whipping cream in a mixer bowl until stiff peaks form. Add 1 cup prepared horseradish sauce, 1 cup shredded white horseradish, 1 tablespoon sugar and 2 tablespoons wine vinegar and mix well.
Yield: One and One-Half Quarts

Magic Kabob Marinade

Add magic to beef or pork kabobs.

1 teaspoon salt
1/2 teaspoon sugar
1/4 teaspoon pepper
1/2 teaspoon paprika
1/3 cup vinegar
2/3 cup sunflower-seed oil
1 clove of garlic, chopped
1/2 teaspoon Worcestershire sauce
1/4 teaspoon oregano
1 bay leaf

Combine all the ingredients in a tightly covered jar and shake well. Marinate the meat in the refrigerator for 6 to 8 hours.
Yield: One Cup

Marinated Flank Steak

A teriyaki-style marinade tenderizes and spices up this cut of beef for great grilling.

6 green onions
3/4 cup soy sauce
1 1/2 teaspoons ground ginger
1/2 cup vegetable oil
2 tablespoons vinegar
3 tablespoons honey
1/2 teaspoon garlic powder
3 pounds flank steak
1 (2-ounce) package sliced almonds
3 tablespoons butter

Chop the green onions halfway up the green part. Discard the remaining green onions or reserve for another use. Combine the chopped green onions, soy sauce, ginger, oil, vinegar, honey and garlic powder in a large bowl and mix well.
Pierce the steak several times. Place in a foil-lined pan.
Pour the soy sauce mixture over the steak. Marinate in the refrigerator for 3 to 4 hours, turning every 30 minutes.
Remove the steak from the marinade, reserving the marinade.
Grill for 6 minutes per side.
Brown the almonds in the butter in a skillet or saucepan.
Stir into the marinade.
Return the steak to the marinade. Heat in a 350-degree oven until the marinade is hot.
Slice the steak crossgrain. Serve in the marinade.
Serve with wild rice or brown rice.
Yield: Six Servings

Beef Stroganoff

*A wonderful version of an old favorite. Great as a
make-ahead entrée for company dinner.*

1½ pounds sirloin steak, cut into ¼x1-inch strips
1½ tablespoons flour
¼ cup melted butter or margarine
1 medium onion, chopped
2 tablespoons flour
1 can condensed beef bouillon
1 tablespoon Worcestershire sauce
1 teaspoon salt
½ teaspoon dry mustard
2 tablespoons tomato paste
1 cup sour cream
1 (6-ounce) can chopped mushrooms, drained, or 8 ounces fresh

*Dredge the steak in 1½ tablespoons flour. Brown quickly in
the butter in a heavy skillet, turning to cook evenly.
Add the onion. Cook for 3 to 4 minutes or just until the onion is tender.
Remove the steak and onion from the skillet and set aside. Blend 2 tablespoons
flour into the pan drippings. Add the beef bouillon and Worcestershire sauce.
Cook until thickened, stirring constantly.
Add the salt, dry mustard and tomato paste. Blend in the sour cream.
Add the steak, onion and mushrooms and mix well.
Cool quickly and pour into freezer containers. Will keep in the freezer for 3 to 6 months.
To serve, thaw partially. Heat in a double boiler over simmering water.
Serve over parsley, rice, wild rice or noodles.*
Yield: Six to Eight Servings

Beef Liver with Onions and Gravy

When Russell Priest shares a recipe, everyone hushes, reads,
or listens. Decatur's renowned cook and caterer shares his delightful
version of this hearty dish for your family to enjoy.

1 cup flour
1 teaspoon salt
1/4 to 1/2 teaspoon pepper
1 teaspoon flavor enhancer (optional)
2 pounds beef liver, sliced
4 to 6 tablespoons butter, softened
1 quart water
3 to 4 tablespoons butter
1/2 teaspoon salt
1/4 teaspoon pepper
1 teaspoon flavor enhancer (optional)
1/4 teaspoon Tabasco sauce
2 tablespoons beef bouillon
1/2 teaspoon Kitchen Bouquet
2 cups chopped onions
2 to 3 tablespoons cornstarch
1/3 cup water

Mix the flour, 1 teaspoon salt, 1/4 to 1/2 teaspoon pepper and 1 teaspoon
flavor enhancer together. Dredge the liver with the flour mixture.
Place the liver on a broiler pan. Spread with 4 to 6 tablespoons butter. Broil
until tender and lightly browned, turning once.
Mix 1 quart water, 3 to 4 tablespoons butter, 1/2 teaspoon salt, 1/4 teaspoon
pepper, 1 teaspoon flavor enhancer, Tabasco sauce, beef bouillon, Kitchen Bouquet
and onions in a saucepan or skillet. Simmer until the onions are tender. Stir in a
mixture of 2 to 3 tablespoons cornstarch and 1/3 cup water.
Place the liver in a baking dish. Pour the onion mixture over the top.
Steam, covered, for 35 minutes.
Note: The liver may be cooked on the grill or in a heavy skillet.
Yield: Six to Eight Servings
Russell Priest, Russell's Place

Eggplant Parmigiana

A superb blending of tastes and textures. The addition of meat to the traditional parmigiana recipe elevates this creation from side dish to entrée.

1/2 cup chopped onion
2 cloves of garlic, crushed
2 tablespoons olive oil
8 ounces ground chuck
1 (35-ounce) can Italian plum tomatoes
1 (6-ounce) can tomato paste
2 teaspoons oregano
1 teaspoon basil
1 1/2 teaspoons salt
1/4 teaspoon pepper
1 tablespoon brown sugar

2 eggs, beaten
1 tablespoon water
1/2 cup Italian bread crumbs
1/2 cup grated Parmesan cheese
1 large unpeeled eggplant, cut into
1/4-inch slices
1/3 cup olive oil
3/4 cup grated Parmesan cheese
1 (8-ounce) package sliced mozzarella
cheese

For the sauce, sauté the onion and garlic in 2 tablespoons olive oil in a skillet until tender. Add the ground chuck. Cook until browned, stirring frequently. Add the undrained tomatoes, tomato paste, oregano, basil, salt, pepper and brown sugar. Simmer, covered, for 1 hour or longer.

For the eggplant, mix the eggs and water in a bowl. Mix the bread crumbs with 1/2 cup Parmesan cheese. Dip the eggplant into the egg mixture, then into the crumb mixture. Heat 1/3 cup olive oil in a skillet. Add the eggplant. Fry until golden brown and crisp. Drain on paper towels.

To assemble, layer half the eggplant, half the 3/4 cup Parmesan cheese, half the mozzarella cheese and half the sauce in a 9x13-inch baking dish. Repeat the layers.

Bake at 350 degrees for 25 minutes or until the cheese is melted.

May be prepared ahead and frozen. Bake, covered with foil, for 45 minutes.

Bake, uncovered, for 15 minutes longer.

Yield: Eight Servings

Plantation Stuffed Peppers

This family favorite can be prepared ahead and frozen for up to two or three months. Working couples and busy moms alike will enjoy popping these out of the freezer for dinner when time is short.

1 pound ground beef
1 cup chopped onion
1 clove of garlic, chopped
2 teaspoons chili powder
1 teaspoon salt
1/2 teaspoon pepper
2 cans tomato soup
8 ounces sharp process cheese, shredded or sliced
1 1/2 cups cooked converted rice
8 medium green bell peppers

Brown the ground beef with the onion and garlic in a skillet, stirring until the ground beef is crumbly. Add the chili powder, salt, pepper and soup and mix well. Simmer, covered, for 10 minutes. Add the cheese. Cook slowly until the cheese melts, stirring occasionally. Stir in the rice. Let cool.
Cut the peppers into halves lengthwise. Remove the membranes and seeds. Cook the peppers in boiling salted water to cover in a saucepan for 3 minutes or just until tender; drain well. Let cool.
Place the peppers on a baking sheet or in a shallow baking pan. Stuff with the rice mixture. Freeze until firm. Wrap the peppers individually in foil or plastic wrap and return to the freezer.
To serve, thaw partially. Remove the wrapping and place the peppers in a shallow pan. Bake, covered with foil, at 400 degrees for 30 to 45 minutes or until heated through.
Yield: Eight Servings

Lemon Veal Parmesan

Wonderful! If veal scallops are not available, substitute boneless chicken breasts. Serve with asparagus and hollandaise sauce and a favorite white wine for special meals. Pictured on page 118.

1/2 to 3/4 cup flour
8 large or 12 medium veal scallops, pounded thin
2 tablespoons grated lemon zest
2 tablespoons grated Parmesan cheese
1 teaspoon freshly ground pepper
1 teaspoon salt
1/4 cup lemon juice
6 tablespoons unsalted butter, preferably clarified
3 tablespoons vegetable oil
8 to 12 very thin lemon slices
2 tablespoons chopped parsley

Flour the veal lightly, shaking to remove any excess. Mix the remaining flour with the lemon zest, cheese, pepper and salt.
Dip the veal in the lemon juice, then into the flour mixture.
Heat the butter and oil in a skillet until the mixture stops foaming.
Add the veal. Sauté quickly over high heat until lightly browned. Add the lemon slices and parsley. Press the lemon slices with the back of a spoon to extract extra juice.
Remove the veal to a warm platter. Spoon the pan juices over the veal.
Yield: Six Servings

On the Side

Vinegar brought to a boil in a new skillet will help prevent foods from sticking thereafter.

Third-Generation Osso Buco
à la Milanese

This Italian recipe meets our pages after three generations of preparation! While in Milan it is traditionally served with a side dish of polenta, down South it is equally enjoyed with a side dish of saffron rice. As veal shanks may be hard to come by in the supermarket, call ahead to plan a magnifico meal.

6 veal shanks
Salt and lemon pepper to taste
1/2 cup flour
1/3 cup olive oil
2 cloves of garlic, crushed
1 medium onion, finely chopped
1 carrot, finely chopped
1 rib celery, finely chopped
1/2 cup dry white wine
1 tablespoon tomato paste
1 large or 2 small vegetable bouillon cubes, crushed

Sprinkle the veal with salt and pepper. Dredge in the flour.
Heat the olive oil in a large deep skillet. Add the garlic. Sauté just
until the garlic changes color.
Add the veal. Cook over medium heat until evenly browned.
Remove the veal and keep warm.
Add the onion, carrot and celery to the skillet. Sauté until the onion is lightly
browned. Add the veal to the skillet. Stir in the wine, tomato paste and bouillon
cube crumbs. Reduce the heat. Simmer, covered, for 1 1/2 hours or
until the veal pulls away from the bone.
Yield: Six Servings

Butterflied Leg of Lamb

Lamb is fabulous on the grill. Try this delicately seasoned marinade
a butterflied cut—a nice change from kabobs. Save more time and
uble by having the butcher butterfly the lamb before taking it home.

1 cup dry red wine
3/4 cup soy sauce
4 large cloves of garlic, crushed
1/2 cup chopped fresh mint
ablespoon coarsely ground pepper

2 tablespoons slightly bruised fresh
rosemary, or 1 tablespoon dried
1 (4- to 5-pound) leg of lamb,
butterflied

Combine the wine, soy sauce, garlic, mint, pepper and rosemary in a bowl
and mix well. Pour over the lamb in a shallow nonreactive baking pan.
Marinate, covered, in the refrigerator for 6 hours, turning frequently.
rain, reserving the marinade. Grill the lamb 4 inches above hot coals for 20
minutes per side or to desired degree of doneness, basting frequently
ith the reserved marinade. Cut into very thin slices. Serve immediately with
corn on the cob, sliced summer tomatoes and a green salad.

Yield: Eight Servings

Roast Leg of Lamb

erved with Mint Sauce (at right) or mint jelly, this dish is a spec-
acular entrée. Add a Middle Eastern touch to the meal and serve
with a rice pilaf, tabouli or Greek salad, and pita bread.

1 (6 1/2-pound) leg of lamb
3 cloves of garlic, cut into slivers
1/2 cup fresh lemon juice

1 1/2 teaspoons dried rosemary
1 1/2 teaspoons coarse pepper
Salt to taste

Cut small evenly spaced slits in the lamb just large enough for the garlic
slivers. Fit the garlic into the slits. Rub the lamb with the lemon juice. Pat
ith the rosemary and pepper. Sprinkle with salt. Place the lamb in a roasting
an. Place in a 400-degree oven. Reduce the oven temperature to 350 degrees.
oast for 1 1/2 hours for medium-rare. Let stand for 10 minutes before carving.

Yield: Six to Eight Servings

Mint Sauce

3/4 to 1 1/2 cups sugar
1 cup cider vinegar
1/4 cup finely chopped fresh
mint leaves

Add the sugar to the vinegar in a
bowl 1/4 cup at a time, stirring
until no more sugar will dissolve.
Add the mint leaves and mix
well. Chill until serving time.
Keeps indefinitely.
Yield: One and One-Half to
Two Cups Sauce

Barbecued Pork

Take a six- to eight-pound Boston butt or fresh picnic shoulder, remove most of the skin and fat, and cover with red (cayenne) pepper (be generous). your taste runs to moist meat, trim less fat and/or cook with the fat side up whole pork shoulder may be used, but requires large cooking facilities.

Place the pork fat side down on a "boat" of several layers of aluminum foil. Fold up the sides to catch the fat produced while cooking. Occasionally spoon the fat onto the coals to produce the smoke which imparts the distinctive flavor of barbecue.

If you have a two-burner gas grill, light one side, turn it as low as possibl and place the pork on the other side. The temperature is about right when t fat smokes heavily but doesn't often flame when spooned onto the coals. Clo the lid and ignore for eight to twelve hours (except for spooning off the fat, The time will depend on how dry or moist you like your meat.

A charcoal grill may be used if it has a cover. The charcoal should be placed at one end, the pork at the other. Many add damp chips hardwood, usually hickory, to the coals several times during the cooking process so that the meat is often surrounded by the hardwood smoke. Temperature is controlled by the addition of more charcoal during the day Traditionalists who love to drink a lot of beer while "working" will want to use this method. Be sure to spoon the fat onto the coals now and then to produce ample smoke.

If you have no grill, an oven on bake at 275 degrees will produce results that will receive the same raves IF you tell no one it was cooked in o oven. Use a broiling pan, not the "boat." Oven thermostats differ and gas grills differ in heat production. Give yourself time for flexibility on your firs try. This will feed ten to twelve or so; it keeps fairly well in the refrigerator freezer to eat later if reheated in the microwave.

Barbecue should ALWAYS be picked and the meat pulled apart into small clumps or it won't taste like proper barbecue. It is NEVER carved. Whethe

served as an entrée or on a bun with coleslaw and mayonnaise or
Miracle Whip, a little red or white sauce (page 133) should be sprinkled
on the individual servings.

Note: Ribs and chicken are almost as simple but do require a little more attention.
They can either be cooked over charcoal or on a gas grill. Ribs are cooked more slowly,
chicken a little hotter. Ribs are easier and much quicker if parboiled (20 to 25 minutes
or until all the pink is gone) before cooking on the grill. Chicken should never be
skinned or it will be too dry. The ribs are cooked over the coals to allow the fat to drip
down; the chicken likewise. When they are good and brown with a few flecks of black,
they are done (45 minutes for parboiled ribs, 45 to 60 minutes for chicken).

Anne Pollard's basting sauce (page 132) is required on chicken and ribs.

Coleslaw

Coleslaw is always served with barbecue. This recipe was handed down to me by my mother, but is modernized for today's cook and kitchen. Using the grating attachment of a food processor or chopping wedges of cabbage for a few seconds in a blender ⅔ full of water makes short work of the grating chore and keeps blood and bits of the tips of your fingers out of the cabbage. I have determined that men are not genetically able to use those rectangular metal grating devices without incurring serious bodily injury.

For each cup of DRAINED grated cabbage, use:

⅛ cup white vinegar	⅛ teaspoon salt
⅛ cup water	2 to 4 drops of Tabasco sauce
¼ cup sugar	

Don't pack the cabbage when measuring; an average head of cabbage is about 6 to 8
cups when grated. Mix the additions, boil until the sugar and salt are dissolved, allow
to cool, add to the cabbage and stir. Allow to sit overnight in the refrigerator.
Yield: Variable

Barbecue, Barbeque, Bar-B-Que or Bar-B-Q

West Indian in origin (probably Haitian), barbecue is believed to come from the Spanish "barbacoa," a framework of sticks on which meat was basted with a sauce while being cooked over coals.

From Haiti, the Creole pronunciation and current meaning spread through the Caribbean and came to us before the Civil War through the slaves of the South. (Haiti was Spanish before it became French.)

Anne Pollard's Famous Basting Sauce for Ribs and Chicken

Although this takes time to prepare, it's absolutely the finest recipe in North America by one of the South's finest cooks.

³/4 cup chopped onion
¹/4 cup vegetable oil
1 clove of garlic, minced
1 cup honey
1 cup catsup
1 cup red wine vinegar

¹/2 cup Worcestershire sauce
1 tablespoon dry mustard
1¹/2 teaspoons salt
1 teaspoon oregano
1 teaspoon pepper
¹/2 teaspoon thyme

Sauté the onion in the oil until the onion is clear. Add everything else and cook on low heat for 15 to 20 minutes. Stir a little while cooking. Baste the ribs or chicken often while cooking so a layer of the sauce builds up on the surface. Toby Sewell has great results with ribs by using pork baby back bo ribs and baking them at 400 degrees for 40 minutes before putting them o the grill. After 20 minutes or so of being basted on the grill they are perfec Try adding ¹/4 to ¹/2 cup brown sugar if you like a sweeter sauce.
Yield: Three Cups Sauce

All-Purpose Barbecue Sauce

Quite different from Anne's recipe but traditional and wonderful.

1 onion, chopped
¹/2 cup butter
2 lemons, cut into halves
2 cups catsup
¹/2 cup Worcestershire sauce

2 tablespoons vinegar
6 tablespoons brown sugar
1 teaspoon salt
1 teaspoon (or more) Tabasco sau
Cracked pepper to taste

Sauté the onion in the butter. Squeeze the juice from the lemons into the p then throw in the lemon halves. Add the remaining ingredients. Simmer for minutes. Baste the ribs or chicken often when they begin to brown. When th are very brown with a few flakes of black on the surface, they are done.
Yield: Three Cups Sauce

Red Sauce for Barbecued Pork

(Or for beef, which is not nearly as good and was never approved by God for barbecue.) Not usually used as a basting sauce, but a seasoning to be sprinkled on individual servings.

3/4 cup vinegar
1/4 cup honey
teaspoons red (cayenne) pepper

1/8 teaspoon salt
2 tea bags

Boil the vinegar, honey, pepper and salt. Add the tea bags and steep until cool. You may add additional red pepper, but try it first. If honey is not available, use 1/4 cup water and 4 teaspoons sugar. The honey and sugar are not universally accepted. You may delete.

Yield: One Cup Sauce

Weise Troup's Famous Barbecue Sauce

The sauce debate continues: thick or thin? This notable sauce is stick-to-your-ribs wonderful and is considered by many to be North Alabama's best tasting.

4 cup chili sauce or tomato sauce
3/4 cup water
1/2 cup Worcestershire sauce
1 teaspoon paprika
1 teaspoon sugar

1 cup vinegar
1 cup catsup
1 teaspoon dried mustard
1 teaspoon salt
1/4 cup unsalted butter

Bring all the ingredients to a boil in a saucepan, stirring constantly. Boil for 5 minutes, stirring constantly. Remove from the heat and let cool. Store in canning jars. Refrigerate after opening.

Yield: One Quart Sauce

White Sauce

(Stolen from Sammy Stone, who says he stole it from someone else, but can no longer remember from whom.) Vary to suit your taste.

1/2 cup white or red wine vinegar
1/4 cup water
1 teaspoon (or more) pepper
2 tablespoons sugar, or to taste
1/2 cup mayonnaise

Add more or less mayonnaise for a thicker or thinner sauce and/or less water for a stronger sauce. You may add MORE, not less, pepper. Many insist it's not right without as much as 1 to 1 1/2 tablespoons pepper. Some say just the IDEA of adding sugar is barbaric. I like the sugar. But then Stone once said I was barbaric because I tended to take my evening meal before 8:30. Primarily used on chicken, White Sauce has also been sprinkled on just about everything else from pork (in lieu of red sauce) and ribs to biscuits and rolls.

Yield: One Cup Sauce

Ribs

There are three basic types of ribs: spareribs, cut from the brisket area; baby back ribs, cut from the loin; and country-style ribs, cut from the sirloin. Spareribs have the least meat (buy about one pound per person), baby back ribs a little more meat (¾ pound), and country-style the most meat (½ pound). If you have a number of guests, you might buy one extra slab or a few extra baby back ribs for seconds. Only pork ribs are nonpoisonous—all others will assuredly impart loathsome social diseases to the unfortunate diner.

Quick and Easy Ribs

Like all these recipes, this one makes the preparation of an epicurean delight to a number of guests quick and simple. Caution: Guests who haven't eaten since lunch may become an annoyance if the breeze blows the aroma in their direction.

Place the ribs in a broiling pan (if using spareribs or country-style ribs, c. the slabs to fit the pan) and pour over them a basting sauce made of half water and half cider or red wine vinegar. For up to 6 pounds of ribs, 2 cups this basting sauce is plenty. Cover the pan with a lid or aluminum foil. Pla it in an oven at 275 degrees for 45 minutes for baby back or country-style r or 1 hour to 1 hour and 15 minutes for spareribs. Baste the ribs a time or tv with the water and vinegar while cooking. While the ribs are cooking, prepo a barbecue cooking sauce by combining the following in a saucepan:

1½ cups catsup	½ cup packed brown sugar
1 cup cider vinegar	⅛ teaspoon Tabasco sauce
½ cup butter	¼ teaspoon salt
¼ cup prepared mustard	3 lemons, peelings and all
⅓ cup Worcestershire sauce	

Stir, adding a little water for a less spicy sauce. Simmer until the ribs are done. Remove the ribs, pour out the basting sauce and place the ribs on a g or charcoal grill at low to medium heat. Cook for 30 to 40 minutes, turnin several times and slopping on the cooking sauce. Try not to let the coals cat fire or the sauce will turn to a black crust, which really isn't so bad-tasting it is bad-looking. And, as we all know, PRESENTATION is soooo important someone who is soon to eat with his hands. Tip: Buy one of those little met oven thermometers and place it in the grill; 250 to 275 degrees is about foolproof for cooking your meat. Try cooking spareribs all day at 190 to 20 degrees without first parboiling. Time-consuming, but maybe the best tastin

Yield: Four Cups Sauce

Adams' Ribs

1 tablespoon garlic powder
1 tablespoon Creole seasoning
(he uses Zatarian's)
1 tablespoon Worcestershire sauce
2 tablespoons pepper
7 to 9 pounds pork spareribs

Mix the first four ingredients and thoroughly rub into the ribs. Grill with the lid down at 300 to 325 degrees for 3 hours or so, turning after 1 hour. After 2 hours, turn and baste several times until done.
Yield: Ten to Twelve Servings

Basting Sauce

¼ cup packed brown sugar
¼ cup Worcestershire sauce
¼ cup prepared mustard
¾ cup catsup
2 tablespoons black pepper
to 2 tablespoons cayenne pepper
or crushed dried red pepper
3 cups red wine vinegar
1 cup water
1 cup white wine (remainder in bottle must be judiciously consumed while cooking or the ribs won't look quite right when done)

Combine the ingredients. Cook over medium heat for 1 hour.
Yield: Six Cups Sauce

Serving Sauce

1 tablespoon butter or margarine
1 medium to large onion, finely chopped
½ tablespoon minced garlic
1 cup catsup
½ cup white vinegar
¼ cup lemon juice
¼ cup steak seasoning
(he uses Dale's)
2 tablespoons brown sugar
1 tablespoon Cajun seasoning (he uses Luzianne's)
2 tablespoons liquid smoke

Melt the butter in a skillet. Stir and cook the onion until clear. Add the remaining ingredients and cook for 15 minutes longer.
Yield: Two and One-Half Cups Sauce

Justice Adams

The recipe of Mr. Justice Oscar W. Adams, the first of his race to be elected to the Alabama Supreme Court—and one of my favorite justices, as he once reversed and rendered the decree of a circuit judge who had the temerity to rule against me. The Judge's ribs are a three-step process: preparation of the ribs before cooking, preparation and use of a separate basting sauce while cooking, and application of a seasoning sauce to be applied before serving.

Andrea Chenault's
Three-Step Ribs

This recipe won first prize at the Morgan County Cookoff. The special sauce recipe was handed down to Andrea from her grandfather.

4 pounds spareribs (allow at least ½ pound per person)
2 teaspoons hickory-flavored salt or liquid smoke

3 cups water
1 cup (about) hickory wood chips
Barbecue Sauce

STEP ONE: *Prepare the grill—15 minutes on high on a gas grill. Charcoal is ready when evenly covered with gray ash. Portion ribs into sections that will fit in a large baking pan. When gas grill or coals are ready, sear the rib portions on both sides.*

STEP TWO: *Preheat the oven to 375 degrees. Line a large baking pan with heavy-duty foil. Position the ribs in the pan. Mix the salt and water and pour into the pan with the ribs. Cover the pan tightly with heavy-duty foil; two layers may be necessary. Bake for 1 to 1½ hours or until the meat begins to pull easily from the bones.*

While baking the ribs, prepare the Barbecue Sauce:

½ cup margarine
1 small onion, finely chopped
1½ cups white vinegar
1 cup catsup
¼ cup Worcestershire sauce

1 tablespoon Tabasco sauce
1 tablespoon salt
3 tablespoons prepared mustard
Juice of 1 lemon

Mix all the ingredients in a saucepan and bring to a boil. Reduce the heat and simmer for 1 hour. The sauce may be prepared in advance and refrigerated if necessary.

STEP THREE: *Combine the wood chips with enough water to soak. Bring a gas grill to medium heat or add charcoal to "rebuild" the fire in the grill. When the coals are ready (a slow fire is preferable for this step), sprinkle evenly with the wood chips. Return the ribs to the grill and begin basting with the sauce, taking care not to burn. Turn and baste until the ribs are thoroughly drenched in sauce.*

Yield: Six to Eight Servings

Boneless Pork Loin with Tangy Sauce

Becky Conroy suggests serving this delicious pork dish with El Mirador Rice, page 208.

3 tablespoons garlic powder
3 tablespoons chili powder
4 pounds pork loin, boneless
Tangy Sauce

Mix the garlic powder and chili powder together. Rub over the pork loin. Place the pork loin in a roasting pan. Bake at 350 degrees for 2 hours or until cooked through. Drizzle Tangy Sauce over the pork loin 20 minutes before the end of the cooking time. Serve any excess sauce on the side. May add pan drippings to the sauce.
Yield: Eight to Ten Servings

Tangy Sauce

1 cup apple jelly
1 cup catsup
2 tablespoons cider vinegar
2 teaspoons chili powder
Salt to taste

Combine the jelly, catsup, vinegar, chili powder and salt in a saucepan. Bring to a boil, stirring frequently.
Yield: Two Cups Sauce
Becky Conroy, Decatur Country Club

Choucroute for Pork and Sausage

A hearty sauce for German sausages, roast pork, game, or smoked meats for hungry fall or winter appetites.

1 pork knuckle or 8 ounces bacon
1 tart apple or baking apple, peeled, sliced
1 small can crushed pineapple
1/4 to 1/2 cup juniper berries
10 peppercorns
1/4 teaspoon caraway seeds, or to taste
2 jars sauerkraut, rinsed
2 bay leaves
1 small onion, finely chopped
2 cloves
2 cups white wine
1 cup chicken stock

Combine all the ingredients in a heavy Dutch oven or römertopf. Bake at 325 degrees for 2 hours. Add cooked sausages near the end of the cooking time just to heat through.
Yield: Eight to Ten Servings

A Yankee Tale of Country Ham

Yankee, beware! When you move to this region of mild winters and magnolias, you will surely be tempted to try your hand at the local cuisine—sometimes with questionable results. Take a lesson from this migrant who confessed to the following story:

"We moved to Decatur shortly before Christmas and worked furiously to get our new home ready for the holidays. While we planned our Christmas dinner, my husband announced that, as new residents of Alabama, we must include a country ham—a fine idea for our first Southern holiday feast. Little did I know that I would be faced with such a selection! I returned home from my supermarket adventure and proudly presented the biggest I could find. At once I was reprimanded for my grave error:

Grilled Garlic Lime Pork with Jalapeño Onion Marmalade

Pork tenderloins are dressed for success with this fabulous entrée, pictured on page 118.

6 large cloves of garlic, chopped
2 tablespoons soy sauce
2 tablespoons grated fresh gingerroot
2 teaspoons Dijon mustard
⅓ cup fresh lime juice

½ cup olive oil
Salt and cayenne to taste
4 (12-ounce) pork tenderloins, trimmed
Jalapeño Onion Marmalade

*C*ombine the garlic, soy sauce, gingerroot, Dijon mustard, lime juice, olive salt and cayenne in a food processor or blender container. Process until mix Pour into a sealable large plastic bag. Add the pork and seal. Place in a shallow dish. Marinate in the refrigerator for 24 to 48 hours, turning occasionally. Let the pork stand at room temperature for 30 minutes. Remo from the marinade, discarding the marinade. Grill on an oiled rack 5 to 6 inches above glowing coals for 15 to 20 minutes or until a meat thermome registers 160 degrees, turning every 5 minutes. Remove to a cutting board. stand for 5 minutes before slicing. Serve with Jalapeño Onion Marmalade
Yield: Six Servings

Jalapeño Onion Marmalade

1¼ pounds red or yellow onions, finely chopped
Salt and pepper to taste
3 tablespoons olive oil

2 jalapeño chiles, seeded, mince
2 tablespoons honey or sugar
3 to 4 tablespoons red wine vineg
¼ cup water

*C*ook the onions, salt and pepper in the olive oil in a large heavy skillet ov medium heat until softened, stirring constantly. Add the jalapeños. Cook fo 1 minute, stirring constantly. Add the honey. Cook for 1 minute, stirring constantly. Add the vinegar. Simmer until most of the liquid has evaporate stirring constantly. Add the water. Simmer for 10 minutes or until the mixt is slightly thickened and the onions are very tender, stirring constantly.
Note: Wear rubber gloves while working with the jalapeños.
Yield: Six Servings

138

Country Ham

Curing ham could be characterized as a Southern art form, and many a farm would not be considered complete without its smokehouse out back. A slow and arduous process, curing for some of the finest hams takes a year or more. Whatever the method, country ham must be properly soaked and boiled before eating to avoid disastrous results (at far left). Country ham is enjoyed both as a main dish and in biscuits, sandwiches and salads.

Scrub a 14- to 16-pound country ham thoroughly with hot water and rinse well. Place in a large kettle with a tightfitting cover. (If a large kettle is not available, the ham may be cut into halves and each half cooked separately.) Cover the ham with cold water. Cover and bring to a boil. Pour off the water. Cover again with cold water. Cover and bring to a boil. Reduce the heat. Simmer, covered, for 4 to 6 hours or until a meat thermometer inserted into the center at the thickest part of the lean meat reaches 170 degrees. Remove the ham from the kettle. Let stand for 15 to 20 minutes for the juices to be absorbed before slicing. Serve hot or cold.

For Baked Country Ham, remove the ham from the kettle 30 minutes before it is cooked through. Remove any rind, being careful not to remove the fat. Score the fat with diagonal diamond-shaped cuts. Place whole cloves in the center of the diamonds. Place fat side up on a rack in a shallow roasting pan. Mix 1 cup packed brown sugar, 1 tablespoon flour and 1 teaspoon dry mustard in a bowl. Stir in 2 tablespoons vinegar. Spread over the ham. Bake at 300 degrees for 30 to 40 minutes or until the ham is cooked through and the glaze is set.

Yield: Twenty to Thirty Servings

"I had bought a fresh ham—not a country one. After an animated discussion on communication skills and one more trip to the store, he returned home with a large sack. We unwrapped the strange looking thing, stared in amazement, and searched unsuccessfully for baking instructions. Christmas morning, we scrubbed off the mold, washed the ham, and placed it in the oven to warm. Several hours later, with great ceremony, the meat was carved and tasted. The salt was enough to raise the blood pressure of the entire city! So, we tried boiling the thing for several hours and carved again. This time it was palatable— but not for my palate. So much for country ham!"

An Anonymous Yankee

Moral of the Story: If you do not have a good Southern cook at hand to direct your hamming, follow these instructions.

Grilled Dove

Rick Paler of Huntsville's Green Bottle Grill shares his mother's game bird recipes that will be sure to please.

3 to 4 doves, dressed
Salt and pepper to taste
Buttermilk
Bacon

Season each dove inside and out with salt and pepper. Soak in buttermilk for 12 hours to overnight. Remove from the buttermilk and wrap completely in bacon, securing with wooden picks.
Place water-soaked hickory chips in hot coals. Push the coals to 1 side to allow for indirect cooking of the dove.
Place breast side down on the cool side of the grill. Close the lid and open the vent above the dove. Grill for 40 minutes or until cooked through, turning once.
Yield: One Serving
Rick Paler, Green Bottle Grill

Grilled Quail

2 quail, dressed
Soy sauce or Dale's Seasoning Sauce
Olive oil
Salt, pepper and garlic to taste
Fresh bay leaves, rosemary and thyme

Marinate the quail in soy sauce or Dale's Seasoning Sauce in the refrigerator overnight. Remove quail from the marinade.
Rub each bird with olive oil. Season with salt, pepper and garlic to taste. Stuff quail with herbs as desired.
Grill using the directions for Grilled Dove (above), basting with the remaining marinade midway through grilling.
Yield: One Serving
Rick Paler, Green Bottle Grill

On the Side

Gravy lumps can be avoided if you add a pinch of salt to the flour before mixing it with water.

Dyrc's Duck

The call of the wild seizes most Southern men at some point
in their lives. Devoted wives, good cooks and some of the hunters themselves,
have developed wonderful recipes that celebrate the success of the hunt
with a great meal. This is one such recipe.

2 to 4 ducks, cleaned
Salt and black pepper to taste
Flour
Vegetable oil
2 (10-ounce) cans French onion soup
1 soup can water
1 soup can white wine
Bay leaves to taste
Thyme to taste
Cumin and lemon pepper to taste
2 (10-ounce) cans cream of mushroom soup

Leave the skin on the ducks. Season inside and out with salt
and black pepper. Coat with flour.
Cook the ducks in a small amount of oil in a Dutch oven until browned.
Add the French onion soup, water and wine. Add additional salt
and black pepper, bay leaves, thyme, cumin and lemon pepper.
Bake, covered, at 350 degrees for 2 hours, turning after 1 hour.
Add the mushroom soup and enough water to reach 3/4 of the way
up the ducks. Season with additional cumin.
Bake for 2 hours longer or until the meat falls away from the bone.
Serve over a bed of wild rice.
Yield: Four to Eight Servings

Fall Haul

Before accepting a hunter's "fall haul," try to find out how the meat has been handled and how much time will have elapsed from the time of the demise to the time of the dinner. Properly field-dressed game that goes quickly to the freezer or grill reflects the flavor of meat from an animal that feeds naturally and exercises freely. Game that is carelessly handled can have the offensive wild flavor of "road kill."

Grilled Venison and Vegetables

A good marinade often saves venison meals from disaster in the kitchen. This kabob recipe is a great way to use up all that meat in the freezer. Serve over a bed of white or wild rice. For even easier preparation, use one cup of your favorite bottled spicy Italian-style salad dressing for the marinade.

1/2 cup red wine vinegar
1/4 cup honey
1/4 cup soy sauce
2 tablespoons catsup
1/8 teaspoon pepper, or to taste
1/8 teaspoon garlic powder, or to taste
1 1/2 pounds boneless venison steak, cut into 1 1/4-inch cubes
8 to 12 small new potatoes
8 to 12 cherry tomatoes
8 to 12 fresh mushrooms (optional)
1/2 medium green pepper or sweet red pepper, cut into 1 1/2-inch pieces
1 to 2 small zucchini, cut into 1-inch chunks
1 large onion, cut into wedges

Combine the vinegar, honey, soy sauce, catsup, pepper and garlic powder i[n] glass bowl or sealable plastic bag and mix well. Measure and set aside 1/4 cup. Add the venison to the marinade and stir or shake to coat. Cover t[he] bowl or seal the bag. Marinate in the refrigerator for 4 hours. Parboil the potatoes in boiling water in a saucepan until partially cooked; drain well Toss the potatoes, tomatoes, mushrooms, green pepper, zucchini and onio[n] with the reserved marinade. Let stand for 1 hour.
Drain the venison, reserving the marinade. Thread the venison and vegetab[le] alternately onto skewers. Brush with the reserved marinade.
Grill over medium-hot coals for 15 to 20 minutes or to desired degree of doneness, turning and basting frequently. Remove from the skewers to serv[e]
Yield: Four to Six Servings

Seafood &
Poultry

Simp McGhee's

Woven into the fabric of Decatur's early
history are various tales of Simp McGhee,
a riverboat captain who regularly put into port
here. In addition to conducting shipping business
and overseeing his saloon, he often visited his
very good friend Miss Kate, Decatur's most
prominent madam.
In 1986, Bob and Ginnie Lind Riddle opened a
restaurant in an old building on Bank Street—
just a block from the site of Miss Kate's
establishment—and named it Simp McGhee's.
Interestingly, the top and the brass rail of the
restaurant's bar are those from the original Simp's.

*Simp McGhee's specializes in seafood and
Cajun fare and serves well as a setting for our
offering of seafood and poultry dishes:
Shrimp Scampi;
Citrus-Baked Cornish Hens;
and Corn Pudding.*

Cilantro Sauce

Serve this sauce with the catfish for a gourmet meal!

2 tablespoons minced fresh
cilantro
¹/₂ cup sour cream
¹/₄ teaspoon pepper
¹/₄ teaspoon salt
2 tablespoons fresh lemon juice

Mix the cilantro, sour cream, pepper, salt and lemon juice in a glass bowl. Chill, covered, for 24 hours to allow the flavors to blend.
Yield: One-Half Cup Sauce

Fried Pond-Fed Catfish

Always available fresh or frozen in Southern grocery stores, catfis has gained national attention in recent years as a mild-flavored healthy fish that can be enjoyed grilled, baked, broiled, and blacken. as well as fried. You can't drive far in the Deep South before passing one of the many catfish restaurants that dot the highways and country roadsides. Many raise their catfish right on the premis in large ponds, although some stalwart fishermen insist on catchin their own in rivers, inlets, ponds, and lakes.

¹/₂ cup yellow cornmeal
2 teaspoons ground cumin
¹/₄ cup flour
2 tablespoons grated lemon peel
¹/₂ teaspoon cayenne
6 catfish fillets
¹/₂ cup buttermilk
2 tablespoons butter
1 tablespoon vegetable oil
Cilantro Sauce (at left)

*Combine the cornmeal, cumin, flour, lemon peel and cayenne in a shallo dish and mix well. Dip each catfish fillet in the buttermilk in a dish, turning coat both sides. Coat each fillet thoroughly with the cornmeal mixture. M store the coated fillets in a covered container in the refrigerator for up to hours. Heat the butter and oil in a heavy skillet over medium heat until the butter is melted. Add the fish. Cook for 5 minutes or until browned and crusty, turning once.
Serve immediately with Cilantro Sauce. Garnish with lemon wedges.*
Yield: Six Servings

Catfish Cakes

Catfish are plentiful in this part of the country. Crabs are not—hence, this cotton country version of the crab cake. Serve as an entrée, or serve one or two on some curly lettuce leaves for a hearty first course.

1½ pounds catfish fillets
1 large potato, peeled
2 eggs, beaten
1 large onion, finely chopped
1 to 2 tablespoons chopped fresh parsley
2 to 3 drops of hot pepper sauce
1 clove of garlic, minced
1 teaspoon salt
½ teaspoon pepper
½ teaspoon dried basil
2 cups finely crushed butter-flavor crackers
Vegetable oil
Tartar sauce (optional)

Poach or bake the fish; drain well. Cover and chill thoroughly. Boil or bake the potato; mash well. Flake the fish into a large bowl. Add the potato, eggs, onion, parsley, hot pepper sauce, garlic, salt, pepper and basil and mix well. Shape the mixture into 8 patties. Coat with the cracker crumbs. Heat a small amount of oil in a large skillet; add the patties. Cook until evenly browned and heated through. Serve with tartar sauce.

Yield: Eight Servings

Terrific Trout or Salmon Basting Sauce

Straight from a fisherman's mouth. This delectable sauce adds extra zest to fresh fish.

2 cups apple juice
1/3 cup light soy sauce
1/4 cup wine vinegar
1 cup finely chopped green onions
2 tablespoons freshly grated ginger
1 tablespoon minced fresh garlic

Mix all the ingredients in a bowl. Brush each side of the fish with the mixture. Bake the fish skin side up in a baking dish at 400 degrees for 10 minutes. Turn the fish and baste liberally. Bake for 5 minutes. Baste the fish with the drippings and bake for 5 minutes longer. May sprinkle the fish with paprika, dill, or another favorite herb or spice instead of basting with drippings. Note: May also be cooked on the grill.
Yield: Three to Four Cups Sauce

Marinated Grilled Swordfish with Mango Relish

The mango is a large orange-yellow juicy-fleshed tropical fruit, no found in many grocery stores in the summer. Peak season is June. The flavor resembles a combination of pineapple and peach, and it often used as a base for chutneys, jams, and jellies. Try this quick and delicious mango relish to serve with this swordfish.

1/4 cup sesame oil
1 tablespoon minced fresh ginger
1 tablespoon soy sauce
1 clove of garlic, minced
1/4 cup chopped fresh cilantro
4 swordfish steaks
Mango Relish (below)

Combine the sesame oil, ginger, soy sauce, garlic and cilantro in a large bowl and mix well. Pour over the fish in a foil-lined pan. Marinate, covered, in the refrigerator for several hours. Remove the fish from the marinade, discarding the marinade. Grill until the fish flakes easily. Serve with Mango Relish. Note: If swordfish is not available, try skinless chicken breasts. Either is healthy and good!
Yield: Four Servings

Mango Relish

1 mango, peeled, finely chopped
2 tablespoons chopped red onion
1/2 cup finely chopped fresh cilantro
Juice of 1 lime

Combine the mango, onion, cilantro and lime juice in a bowl and mix we
Yield: One and One-Half Cups

148

Crab and Artichoke Casserole

The delicate tastes of crab meat and artichokes need very little seasoning. The sauce adds just enough flavor to make this seafood combination really delicious.

1/2 cup butter
3 tablespoons minced onion
1/2 cup flour
1 quart cream, heated to the boiling point
1/2 cup madeira
Salt and pepper to taste
2 tablespoons lemon juice
4 cups fresh or canned crab meat
3 (9-ounce) packages frozen artichoke hearts, cooked, drained
2 1/2 cups shell macaroni, cooked, drained
2 cups shredded Gruyère cheese or Swiss cheese
Paprika (optional)

*Melt the butter in a large heavy saucepan. Add the onion. Sauté until golden brown.
Stir in the flour. Cook over low heat until the flour is pale yellow,
stirring constantly. Remove from the heat. Add the cream, stirring
vigorously. Bring to a boil over medium heat; reduce the heat.
Add the madeira. Season with salt and pepper.
Pour the lemon juice over the crab meat in a bowl and toss lightly.
Combine the crab meat, artichoke hearts, macaroni and cream mixture in a buttered
6-quart casserole. Sprinkle with the cheese. Dust with paprika.
Bake at 350 degrees for 25 to 30 minutes or until heated through.
May be prepared 1 day ahead and stored in the refrigerator.
Bring to room temperature before baking.*
Yield: Ten to Twelve Servings

Crawfish

Crawfish, also called crayfish or crawdads (and sometimes langostinos), are small clawless freshwater crustaceans, similar in appearance to lobsters. They are caught on the muddy bottoms of Louisiana's bayous. When cooked, the tail contains a delicate white meat that is prized as a Cajun delicacy.

Crawfish Etouffée

One of Louisiana's finest culinary creations for a truly Creole me•
If crawfish are not available, shrimp make a fine substitute.

2 teaspoons salt
2 teaspoons cayenne or other
ground red pepper
1 teaspoon white pepper
1 teaspoon black pepper
1 teaspoon dried sweet basil
1/2 teaspoon dried thyme
7 tablespoons vegetable oil
3/4 cup flour
1/4 cup chopped onion
1/4 cup chopped celery

1/4 cup chopped green bell pepp•
2 cups Basic Seafood Stock
(page 151)
1/2 cup butter
2 pounds crawfish tails, peeled,
medium shrimp, peeled, devein•
1 cup finely chopped green onio•
1/2 cup butter
1 cup Basic Seafood Stock
4 cups hot cooked rice

For the seasoning mix, combine the salt, cayenne, white pepper, black
pepper, basil and thyme in a bowl and set aside. For the roux, heat the oil •
large heavy cast-iron skillet over high heat for 4 minutes or until the oil beg•
to smoke. Add the flour gradually, stirring with a long-handled metal whi•
until smooth. Cook for 3 to 5 minutes or until the roux is dark brown,
whisking constantly. Remove from the heat. Stir in the onion, celery, gree•
pepper and 1 tablespoon of the seasoning mix. Continue stirring for 5 minu•
or until the mixture has cooled. For the stock mixture, bring 2 cups Basi•
Seafood Stock to a boil in a 2-quart saucepan over high heat. Add the rou•
gradually, whisking until incorporated. Reduce the heat to low. Cook for •
minutes or until the flour taste is gone, whisking almost constantly (if an•
part of the mixture scorches, stop scraping that part of the pan bottom).
Remove from the heat and set aside. For the etouffée, melt 1/2 cup butter in •
4-quart saucepan over medium heat. Stir in the crawfish and green onion•
Sauté for 1 minute. Add 1/2 cup butter, the stock mixture and 1 cup Basi•
Seafood Stock. Cook for 4 to 6 minutes or until the butter is melted and mi•
into the sauce, shaking the pan back and forth constantly. Stir in the
remaining seasoning mix. Remove from the heat. If the sauce begins to
separate, add 2 tablespoons stock or water and shake the pan until the sau•
recombines. Mound 1/2 cup rice on each of 8 heated plates. Surround the r•
with 3/4 cup of the etouffée. Note: See page 90 for more about making a rou•
Yield: Eight Servings

Low Country Shrimp

The Low Country along the Atlantic coasts of North and South Carolina, is a haven for crab, shrimp, sea turtles, and tourists! This dish from Dean Moore of Simp McGhee's in Decatur combines both sweet and smoky flavors for a wonderful taste sensation!

10 slices bacon
2 cups chopped yellow onions
2 cups chopped ham
3 (16-ounce) cans black-eyed peas
1/4 teaspoon cinnamon
1/4 teaspoon dried thyme
1/4 teaspoon granulated garlic
1/2 teaspoon liquid smoke
1/2 teaspoon cayenne
1/4 teaspoon granulated onion
Salt and pepper to taste
2 tablespoons honey
2 pounds medium shrimp, peeled, deveined
2 cups cooked rice

Cook the bacon in a saucepan until cooked through. Remove and chop the bacon. Cook the chopped onions in the bacon drippings in the saucepan until tender. Stir in the bacon and ham. Combine the black-eyed peas, onion mixture, cinnamon, thyme, garlic, liquid smoke, cayenne, granulated onion, salt, pepper and honey in a stockpot. Simmer over low heat for 30 minutes. Add the shrimp and rice. Cook until the shrimp turn pink. Serve immediately.
Yield: Ten to Twelve Servings
Dean Moore, Simp McGhee's

Basic Seafood Stock

Start with 2 quarts cold water, or enough to cover the other stock ingredients, in a stockpot or large saucepan. Add vegetable trimmings from the recipe you are serving (or 1 quartered medium onion, 1 quartered large clove of garlic and 1 rib celery). Add 1 1/2 to 2 pounds rinsed shrimp heads and/or shells; or 1 1/2 to 2 pounds crawfish heads and/or shells; or 2 1/2 to 3 quarts crab shells; or rinsed fish carcasses with heads and gills removed; or any combination of these. Bring to a boil over high heat. Simmer, gently, uncovered or partially covered, for 4 to 8 hours, adding additional water as needed to maintain 1 quart of liquid in the stockpot. Strain and let cool. Refrigerate until needed. If time is short, using a stock that has been simmered for 20 to 30 minutes is better than using plain water!
Yield: One Quart

Shrimp

A delicacy often enjoyed as an appetizer at inland tables, shrimp are eaten by the cauldron-full in the shrimp boating towns along the South's Gulf Coast. Traditionally, at the commencement of annual Shrimp Festivals, one of the local priests would board a shrimper, winding in and out of the harbor, dispersing holy water in a solemn Blessing of the Fleet. While most of us can ill-afford heaps of shrimp on our tables, we've included a few entrées that show off the wonderful flavor of this delicate shellfish.

Shrimp à la Creole

A Creole sauce is a fine balance of tomatoes, onions, peppers, garlic and cayenne. Throw in shrimp and voilà—Shrimp Creole!

2 tablespoons olive oil
2 cups chopped onions
1/4 cup chopped green bell pepper
1 cup chopped fresh parsley
1/2 cup dry white wine
4 cups chopped fresh or canned tomatoes
1 tablespoon minced garlic
1 tablespoon Worcestershire sauce
1 cup tomato sauce
Salt and cayenne to taste
1/2 teaspoon crushed dried mint
2 pounds shrimp, peeled, deveined

Heat the olive oil in an electric wok or a large skillet over medium-high heat. Add the onions, green pepper and parsley. Sauté until the onions are translucent. Stir in the wine, tomatoes, garlic, Worcestershire sauce, tomato sauce, salt, cayenne and mint. Cook, covered, over medium-high heat until the sauce comes to a boil. Reduce the heat to low. Simmer, covered, for 1 hour. Add the shrimp. Simmer for 30 minutes longer or until the shrimp turn pink, stirring occasionally.
Serve over rice or noodles.
Yield: Eight Servings

Shrimp with Thai Noodles

*Ginger, bean sprouts, and snow peas turn this shrimp
dish into an Asian delight!*

1 pound small shrimp, shelled
4 ounces Oriental noodles or spaghetti
3 tablespoons vegetable oil
2 teaspoons freshly grated gingerroot
3 cloves of garlic, minced
1 red bell pepper, thinly sliced
1/2 cup sliced green onions
6 ounces bean sprouts
1 cup snow peas, sliced diagonally into 1/4-inch strips
1/4 cup grated carrots
3 tablespoons rice vinegar
1/8 teaspoon cayenne
1/2 teaspoon Mongolian fire oil, or red pepper flakes to taste
1 tablespoon soy sauce
1 tablespoon sesame oil
1 to 2 tablespoons minced fresh cilantro
1/2 cup chopped roasted peanuts

*Rinse the shrimp and pat dry on paper towels. Set aside.
Boil the spaghetti in water to cover in a saucepan just until done; drain and set aside.
Heat the vegetable oil in a large skillet. Add the gingerroot and garlic. Sauté
briefly. Add the red pepper and green onions. Sauté until the red pepper and
green onions begin to soften. Remove from the heat.
Rinse the bean sprouts. Microwave on High for 30 seconds or blanch for 1 minute.
Add the bean sprouts, snow peas and carrots to the green onion mixture.
Add the shrimp and spaghetti and stir well.
Mix the vinegar, cayenne, Mongolian oil, soy sauce and sesame oil in a bowl.
Pour over the shrimp mixture, stirring to blend the flavors.
May serve at this point or chill to serve cold.
Arrange the shrimp mixture on a platter. Top with the cilantro and peanuts.
Yield: Four to Six Servings*

Shrimp Scampi

Pictured on page 144, this microwave version of the classic Italian recipe couldn't be easier or more delicious, especially if you love the flavor of garlic. Serve over pasta or rice with a salad and Italian bread for your next dinner party.

3 tablespoons butter
2 cloves of garlic, finely chopped
½ cup white wine

Parsley flakes to taste
1 pound fresh scampi or shrimp, peeled,
deveined

Combine the butter, garlic, wine and parsley flakes in a 1½-quart glass casserole. Microwave on High for 2 minutes. Stir in the scampi. Microwave on High for 4 minutes or until the scampi turn pink. Let stand for 5 minutes before serving.
Yield: Four Servings

Basil Grilled Chicken

A nice change from tomato-based or soy sauce-based barbecue sauces, the aromatic flavor of basil makes a fine basting sauce and herb butter for this grilled chicken dish.

4 chicken breasts, skinned
3/4 teaspoon coarsely ground pepper
1/3 cup melted butter or margarine
1/4 cup chopped fresh basil
1/2 cup butter or margarine, softened
2 tablespoons minced fresh basil
1 tablespoon grated Parmesan cheese
1/4 teaspoon garlic powder
1/8 teaspoon salt
1/8 teaspoon pepper

Rinse the chicken and pat dry. Press 3/4 teaspoon pepper into the meaty sides of the chicken.

Mix melted butter with 1/4 cup basil in a bowl. Brush some of the mixture lightly over the chicken.

Combine softened butter, 2 tablespoons basil, cheese, garlic powder, salt and 1/8 teaspoon pepper in a small mixer bowl. Beat at low speed until well mixed and smooth. Remove to a small serving bowl and set aside.

Grill the chicken over medium coals for 8 to 10 minutes per side or until cooked through, basting frequently with the remaining melted butter mixture.

Serve with the herb butter mixture. Garnish with fresh basil sprigs.

Yield: Four Servings

Cranberry Cinnamon Relish

A tart and spicy accompaniment for poultry.

2 large packages cranberries
2¹/₂ cups sugar
¹/₂ teaspoon cinnamon
2 tablespoons lemon juice
1 jar marmalade

Mix the cranberries, sugar and cinnamon in a bowl. Spoon into a casserole. Bake at 350 degrees for 45 minutes. Remove from the oven and stir in the lemon juice and marmalade. Chill until serving time.
Yield: Six to Eight Servings

Boursin Chicken in Phyllo

Chef Ron Casey of Decatur Country Club wraps herbs and chick in a crispy crust of phyllo—great for dinners or formal luncheons.

8 (4-ounce) boneless skinless chicken breasts
8 ounces boursin cheese, softened
1 clove of garlic, crushed
1 teaspoon caraway seeds
1 teaspoon dried basil
1 teaspoon dried chives
1 teaspoon dried dillweed
3 sheets phyllo dough
Melted butter

Rinse the chicken and pat dry. Mix the cheese, garlic, caraway seeds, bas chives and dillweed in a bowl. Spread 1 tablespoon of the mixture over the center of each chicken breast and roll up. Brush the phyllo with some of the butter. Cut into 8 squares and wrap each chicken breast with the dough. Brush each roll with butter. Place in a shallow baking pan. Bake at 350 degrees for 20 minutes or until the chicken is cooked through.
Yield: Eight Servings
Ron Casey, Decatur Country Club

Broccoli Chicken Roll-Ups

This dish captures "south-of-the-border" flavor while not taxing the cook with a search for unusual or hard-to-find ingredients. Once you try it, prepare to handle requests for repeat performances.

1 (10-ounce) can cream of mushroom soup
1 cup milk
3 to 4 chicken breasts, cooked, boned, chopped
1 (10-ounce) package frozen chopped broccoli, thawed, drained
1 cup shredded Cheddar cheese
1 (3-ounce) can French-fried onions
6 to 8 (7-inch) flour tortillas
1 tomato, chopped (optional)

Mix the soup and milk in a medium bowl and set aside. Combine the chicken, broccoli, half the cheese and half the onions in a large bowl and mix well. Stir in ¾ cup of the soup mixture.
Spread the chicken mixture over the tortillas and roll up. Place seam side down in a lightly greased casserole.
Stir the tomato into the remaining soup mixture. Pour over the tortillas.
Bake, covered with foil, at 350 degrees for 35 minutes.
Remove the foil. Top the tortillas with the remaining cheese and onions.
Bake, uncovered, for 5 minutes longer.
Serve with salsa, a fruit salad or congealed salad for a nicely balanced meal.
Yield: Four to Six Servings

Supper Clubs

Supper clubs are very common in the South. They range from regular excuses to meet and eat with friends and neighbors to elaborate pre-planned menus. Whatever the reason or method, the idea is that everyone contribute to the meal in some way. The host and/or hostess rotates at each meeting; each lends his or her own creativity to the meal and decor. Today's busy lifestyles require much more organization than years ago. What a great way to schedule in dining and relaxation with those we never see enough of!

Chicken with Crab Meat

A wonderful entrée for gourmet supper clubs. It can be prepared ahead of time, which gives this recipe extra appeal to experienced hostesses.

8 boneless chicken breasts
2 tablespoons unsalted butter or margarine
1 teaspoon salt
1/4 teaspoon pepper
Paprika to taste
1/2 cup unsalted butter or margarine
1/2 cup sherry
1 teaspoon garlic salt
1/2 cup catsup
2 (4-ounce) cans sliced mushrooms

1/4 teaspoon dried thyme
1/4 teaspoon cayenne
1 teaspoon salt
1 teaspoon prepared mustard
1/2 teaspoon poultry seasoning
1/4 teaspoon sage
1/4 cup melted unsalted butter or margarine
3 slices white bread, cut into cub
5 tablespoons light cream
12 to 16 ounces crab meat

Rinse the chicken and pat dry. Rub with a mixture of 2 tablespoons butte
1 teaspoon salt, pepper and paprika. Place skin side up in a
9x13-inch baking pan. Bake at 350 degrees for 35 minutes.
Heat 1/2 cup butter, sherry, garlic salt, catsup and mushrooms in a
saucepan. Spoon 1 to 2 tablespoons of the mixture over
each chicken breast. Bake for 10 minutes longer.
Mix the thyme, cayenne, 1 teaspoon salt, prepared mustard,
poultry seasoning, sage and 1/4 cup butter in a small bowl. Toss the brea
cubes with the cream in a large bowl. Add the thyme mixture.
Add the crab meat and toss well.
Stuff each chicken breast cavity with the bread mixture. Bake stuffing
side up for 30 to 35 minutes longer or until the chicken is cooked through
basting frequently with the pan drippings.
Yield: Eight Servings

Chicken with Red and Yellow Peppers

A stir-fry delight that can be prepared while your guests are standing by.

5 whole chicken breasts,
skinned, deboned
2 red bell peppers
2 yellow bell peppers
1 tablespoon unsalted butter
1 tablespoon olive oil
1½ pounds asparagus, trimmed, cut
diagonally into 2-inch pieces
1 tablespoon unsalted butter
1 tablespoon olive oil
½ cup madeira

1 tablespoon chopped fresh thyme,
or 1 teaspoon dried
1 tablespoon chopped fresh rosemary,
or 1 teaspoon dried
1 large tomato, seeded, chopped
2 tablespoons freshly squeezed
lemon juice
¾ cup whipping cream
Salt and freshly ground pepper to taste
¾ cup snipped fresh chives

Rinse the chicken and pat dry. Cut into 1½- to 2-inch cubes.
Core and seed the bell peppers. Cut into 1½- to 2-inch squares.
Heat 1 tablespoon butter and 1 tablespoon olive oil in a wok over medium-high
heat. Add the bell peppers. Stir-fry for 4 minutes or until tender-crisp.
Remove the peppers to a bowl and set aside.
Add the asparagus to the wok. Stir-fry for 5 to 8 minutes or until tender-crisp.
Remove the asparagus and combine with the peppers.
Heat 1 tablespoon butter and 1 tablespoon olive oil in the wok. Add the chicken, in
batches if necessary. Stir-fry for 8 minutes or just until cooked through.
Remove with a slotted spoon and combine with the vegetables.
Add the madeira, thyme, rosemary and tomato to the pan drippings in the wok.
Bring to a boil. Cook until syrupy.
Add the lemon juice. Return to a boil. Stir in the cream. Cook until
thickened, stirring constantly. Season with salt and pepper.
Stir the chicken and vegetables into the cream sauce in the wok.
Cook until the chicken is heated through.
Remove to a serving bowl. Sprinkle with the chives. Serve immediately.
Yield: Six Servings

Lemon Barbecue Chicken

Use chicken wings for a great appetizer. Can be made ahead and served at room temperature.

2½ pounds chicken breasts
1 cup flour
2 teaspoons salt
¼ teaspoon pepper
½ teaspoon celery salt
1 teaspoon paprika
2 tablespoons butter
2 tablespoons vegetable oil
1 small clove of garlic, crushed
½ teaspoon salt
¼ cup vegetable oil
½ cup freshly squeezed lemon juice
2 tablespoons finely chopped onion
1 teaspoon pepper
½ teaspoon dried thyme

*Rinse the chicken and pat dry. Mix the flour, 2 teaspoons salt,
¼ teaspoon pepper, celery salt and paprika
in a nonrecycled paper bag. Add the chicken. Shake until coated.
Remove the chicken, shaking to remove any excess flour.
Combine 2 tablespoons butter and 2 tablespoons vegetable oil in a shallow
baking pan. Heat in a 400-degree oven until the butter is melted.
Place the chicken skin side down in the prepared pan. Bake for 30 minutes.
Mix the garlic with ½ teaspoon salt in a bowl. Add ¼ cup vegetable oil,
lemon juice, onion, 1 teaspoon pepper and thyme and mix well.
Remove the chicken from the oven and turn skin side up. Pour the
lemon juice mixture over the chicken.
Bake for 30 minutes or until the chicken is cooked through, basting
frequently with the pan drippings.*
Yield: Four to Six Servings

Chicken Bola-Gai

Nice and easy Polynesian-style chicken, a pleasant change from everyday fare.

1 chicken, cut up
1/3 cup flour
1 teaspoon salt
1/2 teaspoon celery salt
1/4 teaspoon garlic salt

1/4 teaspoon nutmeg
1/4 cup butter
1 cup pineapple juice
1/4 to 1/2 cup soy sauce
2 tablespoons sugar

*Rinse the chicken and pat dry. Mix the flour, salt, celery salt, garlic salt and
nutmeg in a shallow dish. Coat the chicken with the flour mixture.
Melt the butter in a large skillet over medium heat. Add the chicken. Cook
until evenly browned. Place the chicken in a shallow casserole.
Mix the pineapple juice, soy sauce and sugar in a bowl. Pour over the chicken.
Bake, covered, at 350 degrees for 1 hour or until the chicken is cooked through,
basting 2 to 3 times with the pan drippings.
Serve with rice.*
Yield: Six Servings

Curry

East India's most well-known dish, curry, is a dish of vegetables or meat with a spicy sauce—not a dry dish. The spice, which most Americans buy pre-mixed, is actually a blend of many spices with six of the same basic ingredients: coriander, turmeric, cumin, fenugreek, pepper, and cayenne. Proportions vary in different brands, but the Indian varieties tend to be much hotter than our domestic ones. The traditional Indian wife would grind and mix these spices each day to suit the food she was preparing for her family. With a growing East Indian population in the South, restaurants and Indian grocers are exposing this exciting ethnic cuisine to the region.

Chicken Curry

Dinner guests will enjoy creating their own plates of curry with this East Indian meal. On the buffet line, start with sliced bananas, then add rice and curry (in a chafing dish.) Next, have lots of pretty bowls filled with all the condiments—both sweet and sour. Chutney, peanuts, coconut, and raisins are a must!

1 large chicken or 2 small chickens
Salt and pepper to taste
1 large onion, finely chopped
3 tablespoons butter
1 1/2 to 2 tablespoons curry powder
2 tablespoons flour
1/2 teaspoon salt
1 green apple, cored, chopped
3 to 6 tablespoons whipping cream
1 egg yolk

Rinse the chicken. Combine with boiling water to cover in a large saucepan. Season with salt and pepper to taste. Boil until the chicken is tender. Remove the chicken, reserving 2 cups of the broth. Chop the chicken into bite-size pieces, discarding the skin and bones.
Sauté the onion in the butter in a saucepan until tender and golden brown. Add the curry powder. Cook gently for 15 minutes.
Add the flour, 1/2 teaspoon salt, reserved broth and apple. Cook gently until the sauce is the consistency of light cream. Blend in a mixture of the cream and egg yolk. Stir in the chicken. Heat slowly. At this point, the mixture may be stored in the refrigerator until needed. Do not boil when reheating.
Serve over sliced bananas topped with a bed of rice. Supply chutney, sweet gherkins, pickled walnuts, chopped celery, pineapple chunks, peanuts, olives, hard-cooked eggs, chopped tomatoes, green bell peppers, onion rings, coconut, raisins, grated carrots, grated orange peel, and/or grated grapefruit peel as condiments.
Yield: Four to Six Servings

Southern Fried Chicken with Gravy

1 (2½- to 3-pound) chicken, cut up
1 cup buttermilk
1 cup flour
1½ teaspoons salt
½ teaspoon pepper

Vegetable oil for frying
3 tablespoons flour
1 cup milk
1½ to 2 cups water

Rinse the chicken; pat dry. Place in a large shallow dish. Pour the buttermilk over the chicken. Chill, covered, for 1 hour. Mix 1 cup flour, salt and pepper in a nonrecycled double-strength paper bag. Drain the chicken. Toss in the flour mixture. Shake off the excess. Let stand on waxed paper for 15 minutes. Heat ⅛ to ¼ inch of oil in a skillet. Add the chicken. Fry until browned. Simmer, covered, for 40 to 45 minutes or until the juices run clear, turning occasionally. Cook, uncovered, for 5 minutes longer. Remove the chicken and keep warm. Drain all but ¼ cup of the drippings from the skillet. Add 3 tablespoons flour. Cook until bubbly, stirring constantly. Add the milk and water. Cook until thickened, stirring constantly. Cook for 1 minute longer, adding additional water if needed. Season with additional salt and pepper. Serve the gravy with the chicken.

Yield: Four to Six Servings

Oven-Fried Chicken

2 (3-pound) chickens, cut up
1 cup flour
2 tablespoons salt
2 tablespoons black pepper
2 teaspoons dried thyme
1 cup milk
1 egg

3 egg whites
1 tablespoon Tabasco sauce
2 cups toasted bread crumbs
1 teaspoon white pepper
2 teaspoons paprika
1 teaspoon salt
1 teaspoon dried thyme

Rinse the chicken and pat dry. Remove the skin and any visible fat. Mix the flour, 2 tablespoons salt, black pepper and 2 teaspoons thyme in a bowl and set aside. Beat the milk, egg, egg whites and Tabasco sauce in a bowl and set aside. Mix the bread crumbs, white pepper, paprika, 1 teaspoon salt and 1 teaspoon thyme in a bowl and set aside. Roll the chicken in the flour mixture, dip in the egg mixture and roll in the bread crumb mixture. Place on a waxed paper-lined baking sheet. Chill, covered with plastic wrap, for 1 hour. Place the chicken on a rack in a shallow baking dish. Bake at 350 degrees for 45 minutes or until the chicken is cooked through.

Yield: Six to Eight Servings

Chicken Oriental

The ginger basting sauce is great for large quantity preparation of chicken legs or thighs. Serve with rice and stir-fry vegetables.

2 teaspoons salt
1/4 teaspoon pepper
1 cup frozen orange juice concentrate, thawed

1/3 cup melted butter
2 teaspoons ground ginger
4 teaspoons soy sauce
5 pounds chicken thighs, skinned

Combine the salt, pepper, orange juice concentrate, butter, ginger and soy sauce in a bowl and mix well.
Rinse the chicken and pat dry. Arrange in single layers in 2 oiled 7x11-inch baking pans.
Pour the soy sauce mixture over the chicken.
Chill, covered, overnight.
Bake, uncovered, at 350 degrees for 1 hour or until the chicken is cooked through, basting once with the pan drippings.
Yield: Eight Servings

Stir-Fry Chicken

Authentic Chinese stir-fry with cashews and bamboo shoots. Serve with rice and green tea, and don't forget the fortune cookies for dessert!

1 pound boneless skinless chicken breasts
1 tablespoon light soy sauce
1 tablespoon cornstarch
Vegetable oil for deep-frying
4 ounces cashews or peanuts
1 tablespoon wine
1 tablespoon light soy sauce
1 tablespoon Chinese black vinegar
1 tablespoon sugar
1 teaspoon vegetable oil
1 teaspoon cornstarch
2 tablespoons vegetable oil
1 hot red pepper, soaked, drained
1 teaspoon finely chopped ginger
4 ounces bamboo shoots, chopped
4 ounces frozen green peas, thawed

Rinse the chicken and pat dry. Cut into ¹/₂-inch cubes.
Mix 1 tablespoon soy sauce and 1 tablespoon cornstarch in a shallow dish.
Add the chicken. Marinate for 15 to 30 minutes.
Heat 1 to 2 inches of oil in an electric wok. Add the cashews.
Deep-fry for 1 minute. Remove and let cool.
Remove the chicken from the marinade, discarding the marinade. Deep-fry the
chicken in the wok for 1 minute. Remove the chicken and drain the wok.
Mix wine, 1 tablespoon soy sauce, vinegar, sugar, 1 teaspoon
oil and 1 teaspoon cornstarch in a bowl.
Heat 2 tablespoons oil in the wok. Add the red pepper. Stir-fry until the pepper turns
black. Add the ginger, chicken, bamboo shoots and green peas. Stir-fry for 3 to 4
minutes or until heated through. Add the wine mixture. Turn off the heat. Add the
cashews and mix well. Remove and discard the red pepper.
Yield: Four Servings

Citrus-Baked Cornish Hens

Pictured on page 144. Elegant and romantic for a small dinner party, this dish is melt-in-your-mouth good. You'll enjoy the oohs and aahs. Serve with wild rice and spinach-stuffed tomatoes, preceded by a hearts of palm salad with vinaigrette. For dessert, why not try one of the exotic coffees in the beverage section. Bon appétit!

4 Cornish game hens
1/4 cup apricot preserves
2 tablespoons grated onion
1 tablespoon butter or margarine
1 tablespoon Dijon mustard
1 clove of garlic, minced
Juice and grated peel of 1 lemon
Juice and grated peel of 1 orange

Rinse the game hens and pat dry. Remove the giblets and necks from the hens. Tie the legs of the hens together and fold the wing tips under the backs. Combine the preserves, onion, butter, Dijon mustard, garlic, lemon juice, lemon peel, orange juice and orange peel in a saucepan. Simmer for 5 minutes. Brush the sauce over the hens. Arrange breast side up on a rack in a roasting pan. Bake at 350 degrees for 1 1/4 hours or until cooked through, basting occasionally with the pan drippings. Remove to a platter. Garnish with fresh greens and orange slices.
Yield: Four Servings

Turkey Potpie with Corn Bread Crust

*A wonderful alternative for leftover turkey. Definitely plan to
try this recipe after the holidays!*

2 large carrots, peeled, cut into
3/8-inch slices
Salt to taste
1 large baking potato, peeled, cut into
1/2-inch cubes
6 tablespoons melted unsalted butter
2 medium onions, thinly sliced
6 tablespoons flour
4 cups hot turkey stock, chicken stock or
canned broth
1/2 teaspoon salt
1/2 teaspoon white pepper
1/8 teaspoon hot pepper sauce

4 cups (heaping) chopped cooked turkey
1 cup frozen lime beans, thawed
1/4 teaspoon salt
1/4 teaspoon white pepper
1 cup flour
1 cup white cornmeal
2 tablespoons sugar
1 tablespoon baking powder
1 teaspoon salt
1 egg, slightly beaten
1 cup plus 1 tablespoon milk
3 tablespoons safflower oil or corn oil

*For the filling, add the carrots to enough lightly salted water to cover in a small
saucepan. Cook over high heat for 5 minutes or until tender. Remove the carrots with a
slotted spoon and set aside. Add the potato to the boiling water. Cook for 5 minutes or
until tender. Drain and set aside. Melt the butter in a large heavy saucepan over
medium heat. Add the onions. Cook for 5 minutes or until tender but not browned,
stirring occasionally. Add 6 tablespoons flour. Cook for 1 minute, stirring constantly; do
not brown. Whisk in the stock. Bring to a boil. Boil until the sauce is thickened,
whisking constantly. Season with 1/2 teaspoon salt, 1/2 teaspoon white pepper and hot
pepper sauce. Simmer over low heat for 3 minutes, whisking frequently.*

*Place 1/3 of the turkey in a greased 3-quart casserole or baking dish. Top with
1/3 of the carrots, potato and lima beans. Season with 1/4 teaspoon each salt and
pepper. Repeat the layers with the remaining turkey and vegetables until all are used.
Pour the sauce over the top. Set aside.*

*For the crust, sift 1 cup flour, cornmeal, sugar, baking powder and 1 teaspoon salt into
a large bowl. Whisk the egg, milk and oil in a small bowl until blended. Add to the flour
mixture, stirring just until mixed. Pour evenly over the turkey and vegetables.
Bake at 425 degrees for 35 to 40 minutes or until the crust is golden brown
on top and cooked through in the center.*

May add a small amount of baked ham if you do not have quite enough turkey.

Yield: Eight to Ten Servings

Smoked Turkey

A covered charcoal grill or smoker grill produces a tender and moist bird.
Consider this version for your next holiday dinner.

1 large fresh turkey or frozen turkey, thawed
Salt and pepper to taste
Vegetable oil

Start a fire in the grill using 50 charcoal briquets. When the briquets begin
to turn white, arrange them evenly on either side of the pan so that the
turkey will not be over a direct flame. Place a disposable aluminum pan in the center of
the pan under the turkey to catch drippings. Note: These drippings
will be too smoky to be used for the gravy.
Remove the gizzard, neck and turkey parts and discard or reserve for other uses.
Rinse the turkey inside and out and pat dry. Rub the turkey with salt, pepper and oil.
Do not stuff. Tie the legs together and the wings together with ovenproof kitchen twine.
Place the turkey breast side up in the grill. Cover the top of the turkey
and the wing tips with a foil tent.
Cover the grill and adjust the vents to maintain a medium-hot fire.
Cook the turkey for 11 minutes per pound or until a meat thermometer inserted in the
meatiest part of the breast registers 185 degrees. Add 8 briquets on each side every hour
to keep the fire hot. Remove the foil tent 1 hour before cooking time is complete.
Yield: Fifteen to Twenty Servings

Vegetables &
Side Dishes

Stone Home

When Sammy Stone returned to Decatur
after his college days in New Orleans, he dug the
foundation for a small bachelor's pad on the
grounds of his family's lumber company,
right on the banks of the Tennessee River.
In the thirty-odd years since, Sammy's house has
grown, or rather evolved, almost organically.
With its wonderfully eclectic interior, its view of
the river, its warm fires, and its gracious owner,
it is a welcome retreat—a green, wooded oasis—
in the midst of its industrial neighbors.

*Pictured in front of the entrance to Sammy's are
selections of vegetables and side dishes:
Spinach Artichoke Casserole;
Marinated Grilled Vegetables;
Tomatoes Scoffield; and Marinated Carrots.*

Asparagus

Proper selection and preparation of asparagus is essential for a tender, not woody, taste and texture. When purchased in the supermarket, asparagus should be stored, tips up, in pans of water to retain freshness. Look for tight, well-formed heads. Spears should appear a rich green in color with lavender tips. Do not pick asparagus with woody, dry, or shriveled stems. Although this vegetable can be purchased fresh year round, peak season is in the spring months of April and May. Prior to cooking, remove the woody ends of stalks and scrape any white part of the stalk downward with a sharp knife.

Marinated Asparagus

Take a break from the usual preparation of asparagus with Hollandaise Sauce and try this tangy marinade for thin, fresh, young, tender stalks.

1 pound asparagus spears, cooked, drained
2 cloves of garlic
1/4 cup white wine vinegar
1/4 cup extra-virgin olive oil
1 tablespoon minced fresh dill, or 2 teaspoons dried
1/2 teaspoon grated orange zest
1/2 teaspoon salt
1/4 teaspoon freshly ground pepper
2 orange slices, cut into halves

Arrange the cooked asparagus spears on a serving dish with all the tips pointing in the same direction.
Crush the garlic through a garlic press. Combine with the vinegar, olive oil, dill, orange zest, salt and pepper in a medium nonreactive bowl and whisk until blended. Pour over the asparagus, coating the spears thoroughly.
Marinate, covered, in the refrigerator overnight.
Arrange the orange slice halves in a fan shape over the asparagus.
Garnish with sprigs of fresh dill. Serve at room temperature.
Yield: Four Servings

Asparagus and Ravioli with Lemon Cream Sauce

Fresh asparagus makes this pasta dish one you'll love to try.

1 (16-ounce) package frozen ravioli
Salt to taste
1 pound asparagus, trimmed, cut into ¹/₂-inch pieces
Lemon Cream Sauce

Drop the ravioli into boiling salted water in a large saucepan. Cook using the package directions, adding the asparagus 3 minutes before the cooking time is finished. Cook for 3 minutes and drain well. Pour into a serving bowl. Pour Lemon Cream Sauce over the asparagus mixture, tossing to coat. Serve immediately.
Yield: Four to Six Servings

Lemon Cream Sauce

¹/₄ cup butter
1 cup heavy cream
1 tablespoon grated lemon peel
¹/₂ cup grated Parmesan cheese
1 cup diced cooked ham
¹/₈ teaspoon pepper

Combine the butter, cream and lemon peel in a small saucepan. Cook over medium heat for 5 minutes, stirring frequently. Stir in the cheese, ham and pepper. Cook until heated through, stirring frequently.
Yield: Two and One-Half Cups Sauce

Cooking Dried Beans

This is the way Southern cooks prepare their dried beans. If you'd like to lower the fat, cook in bouillon and eliminate the salt pork or ham. A meal of pinto beans, greens, corn bread, and fried potatoes has been many a Friday night supper in Southern homes.

Combine 1 package of dried pinto beans with cold water to cover in a large saucepan. Add 1 teaspoon baking soda. Soak for 1 hour and drain well. Cover the beans with fresh water. Add salt pork, ham or other seasoning of your choice. Add 1/2 teaspoon baking soda, 1 teaspoon chili powder and 1 teaspoon garlic salt. Cook for 2 to 3 hours or to desired degree of doneness. Add salt if needed when the beans are almost done.
Yield: Eight to Twelve Servings

Confederate Baked Beans

Great for casual dinners, meaty enough for a main dish, and Jack Daniel's is in the sauce!

1 pound ground beef
2 medium onions, chopped
1 large can pork and beans
1 can kidney beans
1 can pinto beans
1 can navy beans
1 can black beans
1 package bacon, crisp-fried, crumbled
1/2 cup catsup
1/2 cup barbecue sauce
1/2 cup packed brown sugar
1/2 cup Jack Daniel's bourbon
1 clove of garlic, crushed
1/4 cup vinegar
1/4 cup brown or Champagne-flavored mustard

*Brown the ground beef with the onions in a skillet, stirring until the ground beef is crumbly; drain well.
Combine the ground beef mixture, pork and beans, kidney beans, pinto beans, navy beans, black beans, bacon, catsup, barbecue sauce, brown sugar, bourbon, garlic, vinegar and mustard in a large bowl and mix well.
Spoon into a 9x13-inch baking pan.
Bake, covered, at 350 degrees for 15 minutes or until heated through.
Yield: Twelve Servings*

Three-Bean Baked Beans

Pictured on page 14. All Southern-style baked beans require a "streak of lean," properly pronounced "streek-a-leen," for that rich flavor. Depending on your butcher, streak of lean is sometimes labeled salt pork or fat back.

1 (4- to 6-ounce) piece of streak of lean or
5 slices bacon, cut into 1/4-inch pieces
1 green pepper, chopped
1 small onion, chopped
2 cloves of garlic, minced
1 tablespoon vinegar
1/4 cup packed brown sugar
1/2 teaspoon liquid smoke
1 can pork and beans
1 can red kidney beans
1 can tiny green lima beans or garbanzo beans

Brown the streak of lean in a large saucepan. Drain half the drippings.
Add the green pepper, onion, garlic, vinegar, brown sugar and liquid smoke
to the saucepan. Cook for 10 minutes.
Add the pork and beans, kidney beans and lima beans. Cook gently for 1 hour.
Yield: Ten Servings

Bountiful Beans

Beans for a very large gathering—and oh so deliciously good and simple to make! Use a very sturdy disposable aluminum roasting pan(s) to bake.

12 pounds pork and beans
6 cups packed brown sugar
2 tablespoons dry mustard
36 slices bacon, cut into pieces
3 cups catsup

Combine the pork and beans, brown sugar, mustard, bacon and catsup
in a roasting pan and mix well.
Bake at 300 degrees for 3 to 5 hours or until the bacon is cooked through.
Yield: Thirty-Six Servings

Green Beans Amandine

A healthier modification of an old favorite.

1 pound fresh green beans
1 teaspoon reduced-calorie margarine
1 tablespoon chopped fresh or
   dried oregano

Freshly ground pepper to taste
3 tablespoons sliced almonds

Trim the beans and cut into 2-inch pieces.
Heat the margarine in a nonstick skillet over medium-high heat. Add the green beans.
Sauté for 2 to 3 minutes, stirring constantly so that the beans cook evenly.
Add the oregano and pepper. Sauté for 20 to 30 seconds or until the
beans are tender-crisp. Sprinkle with the almonds. Serve immediately.
Yield: Six Servings

Green Bean Bundles

A different and delicious way to serve green beans.

1 pound fresh whole green beans
12 to 15 slices bacon, cut into halves

1 cup beef broth or chicken broth
1 tablespoon lemon juice

Cook the green beans in water to cover in a saucepan until tender.
Drain and rinse the beans. Arrange in bundles of 8 to 10 beans each. Wrap
each bundle in 1/2 slice bacon. Secure each with a wooden pick.
Place in a 9x13-inch baking dish.
Combine the beef broth and lemon juice in a bowl and mix well.
Pour over the green beans.
Bake at 350 degrees for 30 minutes or until the beans are tender, turning after
15 minutes. Remove carefully to a serving platter. Garnish with pimento strips
and fresh parsley. May be prepared ahead and stored in the refrigerator until needed.
Cook just before serving.
Yield: Eight Servings

Red Beans and Rice

Chef Dean Moore's recipe is the Monday night special at Simp McGhee's restaurant in Decatur.

4 cups dried red beans
4 quarts water
½ teaspoon celery salt
1 teaspoon ground black pepper
½ teaspoon granulated onion
2 tablespoons Worcestershire sauce
½ teaspoon ground cumin
½ teaspoon cayenne
¼ teaspoon leaf thyme
¾ teaspoon granulated garlic
Hot sauce to taste
1½ cups chopped celery
1½ cups chopped bell pepper
1½ cups chopped yellow onions
1 cup diced ham
2 cups sliced smoked sausage
Cooked white rice

Sort and rinse the beans. Combine the beans, water, celery salt, black pepper, granulated onion, Worcestershire sauce, cumin, cayenne, thyme, garlic and hot sauce in a large stockpot. Cook until the beans are tender, stirring occasionally.
Add the celery, bell pepper, onions, ham and sausage. Simmer for 45 to 60 minutes or until the vegetables are tender. Spoon into a large bowl. Top with the rice.
Garnish with chopped green onions.
Yield: Ten Servings
Dean Moore, Simp McGhee's

Broccoli Casserole

Diced water chestnuts add a nice subtle crunch to this family favorite!

3 eggs
2 (10-ounce) packages frozen broccoli, thawed, drained
2 to 3 cups shredded sharp cheese
1 can water chestnuts
6 tablespoons margarine
2 tablespoons flour
1/2 cup water
1/8 teaspoon onion salt, or to taste
1/2 cup melted margarine
1 sleeve saltine crackers, crushed

Beat the eggs in a large bowl. Add the broccoli, cheese and water chestnuts.
Combine 6 tablespoons margarine, flour, water and onion salt in a saucepan.
Cook until the sauce begins to thicken, stirring constantly.
Pour the sauce over the broccoli and mix well. Pour into a large
greased casserole or 2 smaller baking dishes.
Mix 1/2 cup margarine and cracker crumbs in a bowl.
Sprinkle over the broccoli mixture.
Bake at 350 degrees for 1 hour.
May be frozen after baking.
Yield: Eight Servings

Carrots in Parsley Butter

8 medium carrots, scraped, cut into slices
1/2 teaspoon salt
1/4 cup butter
2 tablespoons lemon juice
1 tablespoon chopped parsley

Combine the carrots with water to cover in a saucepan. Bring to a boil.
Cook for 10 to 15 minutes or until tender; drain well. Add the salt,
butter, lemon juice and parsley and mix well.
Serve hot.
Yield: Four to Six Servings

Herb Butter

Herb butters are a pleasing
way to add zip to vegetables and
breads. Experiment for your favorite
flavor combination.

1 pound butter or margarine,
softened
2 tablespoons chopped
fresh parsley
1 tablespoon chopped fresh basil
1 tablespoon chopped fresh
tarragon
1 tablespoon chopped
fresh chives

Combine the butter, parsley, basil,
tarragon and chives in a large
bowl and mix well. Store in the
refrigerator in an airtight
container. Serve on potatoes, corn
on the cob or any other vegetables
and hot breads of choice.
Yield: One Pound

Marinated Carrots

Also known as copper pennies, this all-time favorite has proven to be timeless.

2 pounds carrots, peeled, sliced
1 medium onion, chopped
1 bell pepper, chopped
1 teaspoon Worcestershire sauce
1 can tomato soup
1 cup sugar

3/4 cup vinegar
2 tablespoons vegetable oil
1 teaspoon dry mustard
1 teaspoon salt
1 teaspoon pepper

*Cook the carrots in water to cover in a saucepan until tender;
drain and cool. Spoon into a large bowl.
Combine the onion, bell pepper, Worcestershire sauce, soup, sugar, vinegar, oil, mustard,
salt and pepper in a medium saucepan. Bring to a boil, stirring until the sugar is
dissolved. Simmer over low heat for 20 minutes or until the onion and bell
pepper are tender. Cool to room temperature. Pour over the carrots.
Marinate, covered, in the refrigerator for up to 2 weeks.*
Yield: Twelve Servings

Corn Pudding

*Definitely Southern and definitely good. The next best thing to living beside
a field of corn. Prepare it—they will come and they will eat!*

2 cups fresh, frozen or canned corn kernels
1 tablespoon flour
3 tablespoons sugar
1 teaspoon salt
2 eggs
3/4 cup milk
2 tablespoons melted butter

*Combine the corn, flour, sugar, salt, eggs, milk and butter in the order listed in a bowl.
Pour into a 1-quart baking dish. Place the baking dish in a larger pan of water.
Bake at 350 degrees for 30 to 45 minutes or until heated through.
May be prepared ahead and baked when needed.*
Yield: Four to Six Servings

Corn with Savory Lime Butter

8 ears of fresh corn
Salt to taste
1/2 cup butter, softened
1 tablespoon snipped fresh savory, or 1 teaspoon dried
1 teaspoon finely shredded lime peel

Remove the husks from the corn. Scrub with a stiff brush to remove
the silks and rinse well. Combine the corn with lightly salted boiling water
to cover in a saucepan. Cook for 5 to 7 minutes or until tender. Mix the butter,
savory and lime peel in a small bowl. Serve the lime butter with the hot corn.
Cover any leftover butter and store in the refrigerator. May substitute 1 teaspoon
crushed dried thyme for the savory.
Yield: Eight Servings

Johnston Street Garlic Pickles

This local cafe shares their favorite recipe for this crispy, crunchy,
garlicky, and oh-so-sweet pickle, which is always served on the lunch plate with
chicken salad and other favorites. A marvelous addition to the
"city slicker" cook's collection because the pickle preparation starts at the
grocery store, not the cucumber patch!

1 gallon plain sour pickles, drained, cut into 1/2-inch slices
12 to 15 cloves of garlic
3/4 cup whole peppercorns
3/4 cup whole mustard seeds
4 cinnamon sticks
5 pounds sugar

Place the pickles in a ceramic container. Add the garlic, peppercorns,
mustard seeds and cinnamon sticks. Pour the sugar over the pickles.
Let cure for 3 weeks, stirring once each day. Store in jars in the refrigerator.
Do not use until cured completely.
Yield: Four Quarts
Betty Brandon Sims, Johnston Street Cafe

Mushroom Casserole

Any type of mushrooms will make this casserole a hit. Pictured on page 8, it makes a great dish for nighttime entertaining.

1/4 cup butter or margarine
1 1/2 pounds fresh mushrooms, sliced
1 large onion, chopped
1/2 cup chopped celery
1/2 cup chopped green pepper
1/2 cup mayonnaise or mayonnaise-type salad dressing
8 slices white bread, cut into 1-inch pieces
2 large eggs, slightly beaten
1 1/2 cups milk
1 (10-ounce) can cream of mushroom soup
1 cup freshly grated Romano cheese

Melt the butter in a large skillet or Dutch oven. Add the mushrooms, onion, celery and green pepper. Cook over medium heat until tender, stirring constantly; drain well. Stir in the mayonnaise.

Place half the bread in a lightly greased 9x13-inch baking dish. Spoon the mushroom mixture evenly over the bread. Top with the remaining bread.

Combine the eggs and milk in a bowl and mix well. Pour over the bread.

Chill, covered, for 8 hours or longer.

Pour the soup over the top. Sprinkle with the cheese.

Bake at 350 degrees for 1 hour or until bubbly and heated through.

Yield: Six Servings

Okra and Tomatoes

Southern necessities, like air conditioning and front porches—such recipes as these are passed from generation to generation.

4 slices bacon
1 medium onion, chopped
2 cups sliced fresh okra
1 1/2 cups fresh corn kernels

4 medium tomatoes, peeled, chopped
1/2 teaspoon salt
1/2 teaspoon pepper

*Cook the bacon in a large skillet until crisp. Remove and crumble the bacon.
Drain all but 2 tablespoons drippings from the skillet.
Cook the onion in the reserved drippings in the skillet over medium heat until tender,
stirring constantly. Add the okra. Cook for 5 minutes, stirring constantly. Add the corn,
tomatoes, salt and pepper. Simmer, covered, for 15 minutes, stirring occasionally.
Sprinkle with the bacon.*
Yield: Six to Eight Servings

Fried Okra

1 pound fresh okra, cut crosswise
into 1/2-inch slices
2 to 3 quarts lightly salted ice water
2 cups yellow or white cornmeal

1/2 teaspoon salt
1/4 teaspoon freshly ground pepper
Vegetable oil for frying

*Soak the okra in the ice water in a large bowl for 15 minutes. Drain well.
Combine the cornmeal, 1/2 teaspoon salt and pepper in a medium bowl,
stirring with a fork until mixed.
Heat 3/4 inch oil to 350 degrees in a heavy medium saucepan over medium-high heat.
Dip the okra into the cornmeal mixture, shaking to remove any excess.
Fry the okra in 3 batches in the hot oil for 8 minutes per batch or until crisp and
light golden brown. Remove quickly with a slotted spoon to paper towels to drain.
Remove to a foil-lined baking sheet and keep warm in the oven.
Sprinkle with additional salt and pepper. Serve warm.*
Yield: Six Servings

Vidalias

Vidalia onions are grown in a twenty-county area of southeast Georgia near the city of Vidalia and are Georgia's acclaimed state vegetable. The Vidalia (pronounced Vi-day-lee-ah) is not a variety of onion. It gets its distinctive sweetness from the soil that is predominant in this part of the state. As the story goes, it took a Yankee, stopping by the local farmers market in Vidalia, to bring the onions to international fame. Little did the locals realize at that time that they had something special. Thanks to the wonders of the interstate highway system, Vidalias are now enjoyed at tables and on hamburgers all over the country. They are usually harvested in May through June and are as anxiously awaited by shoppers as the day-after-Christmas sales.

Vidalia Onion Casserole

Warning! This recipe is so good that you'll be miserable when Vidalias are not in season.

4 large Vidalia onions, sliced into rings
1/4 cup unsalted butter, softened
1 1/2 sleeves butter crackers, crushed
1/4 cup unsalted butter, softened
8 ounces Cheddar cheese, shredded
Salt and paprika to taste
3 large eggs, beaten
1 cup milk

Sauté the onion rings in 1/4 cup butter in a skillet.
Combine the cracker crumbs with 1/4 cup butter in a bowl and mix well. Spread a layer of the crumb mixture in a greased 9x13-inch baking pan, reserving 1/4 cup crumb mixture.
Spread the onion rings over the crumb layer. Sprinkle with the cheese. Season with salt and paprika.
Combine the eggs and milk in a bowl and beat well. Pour over the onion rings. Top with the reserved crumb mixture.
Bake at 350 degrees for 35 to 40 minutes or until the mixture is heated through and the onions are tender.
Yield: Eight Servings

Roasted Vidalia Onions with Balsamic Apricot Glaze

Caterer Russell Priest gives the best onions in the universe red-carpet treatment as an accompaniment to roasted beef tenderloin, pictured on page 8.

2 medium Vidalia onions, cut into halves lengthwise
2 tablespoons extra-virgin olive oil
Balsamic Apricot Glaze

Arrange the onion halves in a single layer in a 9x9-inch baking dish. Drizzle with the olive oil, turning once to coat evenly.
Pour some of the Balsamic Apricot Glaze over the onions.
Bake at 400 degrees for 10 minutes. Baste with the remaining glaze. Bake for 10 to 15 minutes longer or until tender and lightly browned.
Yield: Four Servings

Balsamic Apricot Glaze

2 tablespoons balsamic vinegar
4 teaspoons apricot preserves
1/2 teaspoon salt
1/8 teaspoon ground red pepper, or to taste

Combine the vinegar, preserves, salt and pepper in a small saucepan.
Bring to a simmer. Remove from the heat.
Yield: Three Tablespoons
Russell Priest, Russell's Place

Dried Hot Peppers

Many Southern cooks grow cayenne peppers, harvest them, and string them to dry. Use a large needle and heavy-duty thread to connect the peppers, tie off in a loop, and hang in the kitchen or other dry storage place. Use throughout the winter season as needed.

Hoppin' John

Around December 31, columnists and commentators remind us of—and ponder over—the Southern tradition of serving this dish wi a side of turnip greens on New Year's Day for good luck. No on seems to know why, yet many a mom or dad has made a long distance call to their offspring, worried that they may have forgotten. Good luck!

2 (10-ounce) packages frozen
black-eyed peas
3 cups boiling water
8 ounces lean slab bacon, cut into
1-inch cubes
1 yellow onion, coarsely chopped
3 cups cooked rice

2 tablespoons bacon drippings
butter or margarine
2 teaspoons salt
1/8 to 1/4 teaspoon crushed hot
red chile peppers
1/8 teaspoon black pepper

Combine the peas, boiling water, bacon and onion in a large saucepan. Simmer, covered, for 30 to 35 minutes or until the peas are tender. Remove the bacon. Add the remaining ingredients and mix lightly
Yield: Six Servings

Turnip Greens

1 pound ham hocks
7 cups water
2 bunches fresh turnip greens
1 teaspoon salt

1 teaspoon sugar
1 small fresh or dried whole re
pepper (optional)

Combine the ham hocks and water in a large Dutch oven. Bring to a bo reduce the heat. Simmer, covered, for 1 hour or until the meat is tender. Cut the turnips from the greens and reserve for another use. Trim the stem from the turnip greens. Tear the greens into bite-size pieces. Add the greens, salt, sugar and red pepper to the ham hocks. Return to a b reduce the heat. Simmer, covered, for 1 to 1 1/2 hours or until the greens a tender. Remove and discard the red pepper. Serve with hot pepper sauce if desired. Yield: Ten to Twelve Servings

Truck Stop Potatoes

Caterer John Harris has pleased the palates and hearts
of many area residents with his skill and unflappable optimistic
personality. John adapted this recipe from a dish served with breakfast
at a truck stop in Idaho. Since its presentation to Decatur appetites,
his most sought-after recipe is generously shared with readers here.
A marvelous addition to brunch or barbecue or just by itself,
but not for those counting fat grams.

5 pounds small red potatoes
2 large onions, chopped
3/4 cup melted butter
2 cups sour cream
3 cans tomato bits, drained
8 ounces Monterey Jack cheese, shredded
8 ounces sharp Cheddar cheese, shredded
Salt and cayenne to taste
2 fresh tomatoes, chopped
1 avocado, sliced
1 bunch green onions, cut into small circles
1 cup sour cream

Boil the potatoes in water to cover in a saucepan just until tender;
drain well. Dice the unpeeled potatoes.
Combine the potatoes, onions and butter in a baking pan and mix well.
Bake at 350 degrees or just until the top begins to brown, stirring
occasionally. Remove from the oven and cool slightly.
Combine the potato mixture, 2 cups sour cream, tomato bits, Monterey Jack
cheese and Cheddar cheese in a bowl and mix well. Season with salt and
cayenne. Spoon into a 3-quart glass casserole.
Bake at 350 degrees until heated through.
Surround with the fresh tomatoes, avocado and green onions.
Spread 1 cup sour cream down the center of the dish.
Serve immediately.
Yield: Twelve to Fifteen Servings
John R. Harris, Jr.

On the Side

Potatoes will bake in a
hurry if boiled in salted water for
ten minutes before popping them
into a very hot oven.

Spinach Artichoke Casserole

A fantastic accompaniment to beef or poultry,
this dish is pictured on page 170.

1/2 cup butter
1 1/2 cups chopped onions
1 cup sliced mushrooms
2 cloves of garlic, minced
3 (10-ounce) packages frozen chopped spinach, thawed, squeezed dry
1 teaspoon Worcestershire sauce
2 cans artichoke hearts, drained, cut into quarters
6 ounces cream cheese or low-fat cream cheese, softened
1/4 cup half-and-half or evaporated skim milk
1/2 teaspoon salt
1/4 teaspoon pepper
1/2 cup bread crumbs
1 teaspoon Tabasco sauce
8 ounces Gruyère cheese or low-fat Gruyère, shredded

Melt the butter in a heavy skillet over medium heat. Add the onions.
Sauté until the onions are translucent.
Add the mushrooms and garlic. Cook until the mushrooms release their liquid.
Add the spinach and Worcestershire sauce. Cook until the
spinach loses its bright green color. Stir in the artichokes.
Add the cream cheese, half-and-half, salt and pepper. Cook
until the cream cheese has melted.
Stir in the bread crumbs and Tabasco sauce. Pour into a greased 6x8-inch casserole.
Sprinkle with the Gruyère cheese.
Bake at 375 degrees for 15 minutes or until the top is golden brown.
Yield: Eight Servings

Yellow Squash Stuffed with Spinach and Cheese

Pretty as a picture (page 8), this is a great way to get your family to eat their spinach!

1 pound yellow squash, cut into 1¹/₂-inch lengths
6 ounces frozen spinach, thawed, squeezed dry
2 tablespoons chopped onion
1 teaspoon minced garlic
¹/₂ cup bread crumbs
¹/₄ teaspoon salt
¹/₄ teaspoon pepper
¹/₄ cup shredded provolone cheese
Melted butter

Remove the seeds from the center of each squash length with a melon baller, leaving the skin and outer pulp intact.
Combine the spinach, onion, garlic, bread crumbs, salt, pepper and cheese in a large bowl and mix well.
Fill each squash piece with the spinach mixture. Drizzle with melted butter.
Arrange in a single layer in a baking pan.
Bake at 325 degrees for 12 minutes or until cooked through.
Yield: Four Servings

Sweet Potato Soufflé

A must for the Thanksgiving table.

3 cups mashed cooked sweet potatoes
1 cup packed brown sugar
1/2 cup sugar
1/2 teaspoon salt
1/2 cup melted butter
2 eggs

1 teaspoon vanilla extract
1/2 cup milk
1 cup packed light brown sugar
1/3 cup flour
1/3 cup melted butter
1 cup chopped pecans

Combine the sweet potatoes, 1 cup brown sugar, sugar, salt, 1/2 cup butter, eggs, vanilla and milk in a bowl and mix well. Pour into a greased casserole.
Mix 1 cup brown sugar, flour, 1/3 cup butter and pecans in a bowl. Sprinkle evenly over the sweet potato mixture.
Bake at 350 degrees for 35 minutes.
Yield: Eight Servings

Sweet Potato Casserole

A less caloric modification of a traditional holiday favorite.

6 large sweet potatoes, peeled, chopped
12 egg whites, slightly beaten
1/2 cup reduced-calorie margarine, softened
1/2 cup evaporated skim milk

1 teaspoon vanilla extract
1 teaspoon cinnamon
1 teaspoon nutmeg
1 cup marshmallows
1/4 cup chopped pecans (optional)

Cook the sweet potatoes in water to cover in a saucepan until tender; drain well.
Combine the sweet potatoes, egg whites, margarine, skim milk, vanilla, cinnamon and nutmeg in a bowl and mix well. Spoon into a baking dish.
Bake at 400 degrees for 20 minutes.
Top with the marshmallows. Sprinkle with the pecans.
Bake for 10 minutes longer or until the marshmallows are browned.
Yield: Eight Servings

Fried Green Tomatoes

Why do folks up North struggle to turn their green tomatoes red after the frost when they could fix them this delicious way? Chef Scott Curry has the perfect answer.

¹/₂ cup sifted flour
³/₄ cup yellow cornmeal
1 egg
2 tablespoons milk
¹/₂ teaspoon salt
¹/₄ teaspoon freshly ground pepper
Vegetable oil for frying
3 firm green tomatoes, cored, cut into 12 slices

Mix the flour and cornmeal in a shallow dish. Combine the egg, milk, salt and pepper in a bowl and beat until blended. Heat ¹/₂ inch oil to 350 degrees in a heavy deep skillet over medium-high heat. Dip the tomato slices in the egg mixture, then into the cornmeal mixture. Shake to remove any excess. Fry the tomatoes in 3 batches in the hot oil for 3 to 5 minutes per batch or until the coating is crisp and light golden brown, turning once. Remove with a slotted spatula to a paper towel-lined baking sheet to drain. Remove to a foil-lined baking sheet. Keep warm in a 200-degree oven. Sprinkle with additional salt and pepper. Serve warm. Garnish with sprigs of fresh thyme.

Yield: Four Servings
Scott Curry, Johnston Street Cafe

Scoffield

A recipe for tomatoes that can be prepared year round, this dish got its name from an English gentleman, Mr. Scoffield, who frequented the home of his friends, the Harrises, on trips from England. Lamenting over the lack of fresh tomatoes three out of four seasons, he prepared this dish for the American family using canned tomatoes. Either way, they are a delicious side dish for any meal.

1 (29-ounce) can tomatoes
¹/₄ cup vegetable oil
¹/₂ cup vinegar
¹/₂ cup sugar
Salt and pepper to taste
¹/₄ to ¹/₂ small onion, scraped

Combine the tomatoes, oil, vinegar, sugar, salt, pepper and onion in a bowl and mix gently. Chill for several hours. Cut the tomatoes into halves. Serve in a bowl. Use a spoon to drink the juice.

Yield: Four to Six Servings

Baked Stuffed Zucchini

Zucchini growers will appreciate this fine recipe for the often over-abundant summer squash.

3 medium zucchini, rinsed
3 tablespoons vegetable oil
1/2 cup chopped onion
1 clove of garlic, minced
1 1/4 teaspoons salt
1/2 teaspoon pepper
1/2 teaspoon oregano
2 cups soft bread crumbs

Cook the zucchini in boiling water to cover in a saucepan for 8 minutes; drain well. Cut into halves lengthwise. Scoop out and chop the pulp, reserving the shells. Heat the oil in a skillet. Add the onion and garlic. Sauté for 5 minutes. Add the zucchini pulp. Sauté for 5 minutes. Add the salt, pepper, oregano and bread crumbs and mix well. Spoon into the zucchini shells. Place in a greased baking dish. Bake at 350 degrees for 20 minutes.
Yield: Six Servings

Ratatouille

Pictured on page 118, a fine accompaniment for grilled meats or quiche and home-baked bread for a nice summer luncheon.

1 unpeeled medium eggplant, cut into 1/4-inch cubes
Coarse salt to taste
8 tablespoons extra-virgin olive oil
2 medium zucchini, cut into 1/4-inch rounds
1 red bell pepper, seeded, cut into strips
1 yellow bell pepper, seeded, cut into strips
1 green bell pepper, seeded, cut into strips

2 large white onions, chopped
4 to 5 cloves of garlic, crushed
2 pounds tomatoes, peeled, seeded, chopped, or 2 pounds canned Italian tomatoes
1 bunch parsley, minced
15 to 20 fresh basil leaves, chopped
Salt and freshly ground pepper to taste

*Place the eggplant in a colander. Sprinkle with coarse salt. Let stand for 30 minutes to drain. Pat dry with paper towels.
Heat 2 tablespoons of the olive oil in a skillet. Add the eggplant. Sauté for 8 minutes or until tender. Remove with a slotted spoon to a large bowl.
Add 1 tablespoon of the olive oil and zucchini to the skillet. Sauté for 8 minutes or until tender. Transfer to the bowl.
Add 1 1/2 tablespoons of the olive oil and bell peppers to the skillet. Sauté for 10 to 12 minutes or until tender. Transfer to the bowl.
Add 1 1/2 tablespoons of the olive oil and onions to the skillet. Sauté for 10 to 12 minutes or until tender. Transfer to the bowl.
Heat the remaining 2 tablespoons olive oil in a deep Dutch oven. Add the garlic. Sauté until browned. Discard the garlic. Add the tomatoes, parsley and basil to the Dutch oven. Cook over medium heat for 10 minutes or until reduced to a thick sauce. Stir in the eggplant, zucchini, bell peppers and onions. Season with salt and pepper.
Serve at room temperature or chilled. Best prepared 1 day ahead.*
Yield: Eight to Ten Servings

Vegetable Frittata

Spectacular as a vegetarian entrée, for serving at a buffet or brunch, or as an appetizer—an all-around great recipe to have at your fingertips for any occasion.

3 tablespoons extra-virgin olive oil
1 large red onion, thinly sliced
3 cloves of garlic, minced
3 medium yellow squash, cut into 1/4-inch slices
3 medium zucchini, cut into 1/4-inch slices
1 red bell pepper, seeded, cut into 1/4-inch slices
1 yellow bell pepper, seeded, cut into 1/4-inch slices
1 green bell pepper, seeded, cut into 1/4-inch slices
8 ounces fresh mushrooms, sliced
6 large eggs
1/4 cup heavy cream
2 teaspoons salt
2 teaspoons freshly ground pepper
2 cups dried French bread cubes
8 ounces cream cheese, chopped
10 ounces Swiss cheese, shredded

Heat the olive oil in a large skillet over medium-high heat. Add the onion, garlic, squash, zucchini, bell peppers and mushrooms. Sauté for 15 to 20 minutes or until tender-crisp.
Whisk the eggs and cream in a large bowl until blended. Season with the salt and pepper. Stir in the bread cubes, cream cheese and Swiss cheese.
Combine the egg mixture with the sautéed vegetables and mix well. Pour into a greased springform pan. Pack tightly. Place the pan on a baking sheet.
Bake at 350 degrees for 1 hour or until the top is firm to the touch, puffed and browned. Cover with foil if the top begins to brown too much.
Serve hot, cold or at room temperature.
Yield: Eight Servings

Stir-Fry Sauce

Stir-frying is a healthy and quick way to prepare delicious meat and vegetable dinners. Even those without woks can use a large skillet with good results. Keep the temperature of the stove on high and continue to toss meat or vegetables quickly. A jar of this sauce in the refrigerator will come in handy when you need a quick meal.

3 tablespoons dark brown sugar
1/3 cup cornstarch
2 teaspoons fresh minced gingerroot, or 2 teaspoons ground ginger
4 cloves of garlic, crushed
1/2 cup naturally brewed soy sauce
1/2 cup sherry
1/4 teaspoon bottled red pepper sauce
3 tablespoons red wine
2 1/2 cups beef broth or chicken broth

Combine all the ingredients in a 1-quart jar and mix well. Store for up to 3 weeks in the refrigerator or freeze in 1-cup portions for later use.
Yield: One Quart Sauce

Crunchy Vegetable Stir-Fry

Enjoy as a side dish with baked or grilled chicken or pork. Look for the five-spice powder in the Chinese aisle of the supermarket or in Oriental markets.

1 bunch broccoli
2 tablespoons vegetable oil
1 small yellow onion, thinly sliced
2 tablespoons vegetable oil
1/3 cup soy sauce
1 tablespoon dry sherry
3 cloves of garlic, pressed
2 teaspoons sugar
1/2 teaspoon five-spice powder
1 (8-ounce) can water chestnuts, drained, sliced
8 ounces mushrooms, sliced
1/2 cup toasted slivered almonds

Cut the broccoli into florets. Peel the stems and cut crosswise into 1/8-inch slices. Rinse and drain. Set aside.
Heat 2 tablespoons oil in a wok. Add the onion. Stir-fry until tender. Remove with a slotted spoon.
Heat the remaining 2 tablespoons oil in the wok. Add the broccoli. Stir-fry for 1 minute. Steam, covered, for 2 to 3 minutes.
Combine the soy sauce, sherry, garlic, sugar and five-spice powder in a bowl and mix well.
Add the soy sauce mixture, water chestnuts, mushrooms and almonds to the wok. Steam, covered, for 1 minute.
Add the cooked onion and toss well.
Yield: Four to Six Servings

Marinated Grilled Vegetables

Pick your favorite vegetables and cook them on the grill for a wonderful taste at your next cookout. Pictured on page 170.

1/2 cup balsamic vinegar
1/4 cup extra-virgin olive oil
2 tablespoons dry white wine
1 tablespoon finely chopped shallot
1/2 tablespoon minced garlic
1/2 tablespoon freshly ground pepper
1 teaspoon kosher salt
4 new potatoes
4 Roma tomatoes, cut into
halves lengthwise
3 small zucchini, cut into
halves lengthwise

2 ears of yellow corn, cut into
3-inch pieces
2 purple onions, cut into 3/4-inch slices
2 portobello mushrooms, cut into quarters
1 pound fresh asparagus, trimmed
1 small eggplant, cut lengthwise into
1-inch slices
1 red bell pepper, cut into quarters
1 yellow bell pepper, cut into quarters
1 tablespoon chopped fresh chives
1 tablespoon chopped fresh rosemary
1 tablespoon chopped fresh parsley

Combine the vinegar, olive oil, wine, shallot, garlic, pepper and salt in a large bowl and mix well. Set aside.

Boil the potatoes in water to cover in a saucepan for 5 minutes; drain well.

Cut the potatoes into halves.

Add the potatoes, tomatoes, zucchini, corn, onions, mushrooms, asparagus, eggplant and bell peppers to the wine mixture, tossing gently to coat.

Let stand for 1 hour, tossing occasionally.

Remove the vegetables from the marinade, reserving the marinade.

Grill, covered, over medium-hot coals for 12 to 14 minutes or until tender, basting occasionally with the reserved marinade and turning once.

Sprinkle with the chives, rosemary and parsley.

Note: It is not necessary to use all these vegetables at one time.

Yield: Variable

Candied Apples

A nice change from sweet potatoes when a touch of something sweet is needed in a menu.

1 can sliced apples
6 tablespoons butter
3/4 teaspoon cinnamon
2/3 cup packed brown sugar

Combine the apples, butter, cinnamon and brown sugar in a bowl and mix well.
Spoon into a baking dish.
Bake at 325 degrees for 2 1/2 to 3 hours or until cooked down.
Yield: Three to Four Servings

Cranberry Apple Bake

A great addition to a brunch or as a side dish. Works as a topping for ice cream, too.

3 cups chopped unpeeled apples
2 cups fresh cranberries
1 1/4 cups sugar
1 1/2 cups rolled oats
1/3 cup flour
1/2 cup packed brown sugar
1/2 cup butter
1/3 cup chopped pecans

Combine the unpeeled apples, cranberries and sugar in a bowl and mix well.
Spoon into a baking dish.
Mix the oats, flour, brown sugar, butter and pecans in a bowl.
Sprinkle over the fruit mixture.
Bake at 350 degrees for 1 hour or until heated through and the apples are tender.
Yield: Eight to Ten Servings

Pineapple Casserole

Perfect with ham at dinner or brunch.

2 cans chunk pineapple
1 cup sugar
5 tablespoons flour

1 1/2 cups shredded cheese
1 sleeve butter crackers
1/2 cup melted margarine

Pour the pineapple into a baking dish, reserving the juice.
Mix the sugar, flour and reserved pineapple juice in a bowl until smooth.
Pour over the pineapple.
Top with the cheese. Crumble the crackers over the pineapple and cheese.
Pour the margarine over the top. Bake at 350 degrees for 1 hour.
Yield: Eight to Ten Servings

Scalloped Oysters

A wonderful side dish most often served at
Thanksgiving or Christmas in Southern homes.

1 1/2 pints fresh oysters
1 1/2 cups cracker crumbs
1/2 cup butter
Salt and pepper to taste
1/2 cup cream

Tabasco sauce to taste
1 cup buttered bread crumbs
1/2 bunch fresh parsley, finely
chopped

Drain the oysters, reserving 1/2 cup liquor. Rinse the oysters gently
under cold water to remove any shells. Drain or pat dry with a cloth.
Layer the cracker crumbs and oysters 1/2 or 1/3 at a time in a baking dish,
dotting each layer with butter and seasoning with salt and pepper.
Pour the cream, reserved oyster liquor and Tabasco sauce into the
baking dish. Top with the bread crumbs.
Bake at 400 degrees for 25 to 30 minutes or until bubbly and
heated through. Sprinkle with the parsley.
Yield: Four to Six Servings

Mango Chutney

The perennial accompaniment to a curry dish, this East Indian condiment is made from chopped fruits and spices and is made either sweet or sour. Mango is a characteristic ingredient, but other varieties are equally good. Try this with our Chicken Curry on page 162.

1 cup cider vinegar
1 cup plus 1 tablespoon sugar
1 large firm mango, sliced
1/3 cup preserved gingerroot
1 clove of garlic, minced
1/2 teaspoon mustard seeds
1/4 teaspoon salt
1/3 cup golden raisins
1/3 cup seedless raisins

Bring the vinegar and sugar to a boil in a heavy saucepan. Add the mango, gingerroot, garlic, mustard seeds, salt and raisins. Cook for 8 to 10 minutes or until the mango is almost tender. Strain and reserve the fruit. Return the syrup to a boil. Cook for 15 minutes or until quite thick and reduced by 1/2. Return the fruit to the syrup. Return to a boil. Pour into hot sterilized jars and seal.
Yield: Three Cups

Corn Bread Dressing with Giblet Gravy

From start to finish, everything you need for that Thanksgiving or Christmas turkey dressing.

4 to 6 cups Corn Bread
6 to 8 slices white bread, slightly dry
1/2 teaspoon sage, or to taste
1/2 teaspoon poultry seasoning, or to taste
1/2 teaspoon salt

Turkey broth from a cooked 12- to 15-pound turkey or canned chicken broth
1 cup chopped celery
1 small onion, chopped

Crumble the Corn Bread and white bread into a large bowl. Stir in the sage, poultry seasoning and salt. Bring the broth to a boil in a saucepan. Add the celery and onion. Simmer until the vegetables are tender. Add by cupfuls to the corn bread mixture unti the mixture is moist throughout and of a loose wet consistency. Adjust the seasonings. Set aside 1/2 cup unbaked dressing for the gravy. Pour the remaining dressing into a 12x15-inch baking pan. Bake at 400 degrees for minutes or until lightly browned. Serve with Giblet Gravy (at left).
Yield: Ten to Twelve Servings

Giblet Gravy

Remove the neck, gizzard and liver from the turkey cavity. Boil in 2 to 3 cups water for 1 hour or until tender. Remove from the broth and let cool. Chop into small pieces and return to the broth. Add 2 chopped hard-cooked eggs. Thicken with 1/2 cup unbaked dressing. Thicken with cornstarch if needed. May add chicken giblets to prepare a larger quantity of gravy.
Yield: Two to Three Cups

Corn Bread

1/4 cup bacon drippings or vegetable oil (optional)
2 cups self-rising cornmeal
1/2 cup self-rising flour

1/2 teaspoon baking soda
2 eggs
1 1/2 cups (about) buttermilk

Grease and heat a large cast-iron skillet or melt the bacon drippings in the skillet for use in the corn bread batter.
Combine the cornmeal, flour, baking soda and eggs in a bowl and mix wel Add enough buttermilk to make a thick batter. Pour into the skillet.
Bake at 450 degrees for 25 minutes or until firm and brown.
Yield: Four to Six Cups

Breakfast Casserole

Weekend guests will love waking up to this breakfast dish. Preparation can begin the night before to allow for early morning baking. Serve with juice, fresh fruits, biscuits or muffins, and coffee.

12 ounces Cheddar cheese, shredded
12 ounces mozzarella cheese, shredded
½ cup sliced green onions
½ cup chopped red bell pepper
4 ounces fresh mushrooms, sliced
¼ to ½ cup melted butter

8 to 12 ounces chopped cooked ham
½ cup flour
1 to 2 cups milk
8 to 10 eggs, beaten
2 tablespoons snipped parsley

Toss the Cheddar cheese and mozzarella cheese together. Spread half the mixture in a 10x15-inch baking dish sprayed with nonstick cooking spray. Sauté the green onions, red pepper and mushrooms in the butter in a skillet. Stir in the ham. Sprinkle over the cheese in the baking dish. Top with the remaining cheese. Beat the flour, milk, eggs and parsley in a bowl. Pour over the cheese. Bake at 350 degrees for 35 to 45 minutes or until the center is set and the top is slightly browned.
Yield: Ten to Twelve Servings

Low-Fat Breakfast Casserole

No flavor is sacrificed in this lower-calorie casserole.

3 cups French bread cubes
¾ cup lean cooked ham, or 1 pound turkey sausage, cooked
2 tablespoons diced red bell pepper
1 cup shredded reduced-fat sharp Cheddar cheese
1⅓ cups skim milk

¾ cup egg substitute
1 egg (optional)
¼ teaspoon dry mustard
¼ teaspoon onion powder (optional)
¼ teaspoon white pepper
Paprika to taste

Arrange the bread cubes evenly in an 8x8-inch baking dish sprayed with nonstick cooking spray. Layer the ham, red pepper and cheese over the bread. Mix the skim milk, egg substitute, egg, dry mustard, onion powder and pepper in a bowl. Pour over the cheese. Chill, covered, for 8 hours. Let stand at room temperature for 30 minutes. Bake at 350 degrees for 30 minutes. Sprinkle with paprika. Serve immediately.
Yield: Six Servings

Sausage and Egg Casserole

Try this for brunch or late-night supper with homemade bread. Delicious!

1 pound fully cooked bulk pork sausage, drained
3/4 cup shredded Swiss cheese
5 slices bacon, crisp-fried, crumbled
3/4 cup shredded mild Cheddar cheese
3 tablespoons chopped onion
3 tablespoons chopped green pepper
1 cup milk
1/4 cup baking mix
2 eggs, beaten
Salt and pepper to taste

Layer the sausage, Swiss cheese, bacon, Cheddar cheese, onion and green pepper in a greased 10-inch pie plate. Place the milk, baking mix, eggs, salt and pepper in a blender container in the order given. Blend for 30 to 40 seconds or until mixed. Pour over the layers in the pie plate; do not stir. Bake at 350 degrees for 30 to 35 minutes or until set and lightly browned. Let stand for 5 minutes before slicing.

Yield: Eight Servings

Breakfast Pizza

Kids and teens will love this brunch idea. Spice it up with hot sausage for those who like to work up a steam in the morning!

1 can crescent rolls
1 pound sausage, browned, drained
1 cup frozen hash brown potatoes
5 eggs, beaten
1 1/2 cups shredded Cheddar cheese
Salt and pepper to taste

Press the rolls into a pizza pan, forming a rim on the edge to hold the eggs. Layer the sausage and potatoes over the roll dough. Pour the eggs over the sausage and potatoes. Top with the cheese. Season with salt and pepper. Bake at 350 degrees for 30 minutes.

Yield: Four to Five Servings

Elegant Eggs

*Elegant eggs become Eggs Extraordinaire when topped with a generous amount
of Hollandaise Sauce. Serve with Truck Stop Potatoes (page 187)—an
unlikely sounding pair—for a wonderful breakfast or brunch.*

1/4 cup butter
1/4 cup flour
1/2 teaspoon salt
1/2 teaspoon pepper
4 cups milk
8 ounces Velveeta cheese, cubed, or 8 ounces Swiss cheese, shredded
1/2 cup finely chopped onion
6 tablespoons melted butter
24 eggs, beaten
1 pound bacon, crisp-fried, crumbled
Salt to taste
4 slices white bread
1/4 cup melted butter
Paprika to taste

*For the sauce, melt 1/4 cup butter in a saucepan. Stir in the flour. Cook over
low heat until the mixture is bubbly and begins to brown, stirring
constantly. Season with 1/2 teaspoon salt and pepper. Stir in the milk gradually. Cook
over low heat until thickened, stirring frequently. Add the cheese. Cook until the
cheese is melted, stirring frequently.*
*For the egg mixture, sauté the onion in 6 tablespoons butter in a skillet until tender.
Add the eggs, bacon and salt to taste. Cook until soft, stirring to scramble.*
*To assemble, spread half the sauce in a lightly buttered 9x13-inch casserole. Spoon
the egg mixture over the sauce. Spread the remaining sauce carefully over the top.*
For the topping, cut the bread into small squares. Dip in 1/4 cup butter.
Arrange over the sauce. Sprinkle with paprika.
Bake at 350 degrees for 25 to 30 minutes or until heated through.
May be prepared 1 day ahead and refrigerated before baking.
Yield: Twenty Servings

Eggs Benedict

A poached egg never looked or tasted so good! A microwave method makes preparation even easier. Pictured on page 20 as the focal point of a lovely patio brunch.

8 cold eggs
4 English muffins, split into halves, toasted, buttered
8 slices Canadian bacon, broiled or pan-fried
3/4 cup Hollandaise Sauce (page 203) or cheese sauce

Bring 2 to 3 inches water, milk, broth or other liquid to a boil in a saucepan or deep omelet pan. Reduce the heat to keep the water gently simmering. Break the eggs 1 at a time into a custard cup or saucer or break several into a bowl. Hold the dish close to the surface of the water and slip the eggs 1 at a time into the water. Cook for 3 to 5 minutes or until cooked through. Lift out the eggs with a slotted spoon. Drain on the spoon or on paper towels. Trim any rough edges if desired. Top each muffin half with 1 slice bacon, 1 poached egg and approximately 1 1/2 tablespoons Hollandaise Sauce. Serve hot.

Yield: Four Servings

Microwave Eggs Benedict

8 slices cooked smoked ham, turkey ham, beef or corned beef
4 eggs
2 English muffins, split, toasted, buttered
1/4 to 1/2 cup Hollandaise Sauce (optional) (page 203)

Layer 2 slices of ham with corners alternating in each of four 6-ounce custard cups. Break and slip 1 egg into each cup. Prick the yolks gently with the tip of a knife or a wooden pick. Place the cups on a microwave-safe pie plate or platter. Cover with waxed paper. Microwave at 30 percent power for 5 1/2 to 6 1/2 minutes, rotating 1/4 turn after each 2 minutes. Remove just before the eggs are cooked through. Let stand, covered, for 1 to 2 minutes or until the eggs are cooked through. Loosen the eggs from the sides of the cups. Slip the eggs onto the muffin halves. Top each egg with 2 tablespoons Hollandaise Sauce.

Yield: Two to Four Servings

Hollandaise Sauce

Hollandaise Sauce can curdle if even slightly overcooked, so pay particular attention to the temperature and to constant stirring while preparing.

3 egg yolks
2 tablespoons lemon juice
1/4 teaspoon salt
1/8 teaspoon paprika
1/8 teaspoon ground red pepper, or to taste
1/2 cup firm cold butter, cut into small pieces

*Beat the egg yolks, lemon juice, salt, paprika and red pepper in a small saucepan.
Add half the butter. Cook over low heat until the butter is melted, stirring rapidly.
Add the remaining butter, stirring constantly. Cook until the butter is melted
and the sauce has thickened, stirring constantly. Remove from the heat.
Chill, covered, if the sauce is not being used immediately.*
Note: Leftover sauce can be covered and stored in the refrigerator for several days.
Stir in a small amount of hot water before reheating.
Yield: Three-Fourths Cup Sauce

Dieter's Hollandaise Sauce

1 egg
2 tablespoons chicken broth
1/4 teaspoon grated lemon peel
1 tablespoon lemon juice
Artificial sweetener equivalent to 2 teaspoons sugar
1/4 teaspoon dry mustard
1/8 teaspoon salt

*Combine the egg, chicken broth, lemon peel, lemon juice, sweetener,
dry mustard and salt in a blender container or small mixer bowl. Process
until blended or beat at medium speed until blended.
Pour into a small saucepan. Cook over low heat just until the sauce is thickened
and begins to simmer, stirring constantly. Remove from the heat.
Cover and chill if not using immediately.*
Yield: One-Third Cup Sauce

Homemade Egg Substitute

Eggs are an essential ingredient in so many recipes. This homemade egg substitute is one way of including them in the diet without the cholesterol-rich yolks.

6 egg whites
1/4 cup instant nonfat dry milk
2 tablespoons water
1 1/2 teaspoons vegetable oil
1/4 teaspoon turmeric

Process the egg whites, dry milk, water, oil and turmeric in a blender or food processor for 30 seconds. Store, covered, in the refrigerator for up to 1 week or in the freezer for up to 1 month.
Yield: One Cup

Oeufs aux Champignons

This recipe is time-consuming, but it can be done ahead and is definitely worth the effort!

12 hard-cooked eggs
1 pint fresh mushrooms, minced
1/4 cup butter
Salt, white pepper and red pepper to taste
Worcestershire sauce to taste
Tabasco sauce to taste
8 ounces bacon, crisp-fried, crumbled
8 ounces sharp cheese, shredded
1/4 cup butter
1/4 cup flour
2 cups milk
2 tablespoons sherry
2 tablespoons minced parsley
Paprika to taste

Peel the eggs; cut into halves lengthwise. Mash the egg yolks in a bowl until smooth. Sauté the mushrooms in 1/4 cup butter in a skillet. Add half the mushrooms to the egg yolks in the bowl. Season heavily with salt, white pepper, red pepper, Worcestershire sauce and Tabasco sauce and mix well. Spoon the mushroom mixture into the egg whites. Press the 2 halves of each egg together. Arrange in a lightly greased 2-quart round casserole. Spoon the remaining mushrooms, half the bacon and half the cheese over the eggs. Heat 1/4 cup butter in a saucepan. Stir in the flour and milk. Cook until smooth, stirring constantly. Season heavily with additional salt, white pepper, red pepper, Worcestershire sauce and Tabasco sauce. Stir in the sherry. Cook until heated through, stirring frequently. Pour over the eggs. Top with the remaining bacon and cheese. May be stored in the refrigerator at this point. Bring to room temperature before baking. Bake at 350 degrees for 25 to 30 minutes or until bubbly and heated through. Top with the parsley. Sprinkle with paprika.
Yield: Eight Servings

Sausage Grits Casserole

Lest any of our non-Southern readers become disappointed, this brunch casserole and its variations feature grits. Try one of these if you have never had them before, and you will know why they are so well liked. For milder flavor, use medium- or mild-flavored sausage if you prefer. Down South, we like it hot!

1 pound hot bulk sausage
1/2 cup chopped onion
1 cup quick-cooking grits
8 ounces sharp Cheddar cheese, shredded

2 eggs, beaten
1/2 teaspoon salt
Pepper to taste
1/4 cup shredded sharp Cheddar cheese

Brown the sausage with the onion in a skillet, stirring until crumbly; drain well on paper towels. Cook the grits using the package directions. Combine the sausage mixture, grits, 8 ounces cheese, eggs, salt and pepper in a bowl and mix well. Pour into a buttered 9x13-inch baking dish. Top with 1/4 cup cheese.
Bake at 350 degrees for 1 hour.
Yield: Eight Servings

Garlic Cheese Grits Casserole

Most good cooks will tell you that grits cannot be frozen (at least, not if you still want to eat them!). This casserole can be frozen before baking, thawed, and then baked.

6 cups water
2 teaspoons salt
1 1/2 cups grits
1/2 cup butter, cut into pieces

3 eggs, beaten
1 pound sharp Cheddar cheese, grated
1 to 3 cloves of garlic, minced
Cayenne to taste

Bring the water and salt to a rapid boil in a saucepan. Stir in the grits gradually with a fork. Cook until all the liquid is absorbed. Stir in the butter gradually. Add the eggs, cheese, garlic and cayenne carefully and mix gently.
Pour into a greased 2 1/2-quart casserole.
Bake at 350 degrees for 1 hour and 20 minutes.
Yield: Eight Servings

Coriander

The coriander plant is also commonly known as cilantro and has found its way into many dishes, from salads to stir-fries. The parsley-like leaves are a staple in Mexican cooking for salsas and guacamoles; Asian cooks use it over soups and noodles and even call it Chinese parsley. It has a very distinctive flavor that causes people to love it or turn up their nose—the latter group may prefer the mild-flavored parsley in their cooking. Make sure you choose healthy green stems; wash them in cold water and shake dry. Store in paper towels or in an opened plastic bag in the refrigerator.

Cashew Sesame Noodles

Try this Oriental-style pasta dish at supper club gatherings with Snow Pea and Napa Cabbage Slaw (page 107) and Grilled Garlic Lime Pork with Jalapeño Onion Marmalade (page 138).

2 large cloves of garlic, chopped
3 tablespoons soy sauce
1 1/2 tablespoons rice wine vinegar
1/4 cup Asian sesame oil
3/4 teaspoon dried hot red pepper flakes, or to taste
1 teaspoon sugar
1/2 cup salted roasted cashews
1/3 cup water
Salt and pepper to taste
1 (16-ounce) package thin spaghetti
5 quarts salted water
1 1/2 cups loosely packed finely chopped fresh coriander sprigs

Process the garlic, soy sauce, vinegar, oil, red pepper flakes, sugar, cashews, 1/3 cup water, salt and pepper in a blender until smooth. At this point, the sauce may be covered and stored in the refrigerator for up to 3 days. Bring to room temperature and stir just before using.
Cook the spaghetti in the salted water in a 6-quart kettle until al dente.
Drain in a colander; rinse under cold water.
Toss the spaghetti, sauce and coriander in a bowl.
Garnish with additional chopped cashews and fresh coriander sprigs.
Yield: Six to Eight Servings

Onion Quiche

The Vidalias make this quiche extra Southern and extra sweet. Serve as a first course or with a green salad for a luncheon meal or supper. This recipe is better than the one published by the purveyors of Vidalia onions!

1½ cups flour
2½ teaspoons baking powder
½ teaspoon salt
½ to 1 teaspoon dried sage, or to taste
5 tablespoons shortening
½ cup milk
4 large Vidalia onions, thinly sliced
¼ cup butter
3 large eggs, beaten
1 cup sour cream
1 cup shredded Swiss cheese
¼ teaspoon salt
½ teaspoon pepper
½ teaspoon Worcestershire sauce
8 slices bacon, crisp-fried, crumbled

For the pie shell, mix the flour, baking powder, ½ teaspoon salt and sage in a bowl. Cut in the shortening until crumbly. Add the milk, mixing until a soft dough forms. Roll into a circle on a floured surface. Fit into a lightly greased 9-inch pie plate.

For the filling, cook the onions in the butter in a saucepan for 7 to 10 minutes or until tender. Combine the onions, eggs, sour cream, cheese, ¼ teaspoon salt, pepper, Worcestershire sauce and bacon in a bowl and mix well. Pour into the pie shell.

Bake at 450 degrees for 20 minutes. Reduce the oven temperature to 325 degrees. Bake for 20 minutes.

Yield: Eight Servings

El Mirador Rice

Serve with Boneless Pork Loin with Tangy Sauce, page 137.

³/4 cup long grain rice
Lemon juice
2 tablespoons vegetable oil
2 medium tomatoes, chopped
2 medium bell peppers, chopped

1 clove of garlic, minced
1 cup heated chicken stock
1 teaspoon cumin
¹/4 teaspoon salt
1 teaspoon pepper, or to taste

Combine the rice with hot water to cover and a small amount of lemon juice in a bowl. Let stand for 5 minutes; drain well.
Heat the oil in a large skillet. Add the rice. Sauté until golden brown.
Add the tomatoes, bell peppers and garlic. Sauté for 5 minutes.
Add the chicken stock, cumin, salt and pepper and stir to mix. Reduce the heat. Simmer, covered, for 15 minutes; do not remove the cover while simmering. Fluff and serve immediately.
Yield: Twelve Servings
Becky Conroy

Puttanesca

A wonderful topping for your favorite pasta. One bite and you'll think, "Mama mia, am I in Italy!"

¹/4 cup olive oil
2 cloves of garlic, crushed
4 medium tomatoes, peeled, chopped
¹/2 cup chopped parsley
12 pimento-stuffed olives, sliced
1 (2-ounce) can anchovy fillets, drained, chopped

1 tablespoon chopped fresh basil
¹/2 teaspoon dried
¹/4 teaspoon chili powder
Salt and pepper to taste

Heat the oil in a medium saucepan. Add the garlic. Cook just until the garlic changes color.
Add the tomatoes, parsley, olives, anchovies, basil and chili powder.
Cook for several minutes. Season with salt and pepper.
Serve over pasta with freshly grated Parmesan cheese.
Yield: Four Servings

On the Side

Add a lump of butter or a few teaspoons of vegetable oil to the water when cooking rice, noodles, or pasta to prevent boiling over and sticking.

Desserts

Shelton Home

Admired for its ornately carved woodwork,
old tile fireplaces, and stained glass windows,
the 1905 Chenault house on Jackson Street,
in the Albany area, has recently become the home
of Clint and Nicole Shelton and their
twin sons, Hudson and William.
We present a selection of our desserts on a table in
the living room, with a view from the bottom
of the stairs. Hold on if the boys are sliding down
the banisters!

Pictured here:
Old English Trifle; Roulage;
Poached Pears with Raspberry Sauce;
Blackberry Cobbler;
and Strawberry Meringue Tarts with coffee.

Carrot Cake with Cream Cheese Frosting

3 cups unbleached all-purpose flour
3 cups sugar
1 tablespoon baking soda
1 tablespoon ground cinnamon
1 teaspoon salt
1 1/2 cups corn oil
4 large eggs, slightly beaten
1 tablespoon vanilla extract
1 1/3 cups puréed cooked carrots
1 1/2 cups shredded coconut
1 1/2 cups chopped walnuts
3/4 cup drained crushed pineapple
Cream Cheese Frosting
Confectioners' sugar

Sift the flour, sugar, baking soda, cinnamon and salt into a large bowl and
mix well. Add the oil, eggs and vanilla and mix well.
Stir in the carrots, coconut, walnuts and pineapple. Pour into two 10-inch or
three 9-inch greased waxed-paper-lined cake pans.
Bake at 350 degrees for 30 to 35 minutes or until a wooden pick
inserted near the center comes out clean.
Cool to room temperature. Spread Cream Cheese Frosting between the layers
and over the top and side of the cake. Dust with confectioners' sugar.
Chill if not served immediately.
Yield: Twelve to Sixteen Servings

Cream Cheese Frosting

6 tablespoons unsalted butter, softened
8 ounces cream cheese, softened
3 cups confectioners' sugar
1 teaspoon vanilla extract
Juice of 1/2 lemon (optional)

Cream the butter and cream cheese in a mixer bowl. Sift in the confectioners' sugar
gradually, beating constantly until mixed well. Stir in the vanilla and lemon juice.
Yield: Three and One-Half Cups

Chocolate Toffee Torte

Known for her fabulous desserts, Becky Conroy tells us this chocolate extravaganza will satisfy your favorite choc-o-hol-ics.

1¼ cups unsalted butter
2½ cups chopped pecans
½ cup sugar
¼ teaspoon salt
½ cup melted unsalted butter
8 ounces semisweet chocolate, chopped
2 tablespoons corn syrup
1 cup whipping cream

2 teaspoons instant coffee
2 teaspoons hot water
1½ cups packed light brown sugar
4 eggs, at room temperature
2 ounces semisweet chocolate, chopped
2 cups whipping cream
2 tablespoons sugar, or to taste

*Let 1¼ cups butter stand at room temperature overnight to become very soft.
For the crust, combine the pecans, ½ cup sugar, salt and ½ cup melted
butter in a bowl and mix well. Press into the bottom of a greased and waxed
paper-lined 10-inch springform pan. Place the pan on a baking sheet. Bake at 350
degrees for 10 minutes. Place in the freezer until cool.
For the fudge layer, combine 8 ounces chocolate, ¼ cup of the softened butter and corn
syrup in a bowl. Bring 1 cup cream to a boil in a saucepan. Add the cream to the
chocolate mixture, stirring until the chocolate and butter are melted. Cool completely.
This mixture may be cooled in the refrigerator, stirring frequently;
the mixture must remain soft enough to pour.
Pour the fudge mixture over the crust. Return to the freezer to harden.
For the toffee layer, dissolve the coffee powder in the water. Cream the remaining
1 cup softened butter and brown sugar in a mixer bowl until light and fluffy.
Beat in the eggs 1 at a time. Add the coffee and 2 ounces chocolate and beat well.
Pour over the fudge layer. Return to the freezer until serving time.
To serve, unmold onto a serving platter.
Beat 2 cups cream in a mixer bowl until soft peaks form. Add 2 tablespoons
sugar gradually, beating constantly until stiff peaks form. Spread over the top
and side of the torte. Garnish as desired.
Note: Use only real unsalted butter and semisweet baking chocolate—
chocolate chips don't work!*
Yield: Twelve to Sixteen Servings
Becky Conroy, Decatur Country Club

Chocolate Raspberry Cream Torte

Raspberries and chocolate combine beautifully in this luscious and elegant torte.

2 cups flour
1 teaspoon baking soda
1/2 teaspoon salt
2 cups sugar
1/2 cup baking cocoa
3/4 cup vegetable oil
1/4 cup buttermilk
2 teaspoons vanilla extract
2 eggs

1 cup boiling water
2 ounces semisweet chocolate, melted
2 tablespoons raspberry nectar
1 1/2 tablespoons butter, softened
2 tablespoons sifted confectioners' sugar
3/4 cup whipping cream, whipped
3/4 cup seedless raspberry preserves
2 cups whipping cream
1/3 cup sifted confectioners' sugar

Combine the flour, baking soda, salt, sugar, cocoa, oil, buttermilk, vanilla and eggs in a mixer bowl. Beat at medium speed for 2 minutes. Stir in the boiling water.
Pour into 2 greased and floured 8-inch round cake pans.
Bake at 350 degrees for 25 minutes or until a wooden pick inserted near the center comes out clean. Cool in the pans on wire racks for 10 minutes.
Remove from the pans to cool completely.
Combine the melted chocolate and raspberry nectar in a small bowl and mix well. Let cool.
Beat the butter at medium speed in a mixer bowl until fluffy. Add 2 tablespoons confectioners' sugar. Beat until blended. Add the chocolate mixture and beat well. Fold in the whipped cream.
Stir the preserves well. Cut each cake layer into halves horizontally.
Place 1 cake layer on a serving plate. Spread with 1/4 cup preserves.
Spread 1/3 of the chocolate mixture over the preserves. Layer 1 cake layer, half the remaining preserves, half the remaining chocolate, 1 cake layer, remaining preserves and remaining chocolate over layers. Top with the remaining cake layer.
Beat 2 cups whipping cream in a mixer bowl until foamy.
Add 1/3 cup confectioners' sugar, beating until soft peaks form. Spread over the side of the cake. Pipe onto the top of the cake.
Note: Raspberry nectar may be prepared by mixing raspberry jam with water.
Yield: Twelve Servings

Mayor's Chocolate Cake

This recipe produces the ideal groom's cake. It is particularly impressive when decorated with frosted grapes.

1 teaspoon baking soda
1 cup buttermilk
3/4 cup shortening
2 cups sugar
1/8 teaspoon salt, or to taste
1 teaspoon vanilla extract
5 eggs
2 cups sifted flour
3 ounces unsweetened chocolate, melted
3/4 cup evaporated milk
1/4 cup water
3/4 cup sugar

1/4 cup chopped seedless raisins
1/4 cup chopped dates
1/4 cup chopped figs
1 teaspoon vanilla extract
1/2 cup chopped pecans or walnuts
1 cup semisweet chocolate chips
1/4 cup butter
1/2 cup sour cream
1 teaspoon vanilla extract
1/4 teaspoon salt
3 cups confectioners' sugar

For the cake, dissolve the baking soda in the buttermilk. Cream the shortening in a mixer bowl until fluffy. Add 2 cups sugar gradually, beating constantly. Add 1/8 teaspoon salt and 1 teaspoon vanilla. Beat in the eggs 1 at a time. Add the flour and buttermilk mixture alternately, beating well after each addition. Stir in the melted chocolate. Pour into a greased and waxed paper-lined 10x15-inch cake pan. Bake at 350 degrees for 35 minutes or until the cake tests done. Let cool. Cut into halves horizontally.

For the filling, mix the evaporated milk with the water. Combine with 3/4 cup sugar in a double boiler. Cook over hot water, stirring until the sugar is dissolved. Add the raisins, dates and figs. Cook until thickened. Stir in 1 teaspoon vanilla and pecans. Keep warm.

For the frosting, melt the chocolate chips and butter in a double boiler over hot water; remove from the heat. Blend in the sour cream, 1 teaspoon vanilla and 1/4 teaspoon salt. Beat in the confectioners' sugar gradually until of a spreading consistency.

Spread the fruit filling between the cake layers. Spread the frosting over the top and side of the cake.

Yield: Twenty-Four Servings

Coconut-Glazed Pound Cake

A make-it-from-scratch pound cake. Yum!

2 cups sugar
1 cup vegetable oil
4 eggs
3 cups sifted self-rising flour
1 cup buttermilk
2 tablespoons coconut extract
1 (4-ounce) package coconut
Coconut Glaze

Cream the sugar, oil and eggs in a mixer bowl until light and fluffy.
Add the flour, buttermilk, flavoring and coconut and mix well.
Pour into a greased and floured bundt pan.
Bake at 350 degrees for 1 hour and 10 minutes. Cool in the pan.
Pierce the cake randomly with a small knife. Spoon a small amount of Coconut Glaze at
a time over the cake, allowing the glaze to be absorbed before adding more.
Let the cake stand for 2 hours in the pan. Remove from the pan and cut into slices.
Yield: Sixteen Servings

Coconut Glaze

2 cups sugar
1 cup water
3 tablespoons butter
1 1/2 tablespoons coconut extract
2 tablespoons corn syrup

Combine the sugar, water, butter, flavoring and corn syrup in a small saucepan.
Bring to a boil. Cook for 5 minutes, stirring constantly.
Yield: Three Cups

Mississippi Mud Cake

It is said that this cake's color resembles the brown-black mud of the mighty Mississippi. This recipe is a traditional one with pecans and marshmallows. Some traditions you don't want to change!

1/4 cup baking cocoa
3/4 teaspoon salt
1 1/2 cups flour
cup butter or margarine, softened
2 cups sugar
4 eggs

1 teaspoon vanilla extract
1 1/2 cups chopped pecans
1 (9-ounce) jar marshmallow creme,
or equivalent amount of miniature
marshmallows
Chocolate Frosting

Sift the cocoa, salt and flour together.
Cream the butter and sugar in a large mixer bowl until light and fluffy. Beat in the eggs 1 at a time. Add the flour mixture gradually, beating well after each addition. Stir in the vanilla and pecans. Pour into a greased and floured 9x13-inch cake pan.
Bake at 350 degrees for 30 to 35 minutes or until a wooden pick inserted near the center comes out clean.
Remove from the oven. Spread with the marshmallow creme while still hot. Cool in the pan.
Spread with Chocolate Frosting.
Note: No baking powder or baking soda is needed in this recipe.
Yield: Twelve Servings

Chocolate Frosting

1/3 cup baking cocoa
cup butter or margarine, softened
1/2 teaspoon vanilla extract
1/8 teaspoon salt

1/3 cup light cream or milk
1 (1-pound) package confectioners'
sugar

Beat the cocoa, butter, vanilla, salt, cream and confectioners' sugar in a mixer bowl until light and fluffy.
Yield: Four Cups

Play Dough

Many a parent will appreciate this recipe on rainy days and Sunday afternoon family time!

3 cups flour
1 1/2 cups salt
2 tablespoons cream of tartar
3 cups cool water
Food coloring as desired
3 tablespoons vegetable oil

Sift the flour, salt and cream of tartar into a large bowl. Add the water, food coloring and oil. Mix with a wooden spoon until the mixture forms a ball, adding a small amount of additional flour if the mixture is too sticky. Knead on a floured surface until you get the "right" dough feel. Store in an airtight container.
Yield: One Quart

Pure Decadence Cake

An extremely rich, moist cake. Use for birthday cake with just the candles—no frosting needed!

1 (2-layer) package yellow cake mix
1 (4-ounce) package vanilla instant
pudding mix
1 bar German's sweet chocolate, grated
4 eggs

½ cup water
½ cup vegetable oil
1 cup sour cream
1 cup semisweet chocolate chips
1 cup chopped pecans

Grease a bundt pan with vegetable oil or spray with nonstick cooking spray. Combine the cake mix, pudding mix, chocolate, eggs, water, oil and sour cream in a bowl and mix well. Stir in the chocolate chips and pecans. Pour into the prepared pan.
Bake at 350 degrees for 45 minutes or until a wooden pick inserted near the center comes out clean.
Cool in the pan for several minutes. Invert onto a serving plate.
Yield: Ten to Twelve Servings

Red Velvet Cake

Very popular in the South, a favorite holiday cake. Why not make three to five cakes at one time and freeze them for all those parties?

2½ cups sifted cake flour
1½ cups sugar
1 teaspoon baking soda
1 teaspoon baking cocoa
1 cup buttermilk
1½ cups vegetable oil
1 teaspoon vanilla extract
2 eggs
1 bottle red food coloring
1 teaspoon vinegar
Red Velvet Frosting

Sift the flour, sugar, baking soda and cocoa into a large bowl. Add the buttermilk, oil, vanilla, eggs, food coloring and vinegar in the order listed and mix well. Pour into 2 greased and lightly floured 9-inch round cake pans. Bake at 350 degrees for 25 minutes or until a wooden pick inserted near the center comes out clean. Cool in the pans for several minutes. Remove to a wire rack to cool completely. Spread Red Velvet Frosting between the layers and over the top and side of the cake. May be baked in one 9x13-inch cake pan. Yield: Twelve to Fifteen Servings

Red Velvet Frosting

½ cup margarine, softened
8 ounces cream cheese, softened
1 (1-pound) package confectioners' sugar
½ teaspoon vanilla extract
1 to 1½ cups chopped pecans

Cream the margarine and cream cheese in a mixer bowl until light and fluffy. Add the confectioners' sugar gradually, beating constantly until creamy. Stir in the vanilla and pecans. Yield: Four Cups

Rum Cake

Two glazes make this old favorite extra moist and extra rich.

1 (2-layer) package yellow cake mix
1 (4-ounce) package vanilla instant
pudding mix
4 eggs
½ cup cold water

½ cup dark rum
½ cup vegetable oil
Rum Glaze
Chocolate Glaze
½ cup chopped pecans

Combine the cake mix, pudding mix, eggs, water, rum and oil in a bowl
and mix until smooth. Pour into a greased and floured 10-inch tube pan.
Bake at 325 degrees for 1 hour. Cool in the pan for 25 minutes. Invert onto a serving
plate. Prick the top of the cake several times.
Spoon and brush Rum Glaze evenly over the cake, allowing the
cake to absorb the glaze. Let cool.
Drizzle with Chocolate Glaze. Sprinkle with the pecans.
Yield: Sixteen Servings

Rum Glaze

½ cup butter
¼ cup water

1 cup sugar
½ cup dark rum

Melt the butter in a saucepan. Stir in the water and sugar. Boil for 5 minutes.
Remove from the heat. Stir in the rum.
Yield: Two Cups

Chocolate Glaze

4 ounces semisweet chocolate

1 teaspoon butter

Melt the chocolate and butter in a heavy saucepan over very low heat.
Yield: One-Half Cup

Boiled Frosting

A light, pure white, fat-free icing. Use on angel food cake and serve with fruit for a very low-fat dessert.

1 cup plus 6 tablespoons sugar
3/4 cup water
1 tablespoon light corn syrup
2 egg whites
1/8 teaspoon salt
2 tablespoons sugar
1 teaspoon vanilla extract

Combine 1 cup plus 6 tablespoons sugar, water and corn syrup in a heavy saucepan. Cook over medium heat until the mixture is clear and the sugar is dissolved, stirring constantly. Cook without stirring until a candy thermometer registers 240 degrees, soft-ball stage. Remove from the heat. Beat the egg whites and salt at high speed in a mixer bowl until soft peaks form. Add 2 tablespoons sugar gradually, beating constantly until blended. Add the syrup mixture gradually, beating constantly. Add the vanilla and beat until stiff peaks form and the frosting is of spreading consistency.

Yield: Four Cups

Mock Caramel Icing

Good for pound cakes and bundt cakes.

1/2 cup butter
1 1/2 cups packed dark brown sugar
1/2 cup milk
Confectioners' sugar

Combine the butter, brown sugar and milk in a saucepan. Boil for minutes, stirring constantly. Add enough confectioners' sugar to make of a spreading consistency, stirring constantly.

Yield: Two and One-Half to Three Cups

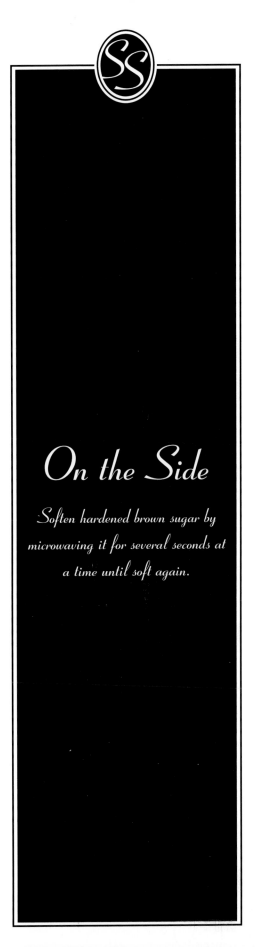

On the Side

Soften hardened brown sugar by microwaving it for several seconds at a time until soft again.

Toffee Crunch Cake

Mary Morgan took her daddy's award-winning English Toffee recipe from the home kitchen into one of Decatur's sweetest business success stories. Morgan-Price Candy Company's toffee and other chocolates and confections are sold locally, and are shipped all over the U.S. The wonderful aroma alone is worth a stop at their shop! Mary shares one of her favorite toffee recipes below.

1 cup sugar
1 cup packed brown sugar
2 cups flour, sifted
1 teaspoon baking soda
1/2 teaspoon salt
1/2 cup butter or margarine
1 cup buttermilk
1 egg
1/2 teaspoon vanilla extract
8 ounces English toffee or 8 Heath bars, chopped
1/2 cup chopped pecans

Combine the sugar and brown sugar in a large bowl. Sift in the flour, baking soda and salt and mix well. Cut in the butter until crumbly.
Measure and reserve 1/2 cup of mixture.
Add the buttermilk, egg and vanilla to the remaining crumb mixture and beat well.
Pour into a greased 9x13-inch cake pan.
Mix the toffee, pecans and reserved crumb mixture in a bowl.
Sprinkle over the cake batter.
Bake at 350 degrees for 30 to 35 minutes or until the cake tests done.
Yield: Twelve Servings
Mary Morgan, Morgan-Price Candy Company

Florentine Cookies Amaretto

*A fanciful oatmeal cookie that looks like lace and is sandwiched
with a chocolate amaretto filling. Wow!*

2/3 cup butter
2 cups quick-cooking oats
1 cup sugar
2/3 cup flour
1/2 cup finely chopped almonds
1/4 cup corn syrup
1/4 cup amaretto
1/2 teaspoon salt
3 tablespoons butter
1/4 cup amaretto
1 1/2 cups semisweet chocolate chips

For the cookies, melt 2/3 cup butter in a medium saucepan.
Remove from the heat. Stir in the oats, sugar, flour, almonds, corn syrup, 1/4 cup
amaretto and salt. Drop by rounded teaspoonfuls 3 inches apart onto foil-lined
cookie sheets, spreading to make thin cookies.
Bake at 375 degrees for 8 to 11 minutes or until golden brown.
Cool completely on the cookie sheets.
For the filling, heat 3 tablespoons butter and 1/4 cup amaretto in a heavy medium
saucepan over low heat until the butter is melted. Remove from the heat. Stir in the
chocolate chips. Cool to room temperature.
Peel the foil from the cookies. Spread the filling over the flat side of half the cookies.
Top with the remaining cookies. Cut into squares.
Yield: Two and One-Half Dozen

Peanut Butter Fudge

Making fudge is one of America's favorite pastimes. The addition of peanut butter makes this recipe uniquely Southern.

½ cup milk
2 cups sugar
2 tablespoons butter
3 tablespoons light corn syrup
½ cup plus 1 tablespoon peanut butter
1 teaspoon vanilla extract

Bring the milk, sugar, butter and corn syrup to a boil in a 2-quart saucepan. Cook to 234 to 240 degrees on a candy thermometer, soft-ball stage, stirring frequently. Remove from the heat.
Add the peanut butter and vanilla. Beat with a hand mixer until creamy. Pour onto a buttered plate. Let cool. Cut into squares.
Yield: Fifteen Servings

English Toffee

A candy favorite you'll want to try. Once you do, you'll make this toffee again and again.

Finely chopped pecans or English walnuts
1 cup sugar
1 cup margarine
3 tablespoons water
1 teaspoon vanilla extract
3 Hershey bars

Sprinkle some pecans into a buttered 9x13-inch pan. Combine the sugar, margarine and water in a saucepan. Cook for 15 minutes or until the mixture is golden brown, stirring constantly. Stir in the vanilla. Pour over the pecans in the pan. Place the candy over the sugar mixture immediately, spreading as the chocolate melts. Sprinkle with additional pecans.
Let stand until set. Chop or break into pieces.
Yield: Ten Servings

Buttermilk Cookies

This wonderful cookie travels well, making it ideal for gift-giving. Great for college student "care packages" at exam time, too!

4¹/₂ cups sifted flour
1 teaspoon baking soda
¹/₂ teaspoon salt
¹/₂ teaspoon nutmeg
1 cup butter or margarine, softened
2 cups sugar
3 eggs
1 cup buttermilk

Sift the flour, baking soda, salt and nutmeg together. Cream the butter and sugar in a mixer bowl until light and fluffy. Beat in the eggs 1 at a time. Add the flour mixture and buttermilk alternately, beginning and ending with the flour mixture and beating well after each addition. Drop by spoonfuls onto a greased cookie sheet.
Bake at 350 degrees for 15 minutes or until lightly browned.
Yield: Four Dozen

Country Chocolate Chip Cookies

This recipe makes three dozen, if you can avoid eating the cookie dough!
Don't forget a glass of cold milk on the side.

2¹/₂ cups flour
3/4 cup each sugar and packed light brown sugar
¹/₂ teaspoon baking soda
1 cup melted butter
1 teaspoon vanilla extract
2 eggs
2 cups semisweet chocolate chips

Mix the flour, sugar, brown sugar and baking soda in a large bowl.
Mix the butter, vanilla and eggs in a small bowl. Add to the flour mixture and mix well.
Fold in the chocolate chips. Drop by spoonfuls onto a nonstick cookie sheet.
Bake at 325 degrees for 8 to 10 minutes or until browned.
Yield: Three Dozen

Spiced Pecans

Great for gift baskets, especially at holiday time.

1/2 teaspoon salt
1 1/2 teaspoon cinnamon
3/4 teaspoon allspice
1 cup sugar
1 tablespoon melted butter
1 egg white, beaten
1 pound pecan halves

Mix the salt, cinnamon, allspice and sugar together. Spread 1/4 of the mixture in a shallow 10x15-inch baking pan. Stir the melted butter into the egg white. Stir in the pecans. Add the remaining sugar mixture, stirring to coat the pecans well. Spread in the baking pan. Bake at 300 degrees for 15 to 20 minutes or until the pecans are lightly browned. Let cool. May be stored in an airtight container for several weeks.

Yield: One Pound

Chocolate Pecan Crumble Bars

Great for bake sales, potluck dinners, and after-school treats.

1 cup butter, softened
2 cups flour
1/2 cup sugar
1/4 teaspoon salt
1 1/2 cups semisweet chocolate chips
1 (14-ounce) can sweetened condensed milk
1 teaspoon vanilla extract
1 cup chopped pecans
1/2 cup semisweet chocolate chips

Cream the butter in a large mixer bowl. Add the flour, sugar and salt and beat until crumbly. Press 2 cups of the mixture into a greased 9x13-inch baking pan with floured fingers, reserving the remaining mixture.
Bake at 350 degrees for 10 to 12 minutes or until the edges are golden brown.
Combine 1 1/2 cups chocolate chips and condensed milk in a saucepan.
Heat until the chocolate is melted, stirring constantly. Stir in the vanilla.
Spread over the hot crust.
Combine the pecans, 1/2 cup chocolate chips and reserved crumb mixture in a bowl. Sprinkle over the chocolate mixture.
Bake at 350 degrees for 25 to 30 minutes or until set. Let stand to cool.
Cut into bars.
Yield: Two Dozen

Praline Squares

Enjoy the wonderful taste of pecans and caramel in this simple pan cookie.

2 cups packed brown sugar
1 cup margarine
2 eggs, beaten
¼ teaspoon salt
1½ cups flour
1 teaspoon vanilla extract
1 cup chopped pecans

Heat the brown sugar and margarine in a heavy saucepan until the margarine is melted, stirring frequently. Let cool for 10 to 15 minutes.
Beat in the eggs. Add the salt, flour and vanilla and mix well. Stir in the pecans.
Spread in a greased and floured 9x13-inch baking pan.
Bake at 325 degrees for 35 minutes or just until set; do not overbake.
Note: Do not use an electric mixer to prepare this recipe.
Yield: Fifteen Servings

Shortbread

What mama's little baby loves . . . and mama does, too.

1 cup packed light brown sugar
4 cups flour
1 pound butter, softened

Mix the brown sugar and flour in a bowl. Add the butter and mix well.
Pat ½ inch thick on a floured board. Cut into desired shapes.
Place on a nonstick cookie sheet.
Bake at 325 to 350 degrees for 20 to 25 minutes or until lightly browned.
Yield: Three to Four Dozen

Cinnamon Christmas Ornaments

Holiday fun with the children, great gift-wrap decorations, wonderful tree trims for a gift basket.

3/4 to 1 cup applesauce
1 (4-ounce) bottle ground
cinnamon

Combine the applesauce and cinnamon in a bowl and mix until a stiff dough forms. Roll 1/4 inch thick on a floured surface. Cut with cookie cutters. Make a hole at the top of each cookie for a ribbon to go through. Place carefully on a wire rack to dry for several days, turning occasionally. Place on a nonstick baking sheet. Bake at 200 degrees for 1 1/2 to 2 hours or until hard, turning after 1 hour. Let cool. Decorate with ribbons, glitter, sequins, etc.
Yield: One Dozen

Russian Tea Cakes

These are a great Christmastime favorite and a family tradition in many local homes.

2 1/4 cups sifted flour
1/4 teaspoon salt
1 cup butter, softened
1/2 cup sifted confectioners' sugar
1 teaspoon vanilla extract
3/4 cup finely chopped pecans
Confectioners' sugar

Sift the flour and salt together. Cream the butter and 1/2 cup confectioners' sugar in a mixer bowl until light and fluffy. Beat in the vanilla. Add the flour mixture gradually, beating well after each addition until a soft dough forms. Chill thoroughly. Shape the dough into 1-inch balls. Place on a nonstick cookie sheet. The cookies may be placed close together; they do not spread. Bake at 400 degrees for 10 to 12 minutes or until set but not browned. Roll the warm cookies in additional confectioners' sugar. Let cool. Roll in confectioners' sugar again.
Note: These dainties look wonderful stored in fancy biscuit jars or large brandy snifters, or piled on a silver platter.
Yield: Four Dozen

Chess Pie

*Very sweet and very rich, a small slice of this
regional favorite is all you'll need.*

1 recipe (1-crust) pie pastry
1/2 cup butter, softened
2 teaspoons vanilla extract
1 1/2 cups sugar
4 egg yolks, beaten

*Fit the pastry into an 8-inch pie plate, fluting the edge.
Beat the butter and vanilla in a mixer bowl until blended. Add the sugar,
beating until light and fluffy. Add the egg yolks 1/3 at a time, beating
well after each addition. Pour into the pie shell.
Bake at 425 degrees for 10 minutes. Reduce the oven temperature to 325 degrees. Bake
for 40 to 45 minutes or until a knife inserted near the center comes out clean.
Serve warm or cool.*
Yield: Eight Servings

Chocolate Chess Pie

*Chess pie gets even richer with this chocolate
variation of the traditional dessert.*

1/2 cup unsalted butter
1/4 cup baking cocoa
2 eggs
1 small can evaporated milk
2 teaspoons vanilla extract
1/8 teaspoon salt, or to taste
1 unbaked (8-inch) pie shell

*Heat the butter and cocoa in a saucepan until the butter is melted, stirring frequently.
Add the eggs, evaporated milk, vanilla and salt and mix well. Pour into the pie shell.
Bake at 325 degrees for 45 minutes or until the center is set and the
pie crust is golden brown. Let stand to cool.*
Yield: Eight Servings

Red Pear Pie

A delicious preparation for the fruit so beautifully displayed on the front cover. The combination of fruit and nut meats makes this a wonderful addition to the Thanksgiving menu.

2 all ready pie pastries
1 cup sugar
3 tablespoons cornstarch
1 teaspoon cinnamon
4 red pears, peeled, sliced

1 cup fresh cranberries
3/4 cup chopped walnuts
3/4 cup golden raisins
3 tablespoons sugar

Fit 1 of the pastries into a deep-dish pie plate. Mix 1 cup sugar, cornstarch and cinnamon in a bowl. Add the pears, cranberries, walnuts and raisins and toss to coat well. Spoon into the prepared pie plate. Top with the remaining pastry, sealing the edge and cutting 3 vents. Sprinkle with the remaining 3 tablespoons sugar. Bake at 350 degrees for 1 hour.
Yield: Eight to Ten Servings

Pecan Pie

Truly the richest and most delicious of all the traditional Southern pies. This family recipe was even served in lieu of the groom's cake at a wedding reception and was very well received.

3 eggs, beaten
1 cup sugar
1 cup light corn syrup
2 tablespoons flour

1/2 to 1 teaspoon vanilla extract
1/2 cup butter
1 cup chopped pecans
1 unbaked (9-inch) pie shell

Combine the eggs, sugar, corn syrup, flour, vanilla and butter in a saucepan. Heat until the butter is melted, stirring occasionally. Stir in the pecans. Pour into the pie shell. Bake at 400 degrees for 10 minutes. Reduce the oven temperature to 300 degrees. Bake for 30 minutes longer.
Yield: Six Servings

Pumpkin Pie Squares

Break tradition at Thanksgiving and try this new twist to pumpkin pie. Bet the kids won't complain!

1 cup sifted flour
1/2 cup quick-cooking oats
1/2 cup packed brown sugar
1/2 cup butter or margarine
2 cups canned pumpkin
1 (13-ounce) can evaporated milk
2 eggs
3/4 cup sugar
1/2 teaspoon salt
1 1/4 teaspoons ground cinnamon
1/2 teaspoon ground ginger
1/4 teaspoon ground nutmeg
1/4 teaspoon ground cloves
1/2 cup chopped pecans
1/2 cup packed brown sugar
2 tablespoons melted butter or margarine

Combine the flour, oats, 1/2 cup brown sugar and 1/2 cup butter in a bowl
and mix until crumbly. Press into a nonstick 9x13-inch baking pan.
Bake at 350 degrees for 15 minutes.
Combine the pumpkin, evaporated milk, eggs, sugar, salt, cinnamon, ginger,
nutmeg and cloves in a bowl and mix well. Pour over the crust.
Bake at 350 degrees for 20 minutes.
Mix the pecans, 1/2 cup brown sugar and 2 tablespoons butter in
a bowl. Sprinkle over the pumpkin filling.
Bake at 350 degrees for 15 to 20 minutes or until the filling is set.
Cool in the pan on a wire rack. Cut into squares.
Yield: Twenty-Four Servings

Homemade Finger Paints

If you dare!

1 envelope unflavored gelatin
1/4 cup cold water
1/4 cup warm water
1/2 cup cornstarch
3 tablespoons sugar
2 cups cold water
Food coloring
Dishwashing liquid

Soften the gelatin in 1/4 cup cold water for 5 minutes. Add the warm water, stirring until dissolved; set aside. Combine the cornstarch and sugar in a medium saucepan. Stir in 2 cups cold water gradually. Cook slowly over low heat, stirring until well mixed. Remove from the heat and add the gelatin. Divide into separate containers for each color. Add 1 or 2 drops of liquid detergent to each container. Add food coloring 1 drop at a time until the desired shades are attained. Will keep in the refrigerator for up to 6 weeks.

Raspberry Cream Tart

The perfect sweet tart for your sweetheart on Valentine's Day,
or as a wonderful summer dessert.

1 recipe (1-crust) pie pastry
1 1/2 cups fresh raspberries
6 tablespoons sugar
2 eggs
1/2 cup ground blanched almonds
3/4 cup confectioners' sugar
1 cup whipping cream

Line a 9-inch straight-sided French tart pan or flan ring with
the pastry. Prick the bottom several times.
Bake at 425 degrees until partially baked.
Combine the raspberries and sugar in a bowl and mix well.
Spread in a single layer over the pastry.
Combine the eggs, almonds, confectioners' sugar and cream in a large mixer bowl.
Beat until thick. Pour over the raspberries.
Bake at 350 degrees for 30 minutes or until the top is golden brown.
Cool to room temperature before serving.
Yield: Six to Eight Servings

Strawberry Meringue Tarts

Don't wonder about the sour cream. The flavors of meringue, strawberries, and sour cream combine beautifully in these light tarts, pictured on page 210.

3 egg whites, at room temperature
1/2 teaspoon almond extract
1/2 teaspoon cream of tartar
1/8 teaspoon salt, or to taste
1 cup sugar, sifted
1 cup sour cream
40 (about) whole strawberries

Combine the egg whites, flavoring, cream of tartar and salt in a mixer bowl. Beat until frothy. Add the sugar 1 tablespoon at a time, beating constantly until the mixture is glossy and stiff peaks form; do not underbeat.
Drop the meringue by tablespoonfuls onto a parchment-lined baking sheet. Make a small indentation in the top of each meringue with the back of a spoon.
Bake at 250 degrees for 30 minutes. Turn off the oven. Let stand in the closed oven for 1 hour for crispier meringues.
Cool away from drafts.
Spoon 1 teaspoon sour cream onto each meringue. Top with a strawberry.
Note: The meringues may be prepared and baked 1 day ahead and stored in airtight containers.
Yield: Forty Servings

Easy Pie Crusts

2 cups flour
1/4 cup milk
1/2 cup vegetable oil
1/2 teaspoon salt

Sift the flour into a bowl. Make a well in the center. Add the
milk, oil and salt and mix well with a fork.
Divide the dough into 2 balls. Roll each between sheets of waxed paper.
Place in two 8-inch pie plates. Flute the edges with a fork.
Yield: Two Pie Shells

Graham Cracker Crust

1 2/3 cups finely crushed graham crackers
1/4 cup sugar
6 tablespoons melted butter or margarine

Mix the cracker crumbs and sugar in a medium bowl. Make a well in the center.
Add the butter and mix well with a fork.
Press firmly onto the bottom and up the side of a 9-inch pie plate.
For frozen desserts, the crust may be used without baking. For other unbaked
pies, bake at 350 degrees for 7 to 9 minutes.
Yield: One Pie Shell

Bread Pudding
with Jack Daniel's Sauce

A great bread pudding has put many a Southern restaurant on the map. The Green Bottle Grill in Huntsville is no exception. Jack Daniel would be proud.

3 loaves dried French bread
2 cups milk
1/3 cup raisins
5 eggs
1 1/2 cups sugar
2 tablespoons vanilla extract
2 cups half-and-half
2 cups sugar
1 cup Jack Daniel's whiskey
1 cup butter, cut into 1-inch cubes

Cut the bread into 1-inch cubes. Place in a buttered 9x13-inch baking pan. Pour the milk over the bread. Let stand until the bread is quite moist. Top with the raisins.
Combine the eggs, 1 1/2 cups sugar, vanilla and half-and-half in a bowl and mix until blended and smooth. Pour over the bread and raisins and mix well.
Bake at 350 degrees for 45 minutes or until the custard is set.
Heat 2 cups sugar and whiskey in a saucepan over low heat, stirring constantly until the sugar is dissolved. Remove from the heat. Whisk in the butter.
Spoon the bread pudding into warm bowls. Serve with the sauce.
Note: This will keep in the refrigerator for up to 4 days. To serve, reheat the bread pudding and whiskey sauce separately.
Yield: Six Servings
Rick Paler, Green Bottle Grill

Crème Fraîche

Add a dollop of this in soups

or on mousse desserts.

1 cup whipping cream (not
ultra-pasteurized)
1 cup sour cream

*Whisk the cream and sour
cream in a bowl. Cover loosely
with plastic wrap. Let stand in the
kitchen or another reasonably
warm place for 8 to 24 hours or
until thickened. Chill, covered, for
4 hours or longer. The crème
fraîche will become quite thick and
the tangy flavor will continue to
develop in the refrigerator.*
Yield: Two Cups

French Chocolate Mousse

Smooth as silk—an elegant conclusion to your next dinner party.

6 ounces semisweet chocolate
2 tablespoons water
1/4 cup sugar
1/2 cup unsalted butter, cut into pieces
6 egg yolks
1 tablespoon vanilla extract, rum or brandy
1 cup chilled whipping cream, whipped
6 egg whites, stiffly beaten

*Combine the chocolate and water in a double boiler over hot
water. Cook until the chocolate is melted, stirring frequently.
Stir in the sugar. Stir in the butter gradually. Cook until the butter
is melted, stirring frequently. Cool slightly.
Beat the egg yolks in a mixer bowl until thick and pale yellow.
Beat in the cooled chocolate mixture and vanilla.
Fold in the whipped cream.
Fold in the egg whites 1/4 at a time, beating and rotating the bowl
constantly. Do not overmix; there will be clots of egg whites remaining.
Spoon into pots de crème cups, sherry glasses or Champagne glasses.
Chill for 12 hours or longer in the refrigerator or for 4 hours in the freeze*
Yield: Six to Eight Servings

Blackberry Cobbler

Cobbler is a Southern favorite for family picnics, church suppers, or just to enjoy the fruits of summer. The Blackberry Cobbler is pictured on page 210 in an elegant chafing dish for a more formal occasion.

6 cups fresh blackberries
3/4 cup sugar
2 tablespoons cornstarch
2 tablespoons water, or 1 tablespoon water plus
1 tablespoon Chambourd liqueur
1 tablespoon freshly squeezed lemon juice
1 cup flour
1 tablespoon sugar
1 1/2 teaspoons baking powder
1/8 teaspoon salt
1/4 cup cold margarine, cut into pieces
1/2 cup whipping cream
1 tablespoon sugar

For the filling, combine the blackberries, 3/4 cup sugar, cornstarch and water in a large saucepan. Bring to a boil, stirring gently. Cook for 1 minute. Remove from the heat. Stir in the lemon juice. Pour into a 9x9-inch baking dish. For the pastry, combine the flour, 1 tablespoon sugar, baking powder and salt in a large bowl. Cut in the margarine until crumbly. Stir in the cream. Knead 2 to 3 times or until the dough holds together. Roll into an 8-inch square on waxed paper. Cover the fruit mixture with the pastry. Sprinkle with the remaining 1 tablespoon sugar. Place the baking dish on a baking sheet. Bake at 425 degrees for 20 to 25 minutes or until the pastry is golden brown.

Yield: Eight Servings

Peach Raspberry Cobbler

½ cup sugar
1 tablespoon cornstarch
2 tablespoons water
4 cups sliced peeled fresh peaches
1 teaspoon finely shredded lemon peel
1 teaspoon freshly squeezed lemon juice
2 cups fresh raspberries
½ cup butter
Lattice Crust
1 tablespoon sugar

Combine ½ cup sugar and cornstarch in a medium saucepan. Add the water.
Stir in the peaches, lemon peel and lemon juice. Cook until thickened and bubbly,
stirring constantly. Fold in the raspberries. Return to a boil, stirring gently to avoid
breaking the fruit. Pour into a 9x13-inch glass baking dish. Dot with the butter.
Arrange half the Lattice Crust strips 1 inch apart in 1 direction only over the cobbler.
Sprinkle with ½ tablespoon sugar. Bake at 350 degrees for 35 minutes
or until the pastry begins to brown.
Arrange the remaining pastry strips over the cobbler to form a lattice.
Sprinkle with the remaining sugar.
Bake for 35 minutes longer or until the pastry is golden brown.
Serve hot or warm with ice cream.
Yield: Ten to Twelve Servings

Lattice Crust

2 cups flour
1 teaspoon salt
¾ cup shortening
3 to 4 tablespoons cold water

Combine the flour and salt in a large bowl. Cut in the shortening until crumbly.
Add the water 1 tablespoon at a time, mixing with a fork until a soft
dough forms. Shape into a ball. Divide into halves.
Roll each piece of the dough ⅛ inch thick on a lightly floured surface.
Cut into 1x11-inch strips.
Yield: Pastry for One Cobbler or Pie

Roulage

As impressive as its name implies, this marvelous rolled meringue, pictured on page 210, derives its name from the French word rouler, meaning to roll.

6 ounces semisweet chocolate chips
3 to 4 tablespoons water
1/2 teaspoon instant coffee
5 to 6 egg yolks
3/4 cup sugar
5 to 6 egg whites
1/8 teaspoon salt, or to taste
1 pint whipping cream
Vanilla extract, rum or brandy to taste
Confectioners' sugar

Spray a jelly roll pan with nonstick cooking spray. Line with buttered
waxed paper or parchment.
Combine the chocolate chips, water and coffee powder in a saucepan.
Cook over very low heat until the chocolate is melted and the mixture is
thick and creamy, stirring frequently. Remove from heat and let stand until cool.
Beat the egg yolks and sugar in a mixer bowl until thick and light.
Beat the egg whites and salt in a mixer bowl until stiff peaks form.
Stir the cooled chocolate mixture into the egg yolks in a bowl. Fold in the egg
whites. Spread lightly in the prepared pan.
Bake at 350 degrees for 20 to 25 minutes or until a wooden pick inserted near
the center comes out clean. Cool to room temperature.
Line a sheet of foil with a sheet of parchment. Invert the roulage onto the parchment,
removing the foil and parchment from the top. Beat the whipping cream with the vanilla
in a mixer bowl until stiff peaks form. Spread over the roulage. Roll up from the narrow
end. Place on an oblong platter. Sift confectioners' sugar over the roulage or place
additional whipped cream in a pastry bag fitted with a star tip and pipe over the top.
Cut into slices. An alternative method of preparation is to roll the warm roulage first
with parchment or waxed paper on top. Unroll carefully after the roulage has
cooled, remove the paper, spread with the filling and reroll.
Note: For best results when preparing this recipe, it is important to work quickly.
Any crusty side edges of the roulage should be removed with a sharp knife to ease the
rolling. The recipe can easily be doubled for two.
Yield: Fifteen Servings

Dacquoise

Two meringue layers, filled with chocolate cream and topped with whipped cream, make a spectacular dessert for that special occasion or time to impress! Another great dessert from Becky Conroy.

3/4 cup plus 2 tablespoons sugar
3/4 teaspoon cream of tartar
1 cup finely chopped pecans
2 1/4 tablespoons cornstarch
1 cup plus 2 tablespoons confectioners' sugar
6 large egg whites
2 cups heavy cream
4 ounces chocolate chips

*Line 2 baking sheets with parchment paper or nonrecycled brown paper.
Trace an 8-inch circle on each.
Mix half the sugar with the cream of tartar in a small bowl. Set aside.
Mix the remaining sugar, pecans, cornstarch and confectioners'
sugar in a medium bowl. Set aside.
Beat the egg whites in a mixer bowl until foamy. Add the cream of tartar mixture
gradually, beating constantly until very stiff peaks form.
Fold in the confectioners' sugar mixture.
Spread over the circles on the paper. Use a small amount of the
meringue to anchor the paper if needed.
Bake at 250 degrees for 2 hours. Let cool. Peel off the paper. The layers
may be wrapped and frozen at this point for later use.
Boil 1/2 cup of the cream in a saucepan. Pour over the chocolate chips in a bowl.
Stir until the chocolate is melted. Let cool.
Whip 1/2 cup of the cream in a mixer bowl. Fold into the chocolate mixture.
Spread over 1 cake layer. Top with the second cake layer.
Whip the remaining 1 cup cream in a mixer bowl. Spread over the top layer.
Garnish with chocolate curls or shaved chocolate.*
Yield: Eight to Ten Servings
Becky Conroy, Decatur Country Club

Southern Ice Cream Favorites

A smooth, rich and creamy base, best ripened in the ice cream freezer, but will keep in the home freezer if necessary.

Ice Cream Base

2 large eggs
3/4 cup sugar

2 cups heavy cream
1 cup milk

Whisk the eggs in a bowl for 1 to 2 minutes or until fluffy. Whisk in the ar. Whisk for 1 minute longer. Add the cream and milk, whisking to blend.
Yield: One Quart

Strawberry Ice Cream

pint fresh strawberries, sliced
1/3 cup sugar

2 tablespoons lemon juice
Ice Cream Base

Mix the strawberries, sugar and lemon juice in a bowl. Chill, covered, for 1 hour or longer. Mash or purée the mixture and add to the Ice Cream Base. Pour into an ice cream freezer container. Freeze using the manufacturer's directions.
Yield: One Quart

Peach Ice Cream

ups finely chopped ripe peaches
1/2 cup sugar

2 tablespoons lemon juice
Ice Cream Base

Mix the peaches, sugar and lemon juice in a bowl. Chill, covered, for 2 hours or longer, stirring every 30 minutes. Drain the peaches, serving the juice. Return the peaches to the refrigerator. Mix the reserved ch juice with the Ice Cream Base. Pour into an ice cream freezer container. reeze using the manufacturer's directions, stirring in the peaches several minutes before the freezing process is finished.
Yield: One Quart

Butter Pecan Ice Cream

1/2 cup butter
1 cup pecan halves
1/2 teaspoon salt
Ice Cream Base

Melt the butter in a heavy skillet over low heat. Add the pecans and salt. Sauté until the pecans begin to brown. Remove the pecans to a small bowl using a slotted spoon. Drain the butter into another bowl to cool. Stir the cooled butter into the Ice Cream Base. Pour into an ice cream freezer container. Freeze using the manufacturer's directions, stirring in the pecans several minutes before the freezing process is finished.
Yield: One Quart

Flower Cups

Fill these with mousse or sorbet for a pretty, edible dish. Sift 1¹/₃ cups flour with ³/₄ cup confectioners' sugar. Add 3 lightly beaten egg whites, 2 lightly beaten egg yolks, 1 teaspoon grated orange zest and 1 tablespoon Cointreau and mix well. Let the batter stand for 20 minutes. Mark widely spaced 5-inch circles on a greased baking sheet. Drop 1 tablespoonful of batter into the center of each circle, spreading evenly. Bake at 350 degrees for 5 to 6 minutes or until the edges are browning but the centers are still soft. Working quickly, remove the cookies with a spatula and form into cupped shapes, using a large orange as a mold. Cool on a wire rack. Repeat this process until all the batter is used.
Yield: Fifteen to
Twenty Flower Cups

Melon Sorbet

Sorbets are wonderful, fat-free frozen ices that traditionally were served between courses to cleanse the palate, but are now part of the dessert menu, especially after a heavy meal.

8 cups very ripe cantaloupe, honeydew or watermelon
4 cups superfine sugar
¹/₄ cup light corn syrup
Juice of 1 lemon

Process the melon in batches in a food processor or blender until it is liquefied.
Combine with the sugar, corn syrup and lemon juice in a large bowl, stirring until the sugar is dissolved and the corn syrup is evenly dispersed. Pour into a freezerproof container.
Freeze overnight or until quite hard. Break into pieces and store the pieces in airtight jars, leaving a small amount of headspace.
An alternative method is to process the ice-hard sorbet in a food processor or blender until mushy. Pour into a decorative freezerproof glass bowl. Freeze for 2 hours before serving.
Yield: Nine Cups

Poached Pears with Raspberry Sauce

An impressive presentation of this delicate fruit and pastry combination is shown on page 210. Equally delicious with chocolate sauce.

1 recipe pie pastry
6 firm ripe pears, peeled, stems intact
2 tablespoons sugar
1¹/₂ teaspoons cinnamon

1 bottle sauterne or other
sweet white wine
Raspberry Sauce

Roll the pastry dough ¹/₄ inch thick on a lightly floured surface. Cut into 4-inch squares or circles. Shape each piece of dough over an inverted muffin cup to form a flat-bottomed "bowl." Cut out six 1-inch-long leaf shapes from the remaining dough. Indent the leaves with the flat side of the knife blade to make veins. Arrange on a nonstick baking sheet. Bake at 450 degrees for several minutes or until lightly browned. Let cool. Core the pears from the bottom, being careful to keep the stems intact. Cut ¹/₄ inch from the bottom of each pear to form a flat base. Place the pears in a large saucepan. Sprinkle with the sugar and cinnamon. Add enough wine to cover the pears. Bring to a boil; reduce the heat. Simmer for 10 minutes or until tender. Remove from the heat. Cool to room temperature. Spoon several tablespoons Raspberry Sauce onto each of 6 dessert plates. Center a pastry shell on each plate. Remove the pears from the saucepan with a slotted spoon and place in the center of the pastry shells. Secure 1 leaf to the top of each pear with a wooden pick. May pipe some whipped cream around the base of the pears.

Yield: Six Servings

Raspberry Sauce

1 (10-ounce) package frozen
raspberries, thawed
¹/₂ cup hot water
1 tablespoon lemon juice
¹/₃ cup sugar

1 tablespoon cornstarch
¹/₄ teaspoon salt
2 tablespoons kirsch or other cherry-
flavored liqueur

Drain the raspberries, reserving the juice. Combine the raspberry juice, water, lemon juice, sugar, cornstarch and salt in a medium saucepan. Bring to a boil; reduce the heat to medium. Cook until the mixture begins to thicken, stirring constantly. Add the raspberries. Cook for 3 minutes, stirring constantly. Remove from the heat. Stir in the kirsch.

Yield: Two and One-Half to Three Cups

Sugared Peanuts

*Double or triple this recipe, because one batch won't be enough
for your family or guests. Snackin' good!*

½ cup water	4 cups shelled raw peanuts, with skins
1 cup sugar	Salt to taste

*Combine the water and sugar in a heavy saucepan or small Dutch oven.
Bring to a boil, stirring until the sugar dissolves.
Add the peanuts. Cook over medium heat until the sugar crystallizes and
all the liquid is absorbed, stirring frequently; watch carefully to be sure the peanuts
don't burn. Remove from the heat.
Spread the peanuts in a single layer on a nonstick baking sheet. Sprinkle with salt.
Bake at 300 degrees for 15 minutes. Stir to turn the peanuts. Sprinkle with additional
salt. Bake for 15 minutes longer. Let stand to cool.
Store in an airtight container.*
Yield: Four Cups

Praline Cheesecake

An extraordinary Southern twist to one of America's best known desserts.

1/4 cup melted butter
1/2 cup chopped pecans
1 1/2 cups graham cracker crumbs
24 ounces cream cheese, softened
3 eggs
1 cup packed brown sugar
2 teaspoons vanilla extract
1 cup whipping cream
1/2 cup pecan halves
1/4 cup orange juice
1/2 cup packed brown sugar
2 cups bourbon (optional)

*Combine the butter, chopped pecans and graham cracker crumbs in a bowl
and mix well. Press into a springform pan. Chill thoroughly.
Combine the cream cheese, eggs, 1 cup brown sugar and vanilla in a food processor
container or mixer bowl. Process or beat until smooth. Stir in the whipping
cream. Pour into the prepared crust.
Bake at 475 degrees for 10 minutes. Reduce the oven temperature to 275 degrees.
Bake for 1 hour. Cool to room temperature.
Combine the pecan halves, orange juice, 1/2 cup brown sugar and bourbon in a skillet.
Cook until the pecans are candied, stirring frequently. Arrange over the cheesecake.
Chill for 4 hours to overnight. Remove the side of the pan.*

Yield: Sixteen Servings

Lemon Cups

*Similar to a baked pudding, this dessert can be served in sherbet glasses
for an elegant presentation. Garnish with holly sprigs, lemon slices,
or a dollop of whipped cream and a berry.*

1 tablespoon butter or
margarine, softened
1 cup sugar
1/4 cup flour
1/8 teaspoon salt, or to taste

5 tablespoons lemon juice
Grated peel of 1 lemon
3 egg yolks, beaten
1 1/2 cups milk
3 egg whites, stiffly beaten

*Cream the butter and sugar in a mixer bowl until light and fluffy. Add the flour,
salt, lemon juice and lemon peel and mix well. Beat in a mixture of the egg yolks and
milk. Fold in the egg whites. Pour into 6 custard cups. Place the cups in a large glass
baking dish half filled with water. Bake at 350 degrees for 30 to 45 minutes or until the
custard is set and browned. Cool to room temperature. Chill thoroughly.
To serve in sherbet glass, run a knife around the edge of each custard.
Scoop out carefully and slip into the glasses.*
Yield: Six Servings

Lemon Curd

Also known variously as lemon cheese, lemon filling, and sometimes lemon jelly.

5 large egg yolks
3/4 cup sugar
1/3 cup freshly squeezed lemon juice

Grated peel of 2 (or more) lemons
1/2 cup unsalted butter, cut into pieces,
at room temperature

*Combine the egg yolks, sugar, lemon juice and lemon peel in a double boiler and
whisk until blended. Cook over simmering water for 7 to 8 minutes or until the mixture
is quite thick and light-colored, whisking constantly. Remove from the heat. Whisk in
the butter gradually. Cover and store in the refrigerator for up to 1 month.
Note: Divine and versatile! Spread between layers of white cake and frost with divinity
icing (you can even cover the cake with coconut); spread over meringues and top with
whipped cream and toasted slivered almonds; spread over English muffins for breakfast;
or simply spread on your finger if no one is looking!*
Yield: One and One-Half to Two Cups

Banana Pudding

No family reunion is complete without it.

2 tablespoons (heaping) flour
1/2 cup sugar
2 egg yolks
1 1/4 cups milk
3/4 cup water
1 tablespoon butter or margarine

1/2 teaspoon vanilla extract, or to taste
2 to 3 bananas, sliced
Vanilla wafers
2 egg whites
2 teaspoons sugar

Combine the flour and 1/2 cup sugar in a saucepan.
Beat the egg yolks in a mixer bowl. Add the milk and water and beat well.
Add to the flour mixture and mix well.
Stir in the butter. Cook until slightly thickened, stirring frequently. Stir in the vanilla.
Alternate layers of banana slices and vanilla wafers in an ovenproof bowl.
Pour the custard over the top.
Beat the egg whites in a mixer bowl until soft peaks form. Add 2 teaspoons sugar
gradually, beating constantly until stiff peaks form. Spread over the pudding.
Bake at 400 degrees until the meringue is lightly browned.
Yield: Eight to Ten Servings

Rice Pudding

In Lebanon, the birth of a baby boy is traditionally celebrated with preparation of a festive rice pudding. This Middle Eastern dish can be served hot or cold and is a great family dessert no matter what the occasion.

½ cup long grain rice, rinsed
1 quart milk
1½ cups water
¾ cup sugar

2 teaspoons mazahar or vanilla extract
Cinnamon to taste
½ cup blanched slivered almonds

Combine the rice, milk and water in a medium saucepan. Bring to a boil over medium heat, stirring almost constantly; reduce the heat. Simmer gently until thickened, stirring every few minutes.
Add the sugar. Cook until creamy. Remove from the heat. Stir in the mazahar.
Pour into a bowl or dessert dishes. Sprinkle with the cinnamon. Top with the almonds.
Yield: Four to Six Servings

Old English Trifle

The custard for this jolly old dessert is made in the microwave. With a pound cake from the grocer's freezer, preparation time is quick without any sacrifice in taste or elegance, as you can see from the picture on page 210.

½ cup sugar
½ teaspoon salt
3 tablespoons cornstarch
2½ cups milk
4 egg yolks, beaten
2 teaspoons vanilla extract
1 (8-inch) yellow or white cake layer
1 cup raspberry preserves
¼ to ½ cup sherry
1 cup whipping cream
3 tablespoons confectioners' sugar
½ cup toasted sliced almonds

Combine the sugar, salt and cornstarch in a 1½-quart casserole and mix well. Stir in the milk gradually. Microwave on High for 7 minutes or until slightly thickened. Stir slightly more than half the hot mixture into the egg yolks; stir the egg yolks into the hot mixture. Microwave on Medium-High for 5 to 6 minutes or until thickened, stirring after 2 minutes. Let cool. Stir in the vanilla. Split the cake layer into halves horizontally. Spread preserves between the layers. Cut the preserve-filled cake into 12 pieces. Place half the cake pieces in a 2- to 3-quart trifle dish. Sprinkle with half the sherry. Cover with half the custard. Repeat the layers. Beat the whipping cream with the confectioners' sugar in a mixer bowl until stiff peaks form. Spread over the custard. Sprinkle with the almonds. Chill for 4 hours or longer. Yield: Eight Servings

Wine Guide

$\mathcal{T}$he pairing of good food with fine wine is one of the great pleasu[...] of life. The rule that you drink white wine only with fish and fowl [...] red wine with meat no longer applies—just let your own taste an[...] personal preference be the guide. Remember to serve light wines w[...] lighter foods and full-bodied wines with rich foods so the food a[...] wine will complement rather than overpower each other.

The best wine to cook with is the one you will be serving at [...] the table. The real secret is to cook with a good wine, as the alco[...] evaporates during the cooking process, leaving only the actual fla[...] of the wine. A fine wine with rich body and aroma will insure a[...] distinct and delicate flavor. When used in cooking, the wine shou[...] accent and enhance the natural flavor of the food while adding[...] its own inviting fragrance and flavor.

Appetizer Wines

Sherry, vermouth and flavored wines are considered appetizer wines. Appetizer wines can be served with or without food at room temperature or chilled to around 50 degrees. They are usually served in a 2½- to 4-ounce glass.

Red Dinner Wines

Red dinner wines are usually served at cool room temperature, around 65 degrees, in 6- to 9-ounce glasses.

Rosé Wines

Rosés are served chilled about 50 degrees in 6- to 9-ounce glasses with ham, chicken, picnic foods, shellfish and cold beef.

Semidry White Wines

These wines have a fresh fruity taste and are best served young. Serve with: dove, quail or shellfish in cream sauce; roast turkey, duck or goose; seafood, pasta or salad; fish in an herbed butter sauce.

- Johannisberg Riesling – *(Yo-hann-is-burg Rees-ling)* • Frascati – *(Fras-cah-[...]*
- Gewürztraminer – *(Ge-vert-tram-me-ner)* • Bernkasteler – *(Barn-kahst-le[...]*
- Sylvaner Riesling – *(Sil-vah-nur Rees-ling)* • Fendant – *(Fahn-dawn)*
- Dienheimer – *(Deen-heim-er)* • Kreuznach – *(Kroytz-nock)*

Dry White Wines

These wines have a crisp, refreshing taste and are best served you[...] Serve with: chicken, turkey and cold meats; roast young gamebir[...] and waterfowl; shellfish; fried or grilled fish; ham and veal.

- Vouvray – *(Voo-vray)* • Chablis – *(Shab-lee)* • Chardonnay – *(Shar-doh-n[...]*
- Pinot Blanc – *(Pee-no Blawn)* • Chenin Blanc – *(Shay-nan Blawn)*
- Pouilly Fuisse *(Pwee-yee-Fwee-say)* • Orvieto Secco – *(Orv-yay-toe Sek-o[...]*
- Piesporter Trocken – *(Peez-Porter)* • Meursault – *(Mere-so)*
- Hermitage Blanc – *(Air-me-tahz Blawn)* • Pinot Grigio – *(Pee-no Gree-jo[...]*
- Verdicchio – *(Ver-deek-ee-o)* • Sancerre – *(Sahn-sehr)*
- Sauvignon Blanc *(So-vin-yawn Blawn)* • Soave – *(So-ah-veh)*

Light Red Wines

These wines have a light taste and are best served young.
...ve with: grilled chicken; fowl with highly seasoned stuffings; soups
and stews; Creole foods; veal or lamb.

- Beaujolais – *(Bo-sho-lay)* • Bardolino – *(Bar-do-leen-o)*
- Valpolicella – *(Val-po-lee-chel-la)*
- Moulin-A-Vent Beaujolais – *(Moo-lon-ah-vahn Bo-sho-lay)*
- Barbera – *(Bar-bear-ah)* • Lambrusco – *(Lom-bruce-co)*
- Lirac – *(Lee-rack)*
- Nuits-Saint Georges "Villages" – *(Nwee San Zhorzh)*
- Gamay Beaujolais – *(Ga-mai Bo-sho-lay)*
- Santa Maddalena – *(Santa Mad-lay-nah)*
- Merlo di Ticino – *(Mair-lo dee Tee-chee-no)*

Hearty Red Wines

These wines have a heavier taste, improve with age,
and are best opened thirty minutes before serving. Serve with:
...me including duck, goose, venison and hare; pot roast; red meats
...cluding beef, lamb and veal; hearty foods; cheese and egg dishes,
pastas and highly seasoned foods.

- Barbaresco – *(Bar-bah-rez-coe)* • Barolo – *(Bah-ro-lo)*
- Burgundy – *(Ber-gun-dee)* • Zinfandel – *(Zin-fan-dell)*
- Chianti Riserva – *(Key-ahn-tee Ree-sairv-ah)* • Bordeaux – *(Bore-doe)*
- Côte Rotie – *(Coat Ro-tee)* • Hermitage – *(Air-me-tahz)*
- Taurasi – *(Tah-rah-see)* • Merlot – *(Mair-lo)*
- Syrah – *(Sir-rah)* • Chateauneuf-Du-Pape – *(Shot-toe-nuff dew Pop)*
- Petite Sirah – *(Puh-teet Seer-rah)* • Côte de Beaune – *(Coat duh Bone)*
- Cabernet Sauvignon – *(Cab-air-nay So-vin-yawn)*

White Dinner Wines

White dinner wines are served chilled to about 50 degrees in 6- to 9-ounce glasses. They complement light foods.

Dessert Wines

Port, Tokay, Muscatel, Catawba, Sweet Sauterne, Aurora and Sherry are dessert wines. Dessert wines are served at cool room temperature, around 65 degrees in 2 1/2- to 4-ounce glasses.

Sparkling Wines

Champagne, Sparkling White Zinfandel, Sparkling Burgundy, Sparkling Rosé and Cold Duck are sparkling wines. Sparkling wines are served chilled to 45 degrees with all foods for all occasions.

Decatur General Foundation

The Decatur General Foundation was founded in 1984 to provide charitable support from the community to benefit the projects and programs of Decatur General Hospital, a not-for-profit community hospital in Morgan County, Decatur, Alabama.

Founded by the Ladies Benevolent Society, a charitable and educational organization, Decatur General first opened its doors as the 28-bed Benevolent Society Hospital in 1915. Since then, Decatur General has grown into a complex of healthcare services and programs that include a 250-bed acute care hospital, cancer treatment center, behavioral medicine center, home health service, and an extensive community health and wellness outreach program.

The Foundation has been instrumental to the hospital's growth and change. Generous support from businesses, individuals, and area organizations has been used to help construct the Oncology Center and Cardiac Catherterization Laboratory, as well as to purchase needed equipment and furnishings for all areas of the hospital. Funds are also used to support several ongoing programs, including cancer support services, a personal emergency response system, and employee scholarships.

Proceeds from the sale of this cookbook will be used to benefit Decatur General as it continues to respond to the community's healthcare needs. Although several generations of families have moved through the everchanging doors of Decatur General since 1915, one characteristic has remained constant: The community continues to demonstrate the same caring attitude and commitment to healthcare as the ladies who worked to establish the Benevolent Society Hospital.

Noel Harris Shinn
(the artist)

Noel Shinn began painting in 1993 at the University of Alabama
in Huntsville under the tutelage of professor Mark Marchlinski. The vivid
contrasts and bold designs of her work in oil on canvas have caught
the attention of area galleries and art enthusiasts alike. Representative of
actual objects, her larger-than-life images are more about space, light,
form, and texture, however, than about association with the objects.
Her work is of the realistic, still-life genre, yet it incorporates
some of the stylistic attributes of American abstraction—large-scale,
high-key color, and dramatic gesture.

She was born in Decatur, Alabama, and has lived there most of
her life. She is the office manager of a Decatur law firm, but declares she will
retire one day and devote full time to painting. She is a graduate of Randolph-
Macon Woman's College in Lynchburg, Virginia, and has taken graduate
courses at the University of Alabama in Huntsville. She is a member
of the Decatur General Foundation Board of Trustees, the Board of Directors
of the Huntsville Museum of Art Foundation, and the Acquisitions Committee
of the Huntsville Museum of Art. Her work is exhibited at the Grisham-
Cornell Gallery in Decatur and Artistic Images gallery in Huntsville.

Cookbook Committee

Steering Committee

Diane Landers

Toby Sewell

Noel Harris Shinn

Betty Brandon Sims

Paula Strong

JoAnne L. Newman

Trudy McKnight Grisham

Committee Members

Jane L. Alexander

Gloria Arthur

Kathy Austin

Dana Baggette

Joan Barksdale

Gay Barran

Susan D. Bellan

Janet Berryman

Rhonda Blevins

Stacy Braudaway

Carolyn Cagle

Sue M. Cates

Elizabeth Chandler

Barbara Chapman

Susan Claborn

Becky Conroy

Genia E. Corum

Anne Cornell

Melissa Craig

Wilson Craig

Meg Curry

Mary Davis

Kathy DeLawrence

Kappie Dunn

Bunny Edwards

Carol Edwards

Dona Emens

Mattie Feltman

Rhea Fisher

Brenda Fulmer

Virginia Garrett

Nellie Gates

Etlean Gordon

Deborah Graham

Angie Harris

Katie P. Harris

Peggy Hill

Phyllis Johnson

Holly Keenum

Rita B. Kyle

Deby Lee

Shirley McCrary

Joan Neville

Gina Sparkman Parks

Larry Payne

Beth Pearce

Elizabeth Pilgrim

Kay Pointer

Vivian Pylant

Jeanne Reinhardt

Marlynn Rhyne

Toni K. Roberts

Patsy Roby

Glenda Sartain

Suzanne Scoles-Helms

Nichole Shelton

Noel H. Shinn

Anita Sibrans

Glee Sides

Phyllis M. Slaten

Jane A. Smith

Jeanne M. Smith

Carol SoloRio

Mary Jane Swanner

Loretta Troup

MM Tweedy

Beth Twente

Special Thanks

Artistic Images
Pat Carl
Roger Conner
Mary Cummings
Decatur Transit, Inc.
FRP™
Bob Gibson's BBQ
Glee Interiors
Green Bottle Grill
Grisham-Cornell Gallery
Holiday Inn
Margaret Shinn Holly
Mary and Jesse Hopkins
Hummingbird Antiques
Wally and Barbara Inscho
Judy Jackson
Jimmy Smith Jewelers
Johnston Street Cafe
Robert McWhorter, Jr.
Nebrig-Howell Antiques
Pam's Gift Tree
Riverwalk Antiques
Sam, Frank and Moore
Sykes Antiques
The Decatur Daily
The Plant Place
Lisa Sims Wallace
Brad Whitfield
Scott Willis

Contributor List

Betty B. Allen
Anne Harris Anderson
Annie Arnold
Elizabeth Arthur
Gloria Arthur
James Arthur
Suzi Askew
Kathy Austin
Allison Bailey
Shannon Bailey
Joan Barksdale
Betty Barnes
Sandy Barr
Gay Barran
Susan D. Bellan
Diane Belsky
Jennifer Bentley
Mary Beth Borden
Linda Clark Boyd
Sharon Briscoe
Alicia S. Broadfoot
Leah Rutherford Brown
Charles F. Bryant
Dana Butler
Lane Byrd
Doris Camberon
Ron Casey
Sue M. Cates
Patsy Cathcart
Elizabeth Chandler
Jennifer Chandler
Kathy Childers
Susan Claborn
Gloria Cobb
Charlotte Cochran
Susan Codding
Marie Colley
Becky Conroy
Anne Cornell
I. C. Craig, Jr.
Judy Crosslin
Elaine L. Crowe
Meg Curry
Scott Curry
Billie Ward Davis
Mary Davis
Kathy DeLawrence
Susan Drane

Betty J. Eagle
Dot Evans
Mattie Feltman
Jane Ann Ford
Pat Fulgham
Brenda Fulmer
Jimmie Galbreath
Lucy Garner
Susan Garner
Virginia Garrett
Nellie Gates
Deborah Graham
Peter Graham
Carolyn Green
Dennis Griffith
Trudy McKnight Grisham
Janet Gugliotta
Sam Gugliotta
Myra Harding
Lori Harper
Kay Harrell
Angie Harris
India Harris
Katie P. Harris
Mary L. Harris
John R. Harris, Jr.
Harriette Harrison
Nancy Hayes
Terri Holmes
Christy Hughes
Dama Hunt
Hazel P. Jeffreys
Jo N. Johnson
Phyllis Johnson
Tammy A. Johnson
Bettye K. Jones
Susan Jones
Auretha Karrh
Mary Ann Kincaid
Linda King
Cindy Knight
Rita B. Kyle
Rachel Lamar
Russeau Lamar
Melinda Lancaster
Diane Landers
Renee Landers
Ila Lang

Contributor List

Donna Lawlor
Diane Layton
Deby Lee
Mary Lee
Maryla Lee
Susan Linn
Douglas Ann Livingston
Maxine Looney
Ida Lowery
Tanya M. Mabry
Sharon Martin
Eunice Mathis
Pat Morris McCleskey
Jane McDonald
Mattie McDonald
Wanda McKnight
Margaret Smith McLemore
Sara J. McNelly
Kay McWhorter
Robert McWhorter, Jr.
Charlotte Meredith
James E. Milner
Sue W. Milner
Gail M. Mobley
Becky Moore
Dean Moore
Mary Morgan
Denise P. Morris
Jane Nabors
Joan Neville
Elizabeth Newman
JoAnne L. Newman
Randy Newman
Becky Oliver
Rick Paler
Gina Sparkman Parks
Lyla Peebles
Elizabeth Pilgrim
Jo Ann Pointer
Kay Pointer
Paula Prestwood
Shirley Prestwood
Russell Priest
Velma Prince
Shirley Joseph Reid
Frieda Rhodes
Ruth Riddle
Patsy Roby

Tommye Rowell
Debra Sarrels
Martha Scoles
Suzanne Scoles-Helms
Toby Sewell
Noel Harris Shinn
William Shinn
Gail Shipley
Anita S. Sibrans
Dyrc F. Sibrans, MD
Betty Brandon Sims
Cindy Lovelady Smith
Dewey G. Smith
Jeanne M. Smith
Sherry Smith
Sharon Smoke
Carol SoloRio
Kay Stepp
Sammy Stone
Nina Strall
Paula Strong
Mary D. Sturges
Mary Jane Swanner
Barbara Tedder
Margaret Ann Templeton
Jewell M. Terry
John Terry
Vera Thomas
Betsy Thompson
Debbie Thomson
Lois Thomson
Virginia Thornton
Cathy N. Todd
Loretta Troup
Randy Troup
Nita Tutwiler
Beth Twente
Mike Twente, MD
Faye Underwood
Lou Underwood
Barry G. Uptain
Pat Walls
Arabelle J. Wilder
Pam Williamson
Bridget Woodall
Jan Worthey
Katie Worthey
Margaret M. Ziak

Art and Photography Index

Art—All paintings are by Noel Harris Shinn.
Photography—All photographs are by Ron Manville of YUM, Inc., and Wilson Craig of Decatur General Hospital. Food preparation and styling are by Jim Griffin of YUM, Inc. Prop styling and set design are by Christine Stamm of YUM, Inc.

Recipe Index

Southern Settings

Decatur General Foundation Cookbook
Post Office Box 1461 • Decatur, Alabama 35602-1461
Phone: (205) 341-2187 • FAX: (205) 341-2648

Please send _____ copies of *Southern Settings* $24.95 each $ _____

Postage and handling $ 3.50 each $ _____

Alabama residents add 8% sales tax $ _____

Grand Total $ _____

❏ Mr. ❏ Mrs. ❏ Miss ❏ Ms.

Name _____

Address _____

City/State/Zip _____

Daytime Telephone Number _____

❏ VISA ❏ MasterCard Account Number _____

Signature _____ Exp. Date _____

Make checks payable to: Decatur General Foundation

Southern Settings

Decatur General Foundation Cookbook
Post Office Box 1461 • Decatur, Alabama 35602-1461
Phone: (205) 341-2187 • FAX: (205) 341-2648

Please send _____ copies of *Southern Settings* $24.95 each $ _____

Postage and handling $ 3.50 each $ _____

Alabama residents add 8% sales tax $ _____

Grand Total $ _____

❏ Mr. ❏ Mrs. ❏ Miss ❏ Ms.

Name _____

Address _____

City/State/Zip _____

Daytime Telephone Number _____

❏ VISA ❏ MasterCard Account Number _____

Signature _____ Exp. Date _____

Make checks payable to: Decatur General Foundation

Photocopied orders accepted.

DecaturGeneral
Foundation

1201 7th Street SE · P.O. Box 2239
Decatur, Alabama 35609-2239